The Unravelling of Ernest Metcalfe

By Conrad Jones

A damaged mind can be dangerous

ISBN: 9798524357168
Copyright @Conrad Jones 2021

The Anglesey Murders Series

Unholy Island

A Visit from the Devil

Nearly Dead

A Child for the Devil

Dark Angel

What Happened to Rachel?

Good, Bad and Pure Evil

Circus of Nightmares

Unravelling

The DI Braddick Series

Brick

Shadows

Guilty

Deliver Us from Evil

Nearly Dead

Detective Alec Ramsay Series

The Child Taker

Criminally Insane

Slow Burn

Frozen Betrayal

Desolate Sands

Concrete Evidence

Thr3e

Soft Target Series

Soft Target

Soft Target II 'Tank'

Soft Target III 'Jerusalem'

The Rage Within

Blister

The Child Taker

Unleashed

Hunting Angels Diaries

A Child for the Devil

Black Angel

Blood Bath

The Book of Abominations

Chapter 1

Father Derek Corbin was fishing. It was windy and cold, and the tide had turned. The fish would be moving away from the shore. He hadn't had a bite all afternoon, not that it mattered. Catching fish wasn't the point. Getting out of the vicarage was the point. It was like being in prison. Except there were drugs and alcohol in prison. He wasn't allowed alcohol on the premises at all. Not even in his own room. It was like being a child. Of course, he sneaked the odd bottle back, but it wasn't worth the earache if he got caught.

It all stemmed back to Father Patrick Creegan. Creegan had been the ringleader of a group of men, responsible for decades of historical sexual abuse against minors and the murder of two teenage boys and several young women. The case was a disaster for the Church and Creegan topped himself by covering himself in petrol and igniting it. The police later recovered the bodies of two teenagers who had been missing since the nineties. They were buried at the spot, where he committed suicide. His death and the subsequent enquiry shook the foundations of the Catholic Church all the way to Rome. Since Father Creegan cremated himself, the entire diocese was being scrutinised. The detective in charge of the investigation was like a dog with a bone. There was no way he was letting go of it.

Father Derek Corbin was being watched like a hawk and treated like a pariah, and he was sick to the back teeth of it.

Bishop Hansen didn't speak to him anymore. He spoke about him, even while he was present, as if he wasn't in the room. It was like being back at boarding school, shunned by everyone and not allowed to go home. The bishop frowned at him and shook his head in dismay whenever he talked about him, which was embarrassing and uncomfortable. He was such a drama queen. The huffing and puffing and hushed tones were driving Derek around the twist. It was as if he was to blame for the entire scandal. Father Patrick Creegan, God rest his soul, was the catalyst and the main organiser and he was dead, yet it wasn't enough to make it go away. He was dead but the other participants were not and they were being hunted by the press as if there was no other news to investigate. Father Derek felt like he was taking the brunt of it all. He felt like an unwanted child at a party or the weird uncle that the rest of the family didn't want to talk to at Christmas. Fuck them. Who were they to judge him? Let him without sin cast the first stone. Bunch of hypocrites. Despite their vows, they'd all strayed across the line at some point. Chastity wasn't normal. It was no wonder temptation won them over on occasion, some more than others. He couldn't care less what the bishop thought of him. He wanted them to pay him off and kick him out of the Church completely with enough money to live in anonymity in the sunshine somewhere. Somewhere where the boundaries blurred, and he could do as he pleased without society vilifying him. They had paid priests to vanish before, so he knew it had been done and he had asked every day for them to release him but the bishop was insistent they wouldn't do that again. It was no longer policy. Defrocking him now would be an admission of guilt on their behalf, and it would cost a substantial amount of money. God forbid, he made the Church look any more complicit in the abuse than they were already. Hypocrites, the lot of them.

He reached inside his waterproofs and took out a half bottle of vodka. This was his treat. When he returned to the vicarage, they would ask him if he'd been drinking and he would say yes. So what? If he said no, they would breathalyse him, so there was no point in denying it. He was past caring. How long did he have left on this shit-hole planet, anyway? Too long. The vodka would dull the relentless boredom. Everything he loved to do was a sin or illegal; everyone he loved or cared about was dead or no longer wanted to have anything to do with him. Life was like one long day. One long, boring, repetitive, pile of crud. He was going to confront the bishop one more time and this time, he wouldn't take no for an answer.

'Pay me off or I'm going to the press with my own version of events, and you won't like that. You won't like that one bit. I can embellish the truth better than most. There are names that no one has heard of yet. Names that will shame you and rock the establishment to its foundations. Push me and see what happens or pay me and let me walk away and you'll never hear from me again.' The pompous ass would have to make a decision this time. It would be his choice which way it went.

'Have you caught anything?' A voice disturbed his thoughts. Derek turned his head to see another fisherman, wrapped up against the bitter wind. He was carrying a tackle box and two rods.

'Nothing but a cold,' Derek said, shaking his head. 'The tide has turned now. I'm going to give it another hour before I call it a day.' He held up the vodka. 'I've got a little help to keep the cold out.'

'I don't blame you,' the man said. 'The weather doesn't make the decision to go home a difficult one. I don't think I'm even going to set up. I'd rather spend the afternoon in the pub. I can always tell the wife I fished all day and caught nothing.'

'Good idea. You're right there. I like your style,' Father Derek said. The fisherman put down his tackle box and rods on the rocks. Another man scrambled into view. They spoke briefly and gestured towards the priest, but their words were taken away on the wind. Derek felt uneasy, but he wasn't sure why.

'I think I know your face, but best to be sure,' the man said, matter-of-factly. 'Are you Father Derek Corbin?' The man saw the recognition flash in his eyes. There was no need to answer the question.

'Do I know you?'

'No, but we know who you are.' The man said, approaching. 'And we know what you did.'

His expression didn't change as he approached him, walking quickly. The second man took out his phone and began filming. Derek barely had time to realise what was happening. The man kicked the back of his chair very hard, launching Derek towards the edge of the rocks. He clung to the chair, but it upended and he fell painfully to his knees. A wave crashed against the rocks, soaking him. 'What are you doing, for God's sake?' he squealed.

'I'm doing everyone a favour,' the man said. He kicked Father Derek in the face, breaking three teeth and fracturing his jaw. He grabbed the priest by the ankles and dragged him to the edge. The sea was rough. 'Are you ready to meet your maker and beg for mercy?' he asked as he tossed Father Derek into the water. The priest vanished beneath the foam, appearing briefly before sinking again. The swell was rough and powerful, dragging him down deeper. Derek saw a blurred outline of the man scattering his tackle across the rocks before tossing his chair and rod into the waves. The second man filmed nonchalantly. He couldn't hold his breath any longer. The weight of his saturated clothing dragged him down, then his lungs gave out, and he inhaled stinging seawater. His panic subsided as consciousness faded and darkness overwhelmed him. He feared the darkness, for he knew demons lurked there, waiting for him.

Chapter 2

The light was fading when Philip Trigg and his brother Tom decided to set off for home. They had spent the afternoon crabbing in the Inland Sea, which separates Holy Island from the rest of Anglesey. They started at Four-Mile Bridge and ended up in the woods near the old Tinto foundry. It was cold, and the temperature was dropping as the watery sun faded into the horizon. It would be dark soon, and they hadn't intended to be out this late. The trees were bare and offered little protection as hailstone began to fall. They set off running together, no words needed. It was silently agreed. They would have to brave the shadows of the woods. There was no other way to get to the road home. It was through the brooding half-light of the woods or back along the coast to Four-Mile Bridge, which would take hours. They picked up the pace. Both wanted to be out of the woods before total darkness descended. It was a spooky place on a bright summer afternoon, on a winter's evening it was frightening. All the myths and folktales of the island came to the front of one's mind as darkness approached. All the ghost stories and warnings of devils and demons clambered for space at the front of the queue in their imagination. Their young minds were still afraid of the Bogeyman, though neither would admit it. They were ten years old but wanted to be older. The frightened child inside them drove them on. They were sprinting as fast as their skinny, little legs would carry them. Brambles and saplings grabbed at their ankles, the thorns pierced their socks and scratched their skin. They ignored the pain and ran on. As they ran, tree roots were threatening to trip them. They bobbed and weaved, trying not to lose an eye on a sharp branch. Halfway through the woods, the trees became denser. The light was almost gone now. Their breathing was laboured. Each breath burnt their lungs. Tom was the first to smell the smoke. He frowned as he ran. It carried the cloying stench of burning meat. It reminded him of the barbeques his father lit in the summer. Everything came off the grill burnt at the edges and was flavoured with a hint of lighter fluid. The smell evoked happy memories.

'Can you smell that?' Philip caught the scent too, and he glanced at his brother a second too long. He tripped and stumbled on a rock, twisting his ankle. He fell painfully, bending his right wrist backwards. His cry was loud and sharp. Immediately, Tom could tell he'd hurt himself. He wasn't messing around or being a sissy. There was a difference. He stopped running and went back for his twin.

'Are you okay?' Tom asked, bending over to catch his breath. Philip was lying on his back, holding his ankle with one hand and protecting his other hand by trapping it beneath his armpit. His lips were fixed in a snarl, teeth bared.

'I think I've twisted my ankle,' Philip said. A tear ran down his cheek. He wiped it away quickly, not wanting to appear weak. 'And my wrist hurts. I think I hit a rock.'

'I think so too,' Tom agreed. 'I thought you'd been shot the way you went down.'

'Fuck off,' Phillip said, biting his lip. 'My ankle gave way. I didn't have any choice in falling over. My wrist is really sore.'

'You're such a numpty,' Tom said. 'This could only happen to you.' He frowned. 'Mum says you're clumsy.'

'I'm not clumsy. I just didn't see the rock,' Philip moaned, trying not to cry.

'Don't get upset.'

'I'm not upset.'

'You look like you're going to cry.'

'I'm not fucking crying,' Phillip said, trying not to.

'Good. It's okay,' Tom said. 'I'll help you out. Let's have a look at it.' They rolled up Philip's trousers and looked at the injured ankle and nodded together in agreement that it was hurt. A dark bruise was forming, and it was already swollen. 'That looks sore. Let's get you up and I'll give you a piggyback.'

'I'll try to walk first,' Philip said.

The boys struggled to get him off the floor, but Philip was soon upright. He was choking back the tears, trying not to look like a softie. He hobbled a few yards, but it was too painful to put any weight on.

'It must be broken. I can't walk on it,' Philip moaned.

'Come on, jump up,' Tom said. 'I'll carry you as far as I can and then we'll have to have a rest and start again.'

'Maybe we could make a splint out of a branch,' Philip said, jumping onto his back. 'And tie it to my leg with my belt?'

'I'm Tom Trigg, not fucking Bear Grylls,' he said, puffing beneath the weight. 'We're in Holyhead, not the Amazon jungle.'

'Okay,' Philip moaned. 'I was trying to be helpful.'

'If you want to be helpful, don't come up with any more shite ideas,' Tom stumbled through the trees, trying to keep his breathing steady. 'That would be helpful.'

'What is that stink?' Philip asked. 'The smoke is coming from over there. Someone has set fire to something.'

'There is smoke and the smell of burning and you reckon someone has set fire to something?'

'Yes. What's wrong with that? Funny arse?'

'Nothing at all. I can see smoke and smell burning. Do you think someone has set fire to something?' Tom asked, shaking his head.

'Fuck off.'

'You should go on who wants to be a millionaire.'

'I would win more money than you,' Philip defended himself.

'As long as they use the special needs questions,' Tom said. 'Like, what makes smoke.' His breathing was becoming deeper. Sweat was running down his forehead. 'You could answer, "someone setting fire to something". Don't phone a friend because you haven't got any.'

'Funny arse,' Philip said, giggling. The smoke became thicker. 'Oh my God, it stinks. What do you think it is?'

'Someone has set fire to something,' Tom said, laughing. He stopped and put Philip down while they giggled at each other. It took a few minutes for them to gather themselves. 'Can you hobble for a while?'

'Yes. I'll try.' They heard voices coming from the direction of the smoke. The voices were deep. Men. Not local men. Not Holyhead accents. They knelt and peered through the gloom. 'Get behind that tree.' They scurried closer to the source of the smoke and hid behind a wide oak tree. 'Why are we hiding?' Philip whispered. They giggled and tried to keep from being heard. The men's voices became agitated. An argument ensued. The boys peered around the tree and watched as petrol was poured into a pit, dug into the ground. It was a neat rectangular shape and was already ablaze but the flames appeared to be dying down, starting to smoulder. The smoke was billowing from the hole in the earth. As the petrol landed, flames exploded skyward, leaping into the bare branches above. The smaller branches crackled and burnt, showering sparks into the air.

'You're putting too much on,' one of the men growled. 'It's making too much smoke.'

'Shut up and get the other one from the van.'

'Don't tell me what to do.'

The flames jumped and flickered and the tree limbs caught fire and burnt, adding to the smoke. Tom tapped Philip on the shoulder and pointed to a blackthorn bush to their left. They scurried on all fours and hid in the safety of the thicket. Sharp thorns threatened to pierce their flesh if they encroached too close to the trunk and branches. They could see the men clearly now. There were three of them. Their faces were partially covered by scarves and they were wearing baseball caps pulled low to their eyebrows. They were standing close to the flaming pit, watching it burn. Whatever was in the hole in the ground smelt of burnt sausages and petrol fumes. The men were standing in silence, staring into the flames. Tom pointed to a van. The back doors were open and they could see a blue tarpaulin wrapped in elastic bungees. There were two brightly coloured rucksacks on the floor nearby. The type climbers use in Snowdonia.

'Look at those bungees. Dad uses them to hold the bags on the roof of the car when we go camping,' Tom said. Philip agreed. They were the same. 'I wonder what they're burning?' he whispered.

'I don't know, but it stinks,' Philip said. The men spoke to each other. Something the boys couldn't hear. They went to the van and dragged out the tarpaulin and its contents. It looked heavy. Two of the men were wearing gloves, but the third wasn't. His hands were tattooed. Tom could see a compass and a skull. The men struggled with the bulky package. The two men wearing gloves spoke in hushed voices, but Tom couldn't understand them. It wasn't Welsh. They dropped the bundle next to the pit and it thumped onto the rotting foliage. A muffled squeal came from inside the bundle. One of the men kicked it. The boys stared in horror as the blue tarpaulin began to wriggle and writhe.

'Oh my God,' Philip muttered beneath his breath. 'There's someone in that.'

'Oh, fuck a duck. I know,' Tom agreed, deciding not to point out he was stating the obvious. 'I don't like this. We need to get out of here.' The boys were transfixed as the men picked up the wriggling tarpaulin and dumped it into the burning pit. There was a crackling of flames as the tarp caught and the stifled screams of whoever was inside. One of the men filmed it on his phone. The smell of burning flesh reached them quickly. 'We need to go right now.' Tom slithered away from the scene on his stomach. Philip was an inch behind him. They were clear of the thorns and brambles before they dared to stand up and run. Philip leant on his twin for support, and they hopped and hobbled as best they could. They ducked and weaved through Penrhos Nature Reserve and didn't stop running until they'd reached home.

Chapter 3

Ernie Metcalfe was at work, sitting at his computer while sexting a woman on a mobile phone when his boss wasn't looking. She was saying things he'd never heard her say before. It was like talking to an imposter. She was clearly very hot and horny tonight. Her messages were increasingly depraved. It was clear the meeting she had earlier that day had pushed her to a new high in the relationship. Using sexual language via text was an experiment for him. It was an alien concept.

He sent a very suggestive message, testing her to see her reaction. She'd been coy at first, not wanting to risk anything too sexual online. Her replies began, *wait and see* or *we can try that, naughty boy*, but as the conversation went on, she was double dirty.

He hadn't heard her say anything like it before. In fact, he was finding it hard to imagine her saying those things at all, yet there they were, on the screen right in front of his eyes. It was completely unbelievable. He had never felt so disappointed in all his life. In all the years he'd known her, she'd never talked about sex in such a brazen way. She appeared to be having some kind of epiphany, becoming 'sexually awakened'. That's what she'd said. They were her words, not his. Another message appeared. He nearly choked on his coffee.

The anal sex had hurt her but in a nice way. She wanted to do it again. In fact, she couldn't wait to do it again.

Was this the same woman or had the body snatchers invaded her being and infected her mind with filth? Ernie felt sick to his stomach. Twenty years of his life pandering to her and her anxiety clearly wasn't worth a toss. It had all been for nothing. The sacrifices he had made counted for nothing. Loyalty was something he valued and respected. Respect was obviously something she didn't understand. How could she do this?

He analysed the possible reasons for it and he had to admit, he understood to a degree. Having children hadn't helped their relationship. They just added to the pressure. He had spent twenty years treading on eggshells day after day, week after week, month after month, showing the patience of a saint to keep her happy.

The two-faced, backstabbing bitch.

He couldn't believe it had all come down to this. With hindsight, he could have walked away from her and never given her a second thought but for the kids. His parents had warned him in the beginning that she had issues and would be a handful, but he was a rescuer. It was in his DNA to sacrifice his own feelings and needs for the sake of others. He had looked after her and his children as well as any father could and this was the thanks he got. The fucking bitch had never said any of those things to him. Not even close. She avoided sex with him like he had the plague. He had never asked for anything strange or made her do anything she didn't want to do yet she was taking it up the arse from another man. It was clear that she was more than happy to do it with someone else. Just not him. Her husband. The father of her children. He had made mental dispensations for her lack of sex drive, yet here they were conversing in the most sexually provocative language he could imagine. Because the fucking bitch didn't know it was her husband she was texting.

His wife, Naomi, thought she was conversing with his workmate Hal-fucking-Nelson, and Hal-fucking-Nelson didn't know his phone wasn't in his locker anymore. Not yet. Ernie had picked the padlock and taken it. Then he sent her a message. The sneaky bastards had no idea he was on to them. Neither of them knew he'd been outside his house when Hal had arrived earlier that day, and he was still there two hours later when the slimy bastard had left. Two hours. Two hours he had sat there waiting, knowing that Hal-fucking-Nelson was in his house. In his bed. In his wife. In his wife in ways he had never taken her. Twenty years of his life wasted.

Anger coursed through his veins. His blood began to boil. He sent a reply saying that he couldn't wait to do it again, either.

Bitch. Dirty cheating bitch.

How could she betray him like that after all the sacrifices he had made? He stared at the screen waiting for her to reply. Come on. What depraved filth are you going to send back this time, bitch? He waited, staring at the screen.

Slut.

'You're not using a mobile phone at your desk, are you, Ernie?' his senior officer, Alf Rogers asked, already knowing the answer. 'Mobile phones and digital devices are not allowed at your workstation. It's a breach of Data Protection. You're more than aware of that.'

'It's important,' Ernie said. 'I won't be a minute.'

'It's against procedure and tantamount to gross misconduct,' Alf warned. 'I must insist the phone is handed over immediately.'

'You're not having this phone,' Ernie said.

'You know the procedure. Don't make this difficult.'

'Fuck off, Alf,' Ernie said, without looking up from the phone.

'I beg your pardon?'

'I said, fuck off, Alf.' Ernie glared at him. His pupils dilated. Alf was wary of Ernie. Ernie was more than capable of dismantling a man in minutes. 'I'll repeat that for you. Fuck off, Alf. Was that clear enough or do you want me to spell it for you?'

'Swearing at a commanding officer is tantamount to gross misconduct,' Alf said. 'Anymore of that and I'll have you on a charge.'

'Quoting the employee handbook at any opportunity is tantamount to being an arsehole,' Ernie said. 'Pretend this hasn't happened. Go away and leave me alone. This is a personal matter.'

'I think we need to reflect on what you've just done and said,' Alf said, standing at his desk. He put his hands on his hips and nodded as if he was talking to a naughty child. Patronising wanker.

He had a face you could never get tired of punching. 'If you give me the phone and apologise, right now, I won't need to take this to HR.'

'Fuck off, Alf.'

'You can't tell me to fuck off, Ernie.'

'Can't I?' Ernie said, frowning. 'Watch this.' He put the phone down and stared at his boss. 'Watch my lips carefully. Fuck off, Alf.'

'That's just churlish.'

'Good word, Alf. Fuck off.'

'Don't be ridiculous,' Alf said, becoming frustrated. 'This can be resolved without any disciplinary action being taken. I just need you to follow procedure and abide by the rules. The rules are there to protect us all. Mobile phones and electronic devices are not permitted at the workstation. It applies to everyone.'

'Now is not a good time to be pulling rank, Alf. I understand you have a job to do, but I've just had some bad news,' Ernie said, glaring at Alf. Alf could see the anger in his eyes. It was unlike him to be angry. He could be moody and distant sometimes, but he had done two tours of Afghanistan as part of 2 Para. When he left the army, he struggled and eventually joined the RAF Police. Ernie Metcalfe was an exemplary RAF employee and an outstanding police officer. His record was impeccable. 'I've had some very disturbing news today. Don't make an issue about this,' Ernie said. 'Go away and leave me be. I'm not in the right frame of mind to listen to your bullshit.'

'Okay. If you have had some bad news on a personal level, I can take that into consideration. I think we should calm down. We can keep it here on the shop floor. The brass doesn't need to know about this. It's my job to make sure you follow procedures but I'm also here to support you when there's a problem.' Alf shrugged and pointed a finger. 'This is very out of character for you and you clearly have a problem. So, man to man, let's go into the office and talk this through. I'm sure we can work through this.'

'Okay, Alf,' Ernie said. 'I appreciate that. Let's go into the office and do that.'

The other people in the office watched, amused at the incident. Alf caught a few of the shift smirking at his climbdown. He blushed. They would ridicule his authority again. They always did. He knew several were already sending emails to colleagues on other parts of the base saying Sergeant Metcalfe had just told Flight Sergeant Rogers to fuck off and Rogers shit his pants and backed down. It was the most exciting thing that had happened for ages.

'Before we do go into the office, I'm going to need to take that mobile phone from you,' Alf said, trying to save face. At least a little.

'Don't be an arse, Alf. I'm not handing over this phone,' Ernie said, sighing. He rubbed his forehead at the temples. He could feel a headache coming.

'We can keep this between us, but I need to be seen to take the phone,' Alf said, shrugging. 'Come on, Ernie. Help me out here.'

'I don't think so.'

'It's a Data Protection issue,' Alf said, hands on hip again. Wanker. 'You may have photographed protected information.'

'I haven't.'

'You may have,' Alf insisted. 'It's purely procedure.'

'I haven't photographed anything.'

'You're missing the point. You may have. I'm giving you a direct order.'

'Fuck off, Alf.'

'That's your second life gone,' Alf said. 'Strike three and you're on a charge.'

'Charge this,' Ernie said. He stood up from his desk and picked up his chair, hurling it across the office in the general direction of his superior officer. It missed and shattered against the wall.

'That's gross misconduct,' Alf stammered, ducking against the wall. 'What the hell are you playing at?'

'This is gross misconduct too,' Ernie said, his expression darkened. Ernie grabbed his monitor and ripped it from the desk. He hurled that in the same direction with more luck this time. It struck Alf on the hip. He cried out in pain and hid behind his desk. The screen shattered into a thousand pieces. 'Is that three strikes yet?'

'I'm calling security,' Alf said, ducking behind his desk. 'You've gone too far now.' Ernie picked up his keyboard and aimed it. He threw it like a frisbee, spinning it through the air. It struck Alf on the side of the head before smashing into the wall. Plastic pieces shot in all directions. 'Stop that!' Alf demanded.

'Let's go into the office and talk about it,' Ernie said, picking up the water cooler. Alf was hiding beneath the desk waiting for security to answer. He peered over the desk, phone to his ear. The water cooler exploded on his desk, saturating Alf and everyone within range. 'Do you want some water to take with you?'

'Pack it in!' Alf shouted, soaked to the skin. His clothes were stuck to him. 'Have you lost your mind?'

'Something like that,' Ernie said. He couldn't find anything else to throw, and the anger was subsiding. 'You don't need security, Alf, you wanker.' Ernie put on his coat. He slid the mobile into his pocket. 'I know the way out. I'm taking some leave. This is my formal request for some time off.'

'I'm not accepting your request,' Alf said, standing up. Hands on hips again. Wanker. 'You're out of this team,' he shouted, but Ernie Metcalfe was already gone.

Chapter 4

Sergeants Bob Dewhurst and April Byfelt arrived at the home of Tom and Philip Trigg in Morawelon. It was only six o'clock but it was dark and the street lights burnt yellow. There were no clouds, and a star-studded sky enveloped the world. They climbed out of the patrol car and approached the front door. The property was an end of terrace and obviously owned by house-proud people. It was in immaculate condition and the garden was well kept. A new Toyota was parked outside. The door opened before they could knock.

'Thank heavens, you're here,' the lady said. She looked flustered. 'I'm Brenda. Brenda Trigg. Come in.' She ushered the uniformed officers into the living room. 'The police are here, Morris.'

'I'm Sergeant Dewhurst and this is Sergeant Byfelt,' Bob said. A male in his thirties was standing in the kitchen doorway to his left. He looked uncomfortable. A teenage girl was sitting in an armchair to his right, staring at her phone. She didn't look up or acknowledge their arrival. Two young boys were sitting on the settee, clearly twins. They looked to be distressed. One of them had his foot on a stool, the ankle bandaged with crepe and a bag of frozen peas applied. 'Someone has been in the wars,' Bob said, pointing to the injury. 'How did you get that?'

'I tripped in the woods,' Philip said. 'My wrist hurts more but we've only got one bag of peas.'

'That's why we called you,' Brenda said. 'Isn't it, Trigg?' she said to the male. The male blushed red and nodded. 'This is my husband, Morris.' Bob nodded hello. 'But we call him Trigg. Don't we, Trigg?' Trigg nodded. 'Are you going to tell the police officers why we called them?'

'Take your time,' Bob said. It was clear Trigg wasn't the instigator of the call. 'What is this all about?'

'The boys have been over at the Inland Sea this afternoon,' Trigg said. 'On the way back through the woods, they saw some men burning stuff in a pit.' He paused, looking nervous. 'The boys reckon they saw the men dragging someone from the back of a van and tossing them onto the fire.'

'Are you sure it was a person?' Bob asked, facing the boys. They both nodded. 'Was it a man or a woman?'

'We couldn't see because they were wrapped up in a blue sheet,' Tom said. 'And they had bungee cords wrapped around the sheet. Like the ones dad has on the car when we go camping.'

'You didn't see a person?' April asked.

'Nope. They were wrapped up.'

'So how do you know it was a person inside?'

'We heard them,' Philip said. 'They were shouting but it was hard to hear them.'

'Like as if they were gagged with something,' Tom said. 'Like you see on the telly.'

'What time was this?'

'It was going dark,' Tom said. 'We saw them throw the man into the fire and we got scared. Then we ran home.'

'What makes you sure it was a man?' April asked.

'The voice was deep,' Tom said. Philip nodded.

'They were back here by about ten-past five, in a right state they were. I couldn't make any sense of what they were saying at first,' Brenda said. 'I had to sort out Philip's war wounds first. Trigg came home from work about half-past five and then we called you.'

'We didn't phone the emergency line because the boys have been known to exaggerate,' Trigg said. 'It all sounds a bit farfetched to me. I didn't want to make a fuss and call you out on a wild goose chase.'

'I can understand why your dad is being cautious. Are you telling us the truth?' Bob asked the boys. They both nodded sincerely. 'Where did you see this fire?'

'In the woods near the old Tinto factory,' Tom said. 'We came out of the trees by the five-bar gate on the track that goes to Trearddur Bay.'

'I know where that is,' Bob said. 'How far into the woods were you when you saw the fire?'

'I don't know. Not very far.'

'Do you think you can remember whereabouts you were?' April asked.

'I can, but you don't need us to tell you,' Tom said. 'You'll be able to smell it when you get there.'

'What did it smell like?' April asked.

'Like when my mum burns the chops,' Philip said.

'Or dad lights the barbeque after too many Stellas,' Tom added.

'Cheeky little buggers,' Brenda said, rolling her eyes.

'Okay. We'll go and take a look,' Bob said. 'I hope you're telling us the truth.'

'We are. Do you want me to come with you and show you?' Tom asked.

'No. I know where the gate is,' Bob said. 'We'll call it in and take a look first. We will need to talk to you again.' He turned to the adults. 'Thanks for calling us. We'll take a look into it and let you know what we find.'

'I'm not sure if you're wasting your time,' Trigg said, shaking his head. 'They're at that age, you know, but we thought it was best to tell you.'

'We have to take it seriously,' April said. 'We know they're young but the very nature of what they say they've seen is enough for us to follow it up.' The parents nodded, concerned expressions on their faces. 'Don't worry. We'll let you know what we find.'

The sergeants left the house and went back to their vehicle. They climbed inside and Bob drove it away towards London Road.

'Are we going there before we call it in?' April said.

'I'm loath to call it in and find out someone has been burning rubbish,' Bob said. 'It's only down the road.'

'Rubbish doesn't wriggle,' April said.

'I know. Let's take a quick look first. Then we'll decide. It's a ten-minute drive to the gate he mentioned.'

'They looked to be telling the truth to me,' April said.

'And me,' Bob said. 'But let's be sure before we make fools of ourselves. The Chief has been banging the drum about budgets and wasting money since the circus murders. I don't want him on my case for calling out the troops on the word of a couple of ten-year-olds.'

Chapter 5

Naomi felt alive for the first time in years. She couldn't remember feeling like this ever. Her emotions were like a rollercoaster, hitting unbelievable highs and surging to impossible lows, making her feel sick with anxiety. Hal had come into her life and set it ablaze instantly. It had begun online. She had posted a picture of her and the kids at Penrhos and he commented on how pretty she looked. At first, she was wary of him, thinking maybe he was a sex pest, but they began talking and after a few months, they'd become friends. There was chemistry there too. One day, they met in Tesco by accident and they chatted like a couple of teenagers. The magnetism between them was instant and powerful. The next thing, he was messaging her every day. After a few weeks, she gave him her mobile number, and they talked for a week or so and then they met up at South Stack. He kissed her and her head exploded. She had emotions that she hadn't felt for what seemed like forever. They had sex on the heather and it blew her mind. Never in her wildest dreams could she have imagined having sex outdoors. It was as if all her inhibitions had melted away. The shackles of shyness had been unlocked and cast aside. Since then, it had been a whirlwind. She was ecstatic but terrified. Hal was married with children too. Officers in the RAF Police had to be whiter than white. Anyone found behaving in a way which could bring dishonour to their flight was dealt with severely. RAF Valley was a close-knit community of officers and their families. They were playing with fire and they both knew it, but they couldn't stop seeing each other.

Earlier that day Ernie had left for work. He said he was doing overtime to prepare for a new unit of fighter pilot trainees. Hal messaged her, and she told him the kids were at school and Ernie was at work. She let him into her house and into her bed, and it was the most incredible experience she'd ever had. They had done things she couldn't have imagined and it felt as if every sinew in her body was electrified. Every nerve ending had come to life. She cried as they made love and Hal was confused, but they were tears of joy. Tears of ecstasy. Tears of discovering feelings inside her that she didn't know were there. When he had left, she felt a void in her life. Her emotions crashed, and the guilt suffocated her. She showered for an hour but still didn't feel clean. Hal's odour was all over her, engrained so deep into her pores that she was convinced Ernie would smell his scent. He would know, surely, he would be able to see betrayal in her eyes.

The questions echoed around her mind. How could she do those things with another man? A man she hardly knew. What the hell was going through her mind? She was a married woman with three children and a husband who tried his best to keep his family safe and well looked after. Ernie was a good man. Boring but good. She wasn't in love with him. She wasn't even sure she ever had been in love with him. Sex between them had been functional and uncomfortable. She didn't want to have sex with him. How could she tell the man she'd married and had children with that she didn't want to have sex with him? Worse than that, how could she tell him she'd had sex with another man and it had been mind-blowing? How could anyone say that? It would break him and he didn't deserve to be broken.

Hal worked with Ernie, but they were on different shifts and different teams and hardly spoke to each other. Ernie didn't like Hal. Hal didn't like Ernie. Hal had been messaging her the most erotic things since he'd left and gone to work. She had been sending him replies that made her toes curl with excitement. It was all so exciting that it made her feel young and attractive and alive. It made her feel like a woman. Not a wife, not a mother, not an officer's spouse, but an attractive, desirable woman. It also made her feel sick with guilt. Sick with the thoughts of being caught. What if Ernie found out or Hal's wife found out? What about their children? What about their families? What about the RAF and their senior officers? She couldn't think straight. Her stomach was twisted in knots and her nerves were on edge. She heard a car pull onto the drive and she looked out of the window. Ernie was home from work early. Ernie never came home early.

Chapter 6

Bob turned off the main road onto a service road, which led to the Alpoco plant. Beyond that, it weaved alongside the woods which lined the Inland Sea to Trearddur Bay. There were more craters in the road than on the moon. The car rocked from side to side and dirty water splashed from the potholes onto the windscreen.

'This is the only road in,' April said.

'And the only road out,' Bob added. 'They have closed the access gates to keyholders only now.'

'Since when?'

'Since Jack Josh tried to charge people for crossing his land.'

'That road has been there since before the Romans got here,' April said.

'I bet he charged them too.'

They trundled along the pitted path, trying to avoid the bigger potholes. When they reached the gate, Bob stopped the car and switched the lights to full beam. He aimed the front of the vehicle towards the woods. They could see the silhouettes of trees and nothing more. Dark shadows shifted and merged into an inky black beneath the branches.

'This is where the boys said they came out of the woods,' Bob said. 'There's a path between the trees there. Let's have a look, shall we?'

They climbed out of the vehicle and the cold night air welcomed them along with the unwholesome whiff of burnt meat. Bob reluctantly sniffed at the air. He had been a policeman long enough to recognise the odour. April shook her head. She recognised it too.

'We both know what that is,' April said.

'I'll call it in,' Bob said. 'It looks like the twins were telling the truth.'

Chapter 7

Naomi felt her heart pounding in her chest. Ernie wasn't due home until after midnight. He never came home on his break. Something must have happened. He worked with Hal. Could Hal have told someone and they'd told Ernie? Ernie would be devastated. He was an old-fashioned guy with principles and morals. Her guts felt like they were tying themselves into knots. She felt like she was going to vomit. Her hands were shaking when she heard the key turn in the lock. She caught her reflection in the mirror. Guilty. She looked guilty. The door opened, and Ernie stepped in.

'What are you doing here?' she asked, nervously.

'Charming,' Ernie said. 'I live here. You haven't forgotten me already, have you?'

'No. Of course, not,' she muttered. Her face blushed red. She couldn't lie without blushing. Ernie always told her never to play poker as her facial expressions always gave her away. 'I wasn't expecting you home.' She felt her tongue twist. It was hard to put her words together. 'I'm surprised to see you. You never finish before midnight,' she added. 'Has something happened?' she asked, immediately wishing she hadn't. He knows. *He must know*, she thought. Why else would he be home?

'No. Nothing has happened. I thought I would surprise you,' Ernie said. He held up two carrier bags. 'Takeaway and pinot grigio. They owe me some leave, so I've taken a few weeks off.'

'A few weeks?' Naomi repeated. She felt her heart sink. 'How lovely.'

'I've bought us a Chinese and a few bottles of wine,' Ernie said, holding up the bags like trophies. 'I thought we could have a romantic night in,' he said. He stared at her. His expression was strange. He was staring into her. She felt frightened. Ernie had never frightened her before. He wasn't a scary man. Not until now. Maybe she was just being paranoid. 'We deserve a bit of us time,' he said. She felt his eyes gauging her reaction, searching her eyes for signs of deceit. 'Just you and me. Like we used to in the early days.' His expression was strained. He was smiling, but there was no warmth in his smile. 'That would be nice, wouldn't it?' Naomi wasn't sure what to say. She nodded and half smiled. 'You don't look very pleased.'

'What do you mean?' she mumbled.

'I said, you don't look very pleased,' he said. There was an edge to his words. 'I've gone to a lot of effort to take time off work and bring you a takeaway and some wine. Yet you look like you're about to throw up.'

'Don't be silly,' she said. 'It's a lovely idea. I'm just surprised, that's all.'

'Good,' Ernie said, grinning from ear to ear. There was something behind his eyes. Mischief. Or something much worse. 'What time are the kids due home?'

'What?'

'What time are the kids due home?'

'Your mum will be dropping them off when she's fed them,' Naomi said. 'An hour or so.'

'Good,' Ernie said. He went into the kitchen and took out the takeaway. He turned on the oven and put the foil containers onto the middle shelf. 'I'm going to put this in here to keep warm.'

'Okay,' Naomi said. Her insides were like jelly. Ernie walked over to her and grabbed her by the wrists. 'What are you doing?'

'You and me, are going to bed,' Ernie said, kissing her hard on the lips. She felt like she was going to suffocate. 'It's time we had a bit of mummy and daddy time. Don't you think we should have more intimate time together?' Naomi nodded, stunned like a rabbit in the headlights. He pulled her through the kitchen door towards the stairs. Naomi could see the look in his eyes. She hadn't seen that look before. 'We're going to make the most of an empty house. Take advantage of the time we have alone. That will be nice, don't you think?'

'What if the kids come home early?' she protested. She resisted but he was too strong and she didn't want to have to say no. He was behaving strangely. She was frightened. 'Ernie? What has got into you?'

'What has got into me?' he chuckled dryly. He steered her up the stairs into the bedroom. 'That's ironic. I could ask you the same question.' He closed the door and pushed her onto the bed. 'Get undressed,' he said, smiling coldly. She hesitated, but he glared at her. 'Come on, darling wife. Don't waste any of this precious time we have. It's been way too long.' He undressed while he watched her and took an unopened bottle of lube from his pocket and placed it onto the bedside table where she could see it. He gestured towards it and grinned. 'I've bought a little surprise for you,' he said. Naomi saw it, and the blood drained from her cheeks. Ernie smiled. 'I thought we could try somethings we haven't done before,' he said. 'I'm on holiday, so we've got two weeks to explore and experiment while the kids are at school.' He climbed onto the bed and kissed her hard, forcing his tongue into her mouth. Naomi thought her heart was going to burst in fright. 'Won't that be fun?'

Chapter 8

Detective Inspector Alan Williams heard the armed response unit call the area clear. His long, wax jacket kept the chill out but didn't stop his bald head from feeling the cold. A pea-sized growth on his forehead stood purple and angry. His fine grey hair was cropped to his scalp above his ears. The force helicopter hovered above the Inland Sea, its searchlights focused on a clearing a few hundred yards from the water. Detective Sergeant Kim Davies approached. She looked different. Her blond hair was hanging loose today. She was wearing a long, wool coat, tied at the middle, and a matching scarf. Alan smiled at her.

'Sorry to call you in on your day off, but I thought you would want to see this,' he said. The armed officers appeared from the trees and uniformed officers manned a cordon. 'A couple of kids stumbled across three men burning something in a pit in the woods. They think they saw them dumping someone onto the fire.'

'What makes them think that?'

'It was a long bundle wrapped in a tarpaulin and fastened with bungees. The bundle wriggled, and they heard a muffled shout.'

'And the person was thrown on a fire alive?' Kim asked, frowning.

'Yes.'

'You said, they *think* they saw it?' Kim asked, frowning. DS Richard Lewis caught up with them. 'Hello, Richard,' she added.

'Hello,' Richard said, panting. 'I just got the message about a couple of kids witnessing a murder but it was garbled?'

'Yes,' Alan said. 'They said they saw someone wrapped in a tarpaulin, tied up with bungee cords. They said the bundle was wriggling and they could hear them shouting but it was muffled, like a gag was used and that three men tossed it into a fire pit.'

'Nice,' Richard said. 'The smell in the air would make me agree with your witnesses.'

They walked down the path towards the woods. Pamela Stone was waiting for them. They said their hellos and donned gloves and forensic suits and overshoes. The smell of burnt flesh was stronger and it tainted the air despite the sea breeze.

'Hello, Pamela,' Alan said. 'The ARU have secured the area but haven't encroached on the clearing to preserve whatever is there.'

'Good,' Pamela said. 'The smell doesn't bode well.'

'No,' Alan agreed. 'Let's see for ourselves, shall we?'

'After you,' Pamela said. 'Just in case the baddies have climbed the trees and are waiting for us to go in there before they jump down and stab us to death.'

'Happens all the time here,' Richard said. 'Baddies up trees.'

Alan and Kim exchanged glances. Alan shrugged. 'Sounds perfectly reasonable to me,' he said. 'I'd be more worried about the mantraps hidden in the leaves on the ground. They will snap your leg off. And then there're the snakes. They'll be attracted by the smell.'

'Can you three pack it in, please?' Kim said. She shook her head in despair. Alan was about to reply but she cut him off. 'I worry about you three sometimes. Pack it in.'

They approached the clearing and signalled that the tripod lights could be brought in. Officers carried the equipment along the path.

'Don't stray off the path,' Pamela instructed them. Officers deployed four sets of lights and illuminated the clearing and beyond. 'At least we can see the man traps now,' she muttered. Kim shot a withering glance at her but she ignored it. 'There is our firepit,' she said, pointing.

Alan walked towards the blackened maw. Grey-blue smoke hung in the air. He could feel the intense heat from the smouldering remains of the fire. It was painful to approach. The hole was the size and shape of a grave. He grimaced at the stench. It was stronger there. It was the unmistakable odour of burning, human flesh. The ground around the edge of the pit was blackened. All the leaves and mulch had burnt to cinders. The heat was intense, despite the lack of flames.

'There are footprints all around the pit,' Alan said. He skirted the pit to find a cooler place to approach it. It was difficult to avoid compromising the evidence. 'And there are tyre tracks leading all the way to the edge of the clearing. Follow them and see how they got a van in here,' Alan said to Kim. She headed off into the trees, following the tracks in the direction of the sea. 'Bring some stepping-plates in please.' Officers passed them a stack of plastic steps to build a forensic bridge over the potential evidence. They put them down and stood on them as they neared the pit. Alan had three left when he reached the edge. The heat was too intense to stay there longer than a few seconds. He shone his torch into the smoke-filled hole. A blackened skull looked back at him, the flesh and hair burnt away. A full set of porcelain veneers smiled at him, looking unnatural in the darkness. 'I have a skull and the remains of an adult judging by the size and length.'

'I have exactly the same at this end,' Pamela said. 'We're looking at two victims at least.' She moved the beam of her torch around the rim of the pit. Bricks lined the sides of the pit up to about six inches from the top. 'Those are fire bricks. Old ones,' she said.

'Fire bricks?' Alan mused. 'This was purpose built.'

'Absolutely. A very old one, probably from the eighteen-hundreds. This is a purpose-built crematorium. The bricks are carbonised and cracked in places.'

'Meaning what?' Alan asked.

'Meaning they've been there a long time and exposed to intense heat many times,' she said. Shining her torch around the clearing. 'This is an animal crematorium.'

'I know a few farmers who built these in their fields for disposing of animal carcasses. Especially if disease hit their livestock. I haven't seen one since my father stopped working at the cattle auction. That was in the eighties,' Alan said. 'This area was all farms once. Many years before the aluminium plant was built,' he added. 'This could have been here since the beginning of last century. Obviously, no one knows it's here or it would have been deemed a health and safety risk and filled in.'

'Clearly someone knew it was here,' Pamela said. 'I've seen a couple before in Flintshire. They were built about the turn of the century. Possibly earlier than that,' Pamela said. 'They were used all over the country to get rid of livestock, and some farmers made a little on the side disposing of humans during the Spanish flu epidemic. They act like an oven and stay hot for days. A body can be turned to dust in four to five hours. The evidence I need will be completely destroyed in a few hours,' she said.

'It's too hot to remove anything manually,' Alan said. 'What do you suggest?'

'The fire brigade will have heat resistant equipment. I'll call them now,' Pamela said. 'We need to get those skulls out of there immediately. It might be too late but we can try.' She made the call and explained what they needed. 'There will be a lid to this pit somewhere,' she said. Alan joined in the search. They found a rectangular piece of iron near the edge of the clearing. It was twice the size of the pit and covered in wire mesh. The age of the metal and welding was an indication that it was probably over a hundred years old. Branches and foliage had been weaved through the mesh to camouflage the lid. 'There it is. I'm guessing these two unfortunates are not the first people to be disposed of here.'

'How long on the fire brigade?' Alan asked.

'Fifteen minutes,' Pamela said. 'I just hope it's not too late.'

'Me too. We need to know who these people were,' Alan said. 'And find the bastards who put them here.'

Chapter 9

Ernie lay on his back staring at the ceiling. His skin was coated in a sheen of sweat. He felt like a wild animal satiated. The sex had felt like he was reclaiming what was his. Marking his territory to ward off rival males. It also felt like he was doling out a punishment. His wife was lying next to him in an almost catatonic state. He could hear her breathing and it grated on his nerves. If he could snuff it out without any consequences, he would do it in a heartbeat. She was sobbing silently, her back to him. Her shoulders were trembling. Slut. Ernie ignored her distress. She had brought it on herself. Every action has a reaction. No one falls into bed with someone. There are no accidents. A conscious decision has to be made at each stage. She had made hers and now he had to make his.

'The kids will be back soon,' Ernie said, checking the time. 'I'm looking forward to that Chinese. I've worked up an appetite and you've earned your supper.' Ernie slapped her buttocks hard. Naomi made a sharp whimpering sound. 'Naughty Naomi, I'm going to call you from now on. Obviously, not while the kids are around.' He squeezed her tightly and kissed her neck. He felt her muscles tense at his touch. Slut. 'I feel like we've crossed a boundary today. We should have crossed it years ago but life is about learning.' He smiled to himself, pleased with his performance. The balance was restored. Someone had dared to venture into his domain and take what was his, but it wouldn't happen again. He would make sure of that. 'I want you to see the future the same way I do, Naomi,' he said. He glanced at her but couldn't see her face. 'Are you listening to me?' His wife didn't answer. 'Are you listening to me?' he repeated. His voice was cold and calm and strange. Scary strange. 'Answer me.'

Nothing.

'I said, answer me. Are you listening?' Ernie elbowed her in the ribs.

'Yes. I'm listening,' Naomi said, her voice a whisper. Fear gripped her. Something was very wrong. He had been so rough, like an animal. When she'd said no, she didn't want to do that, he slapped her face and did it anyway. The shock had stunned her into submission. She had done what he asked as if she wasn't there. As if it was happening to someone else. All the time her mind screamed at her. *This is rape. You're being raped by your husband,* but she couldn't scream. Ernie wasn't Ernie right now. She had no idea who he was anymore.

'Listen carefully because I don't want to have this conversation again,' Ernie said.

'I'm listening.'

'This is very important. What I'm going to say needs to be understood completely. So, you need to listen very carefully.'

'I am listening.'

'Good.' He took a breath. 'This is how I see things. We have three daughters, aged ten, eight, and seven. They are a handful to manage,' he said. 'When we were posted here, my parents sold their house and moved to Anglesey to help you with the girls because they know you've struggled with your mental health.' Naomi closed her eyes. It was the truth. 'You do realise that don't you?'

'Yes. Of course, I do.'

'Do you have any idea what a huge commitment they've made?'

'Yes. I'm very grateful to them,' Naomi mumbled.

'Grateful?' Ernie said, shaking his head. 'You couldn't spell the word grateful.'

'I am grateful to your parents,' Naomi repeated. She felt the need to keep him calm. She sensed he was simmering beneath the surface. Did he know?

'If you are grateful, you have a funny way of showing it. I've never met anyone more ungrateful of what they have in all my life.' Naomi didn't reply. 'The girls are growing up fast and they're going to finish school, go to college, and probably want to go to university, which will cost an awful lot of money. Tens of thousands of pounds for each one of them.' He paused to add it up in his mind. 'Then they will want to travel for a while, Australia, Thailand, India, the Americas. All teenagers want to travel for a while, although they won't have the money. They might have some savings but they won't have enough. That will cost a fortune too. They will all want to learn to drive. Lessons cost a fortune and when they pass their tests, they will need cars, and they will need to be taxed and tested and insured. Thousands and thousands of pounds and all the time, we'll be clothing them and feeding them and paying the bills to keep the roof over our heads and the lights burning.' He nudged her in the back. 'Are you following me?'

'Yes.'

'Good. You need to. Once they've got the travelling out of their system, they will sleep around until they meet a complete dick-head and want to be married.' He paused to look at her. 'Are you following this?'

'Yes. I'm following you.'

'That's three weddings we will be expected to pay for. Then they will want houses, mortgages, and deposits, children, and the circle will begin again. Our lives are already mapped out for us. As soon as we decided to have children, our futures were planned. All our choices were made for us. The girls have taken priority over what we want and they always will. Don't you see that?' She didn't answer. 'Our lives will be dedicated to paying for our daughters to begin theirs.' He sat up and shrugged. 'That's our future. Our future. Mine and yours. I'll be working until I'm seventy years of age to support our family and make sure the girls get a good start in life.' He nudged her again. She was sobbing now, her body shaking. 'Can you see that future, Naomi?'

'Yes.'

'That's the future we face. We made vows, until death us do part. Richer or poorer, sickness and health. All that bullshit we signed up for has a moral value. Bringing up our children has a moral value.

Fancies of the mind and body are for the weak and are not permitted in real life. They belong in romance stories in glossy magazines and trashy paperbacks. We don't live in a magazine. We live on planet Earth where our daughters are like three parasites sucking the life from us until we die.'

'Parasites?' Naomi said, shaking her head. 'I don't see them as parasites. I think that's harsh.'

'Oh, she speaks,' Ernie said, sitting up. He grabbed his phone and googled the meaning of the word. '*Parasite. A parasite is an organism that lives on or in a host organism and gets its food from or at the expense of its host.* It can't be any clearer. We will feed and support our children for the remainder of our lives.' He shrugged and lay back down. 'My entire family has chosen to invest their time into bringing up our daughters. My parents have altered their lives to support us and I will be working until I'm nearly dead to provide for you and our children.' He nudged her again. 'Can you see what's wrong with this picture yet?' She sobbed but didn't reply. 'I asked you a question. Can you see what's wrong with this picture?'

'No. I can't see what is wrong,' Naomi said, sniffling.

'I'll tell you what is wrong. Let me explain,' Ernie said. 'Let me ask you a question. What the fuck do you bring to this picture?' Naomi didn't speak. She opened her mouth but no words came out. 'Where's your investment in this future I'm painting for you?'

Naomi didn't answer.

'Are you struggling for an answer?'

'Yes,' Naomi sobbed.

'I'll tell you the answer in a nutshell.' Ernie looked at her and was sickened by her weakness. Selfish bitch. Slut. 'The answer is fuck all. Nothing. Fuck all is what you bring to it. That's about to change.'

'What do you mean?'

'Tomorrow you will go out and find a job. You will work and you will contribute financially to this family. Enough is enough. I'm sick of you sitting around while I work all day. What do you get up to when I'm at work?'

'I cook and clean the house,' Naomi stammered. Fear held her in its grip. Did he know?

'You could clean this house in an hour. You've been cleaning it for ten years and it's not getting any cleaner. So, what else do you do when I'm working?' She didn't answer. 'It's time you had something else to focus on,' Ernie said. 'You need to contribute to this family's future. There's no more dead weight in this relationship. The free ride is over. I gave you an inch, and you took a yard. In fact, you've taken the piss for ten years.' He looked angry as if he was going to say something. His eyes glazed over, and he went quiet. 'You will get a job and you will contribute to our future. Our future. Mine and yours and our daughters.'

'I'm not ready to go back to work,' she sniffled. 'My anxiety is debilitating at times. You know that.'

'Anxiety about what? You need to try harder,' Ernie said. 'I'm not carrying you through the next thirty years because you get a bit anxious about fuck all. I get anxious about you being anxious. The kids get anxious because they see you being anxious. We all get anxious. Anxiety is just part of being human. Get a fucking grip.'

'You know it's more than that,' Naomi said, finding her voice. 'It's not as simple as just pulling myself together.'

'It's as simple as you make it. You're weak, Naomi.' He nudged her hard in the back. 'You can be weak at work and get paid to be anxious. Did you hear me?'

'Yes. I heard you.'

'Good,' Ernie said. 'Just one more thing you need to understand. I chose my future when I married you. I chose my future when we had children. I like my future. My parents have committed to help us bring the girls up. I'm prepared to work until I retire and provide for my daughters and their children too. I have no problem with that but if anyone were to threaten the stability of this family and endanger our future, I would do whatever it takes to protect it.' He waited for her to speak but she didn't. 'Do you understand what I'm saying?'

'Not really.'

'I'll spell it out to you,' he said. 'If I catch you fucking another man, I'll slit your throat and cut your body into pieces and then bury you all over North Wales. I'll make you disappear into the ether quicker than you can blink. I will turn you into a statistic in seconds and not blink an eye or give you a second thought.' He let her digest the threat. She held her breath, unable to speak. 'Do not underestimate me, Naomi. That would be a huge mistake.' Naomi shuddered, her tears soaking the pillow. He heard a car stop outside and the kids coming up the path. 'The kids are home. That's a shame.

I was going to use the lube again. Maybe later, eh?' he said, slapping her buttocks again. 'I'm going to have a shower. You need to straighten your face and put a smile on it. I don't want my mother seeing you upset. Get up and pull yourself together,' Ernie said. He walked into the ensuite and turned on the shower. 'Things are going to change in this house.' He closed the door and Naomi cried until she thought she would suffocate.

Chapter 10

The fire brigade arrived and donned suits that belonged in a contagion movie. They approached the pit to inspect it and decide how to proceed. Pamela Stone was nearby, processing the rest of the clearing while her evidence was roasting in the pit. Alan and Kim were watching, concerned expressions on their faces.

'The heat is too intense even in the protective suits,' Gavin Owen said. He was the lead officer from engine one. 'The bricks are giving off so much heat, it's impossible to put a man in there.'

'We can remove what we can from the edge of the pit using the shovels but there're no guarantees what condition it will be in.'

'I need those skulls intact,' Pamela said. 'I can sacrifice the rest of the bodies if you can recover them.'

'We could dig a trench and cool the bricks with the hoses?' Gavin said. 'But the water will damage whatever is left in there.'

'Can you recover the skulls first?' Pamela asked.

'We can try.'

The firemen attached telescopic poles to their snow shovels. They lowered them beneath the skeletons and tried to lift them without causing further damage. One of the skulls disintegrated as soon as it was touched. The bones were dust, and the teeth disappeared into the blackened ash beneath them.

'Sorry,' Gavin said. 'Let's try the other one.'

The firemen pushed the shovel into the ash beneath the second skull. It fell from the spine and rolled over, landing face up on the shovel. The hollow eyes stared at them accusingly. They waited for a few moments before pulling the shovel away from the smouldering debris. The skull remained intact as they brought it up. They rested it on the forest floor. Pamela waited for the contents to cool down before they gently placed them into a Perspex container. The teeth appeared to be intact. Porcelain veneers glowed white against the blackened bones.

'We may get something from the dental work,' Pamela said. 'I think the bone is too far gone to recover DNA but we won't know until we try. Can you bring up whatever you can please,' she asked. 'We have some debris trays in the van. We'll have to sift through whatever is left in the ashes. Don't hold your breath on this one.'

'I understand,' Alan said. 'We've got boot prints and tyre tracks to be working on for now. Whoever set this fire has detailed knowledge of this island and specifically this area. They have either got family who owned this land or worked on it,' he said. 'Let's organise a briefing in the operations room in an hour,' he said. 'And I want a sketch artist at the Trigg home to work with the twins on the men they saw. I'll give the ACC the good news. This is a double-murder investigation and we have at least three perpetrators to find.

We'll need an MIT drafted together. Fifty detectives should do it. That will hit him right in the budget.'

'Look at the tyre tracks here,' Pamela said, pointing to a deep imprint in a muddy section of ground. 'The wheels were spinning.' She walked further along the tracks. 'The back end of the vehicle fishtailed here.'

'So, they left in a hurry,' Alan said, nodding. 'And they didn't put the lid on the firepit.' Kim looked confused. 'Why not cover the pit before they left?'

'Wouldn't it smother the fire?' Kim asked.

'No,' Pamela said. 'They built breather vents into them. When the lid is placed over it, the heat increases and there's no smoke. The remains would have been dust and ash by the morning. They didn't have time to cover it.'

'Why would they leave in such a hurry?' Kim asked.

'What if they heard a couple of kids running through the woods?' Alan asked. 'They couldn't catch them on foot, so they jumped in the van and chased them.'

'But they didn't catch them,' Kim said.

'They may have seen where they ran to,' Alan said. 'In which case, those boys and their family are in danger. Put a unit on their house.'

Chapter 11

Ernie walked into the living room with a spring in his step. He felt liberated. In control. Although he knew it was a temporary state of mind. The doubts and insecurities would creep back into his head soon. They always did. His self-defence mode would kick into overdrive, threatening to destroy everything he perceived as a threat. But for now, he was in the driving seat even if the destination was uncertain.

The shock of finding out Naomi had been screwing Hal-fucking-Nelson had rocked him to the core, but he had reacted and put himself firmly in charge. It had knocked him off balance, but he had recovered well. He was a fighter. A warrior. Just like when he came back from Afghanistan. They said he was suffering from PTSD, but they didn't know the half of it. What they saw with their eyes was nothing to what was going on inside his head. The turmoil was indescribable. The confusion had driven him to distraction. He had become detached and desensitised to his surroundings. Seeing men blown to bits by IEDs week after week has that effect. That and killing another human with his bare hands. The face of the suicide bomber he'd killed was engrained in his mind. He had to kill her before she could detonate her device. His weapon had been grabbed and thrown aside by her accomplice, and Ernie had used a rock to beat her brains out before she could press the button. With his mind's eye, he could see her face disintegrating beneath the blows, feel her blood speckling his skin. They called his memories PTSD. A disorder. It was self-preservation not a disorder. His brain was compensating for the horror it had encountered at close quarters. He developed a coping mechanism, and he survived. Now he was coping with another crisis. The fact his wife was a slut. He would adapt and survive this situation too. She might not. His entire family was in peril. Their lives were hanging in the balance. That was down to her.

'Where's Mum,' Helen asked, bursting into the room. She was ten going on eighteen. She and her mother were joined at the hip and she was the double of her. The likeness was uncanny. Normally, that endeared him to her, but today he resented it. Slut. 'I've got to tell her about what Pippa Greenway has done. She won't believe it. Where is she?'

'She's having a shower,' Ernie said.

'In the evening?' Helen asked. 'She never has a shower at this time. How weird.'

'Let her have ten minutes to herself.'

'I'm going up to tell her about Pippa,' Helen said, ignoring him. She was gone before he could complain. He could hear her stomping up the stairs. 'She will not believe it.'

'Have they behaved?' Ernie said, kissing his mother on the cheek. She smelt of Coco Chanel. She had always smelt the same for as long as he could remember.

'They always do,' Rose Metcalfe said, smiling. 'They're a credit to you. Such good manners.'

'Where did you go?' Ernie asked.

'We went to the Sea Shanty for tea and ice cream,' Hannah answered. She was eight going on eighteen and also the double of her mother. Slut. 'Hilary didn't eat her chicken, so I had it. Then we had rum and raisin ice cream because granddad said it was his favourite. It was disgusting.'

'It grows on you as you get older,' Ernie said, remembering the first time he had tried it. He thought it was disgusting too. 'How is dad?' Ernie asked. He looked out of the window. His father was sitting in the car, the engine running. 'Why does he do that?'

'He's fine. But he wants to go home to use the toilet. You know what he's like. His stomach is so unpredictable these days. He won't use the toilet anywhere but at home. You know what he's like.' His father waved at him and pointed to his watch. 'Oh, for heaven's sake. Look at him pointing to his watch. Everything has to be run like a military operation. I wanted to speak to Naomi, but he's in such a rush, I'm worried he'll be panicking about making it to the loo. Will she be long?'

'She's had a bit of a dodgy tummy,' Ernie said. 'Something she's eaten, probably. Something she's not used to.' He thought of Hal-fucking-Nelson in her mouth and forced the image away. Slut. His anger level spiked into the red zone. The urge to bash her brains out was overwhelming. If only he could, he wouldn't feel so confused. It would be over with and he could move on. 'I'm sure she'll be fine.'

'Oh dear. I hope she's all right,' Rose said. 'Has she taken anything?'

'I'm sure she's taken a few things,' Ernie said, nodding. His mind drifted. He saw Hal-fucking-Nelson on her and he saw her enjoying it. Slut.

'Are you okay, Ernest?' Rose asked. She touched his face. 'You look a little distracted.'

He snapped back to reality. Positive. Talk about something positive. 'I'm fine. She's been talking about getting a job.'

'Naomi working?' Rose said, shaking her head. 'I didn't think she would be able to. What about her anxiety?'

'I think she's dealing with it.'

'She'll have to be careful. There's no point in rushing back to work if she's not ready.'

'Rushing back to work?' Ernie said, frowning. 'She hasn't worked since Helen was born and she's ten. Ten years isn't rushing back. It's time she went back to work. It's not doing her any good sitting around the house while I'm at work.' Ernie paced the room, looking out of the curtain. 'The devil makes work for idle hands and all that palaver.'

'That's a strange thing to say,' Rose said. Her husband beeped on the horn. 'Is everything okay between you two?'

'Never better,' Ernie said. 'Dad is pointing to his watch again. You had better get off. Thanks for having the girls. They love going for tea with their old grandma.'

'You're not too big to be over my knee,' Rose joked.

'I'll see you on Friday,' Ernie said.

'Friday?'

'You haven't forgotten, have you?'

'Forgotten what?' Rose asked.

'I'm taking Naomi away for a couple of days. You said you would have the girls.' Ernie lied. Rose was becoming forgetful. He could take advantage of that.

'Did I?'

'Yes. You've forgotten, haven't you?'

'Naomi hasn't mentioned anything about going away.'

'It's a surprise. She doesn't know yet.'

'I see. That will explain it.'

'Is it a problem?'

'No. It's never a problem. Your father wanted to go to Llanberis on Saturday, but we can take the girls. It would be a nice run out for them.'

'Will you pick them up from school on Friday?' Ernie asked. 'I'll make sure they have their things with them.'

'Yes. Of course, we can.' Rose sensed something different in her son. 'Are you sure everything is okay?'

'Absolutely. I've never been surer of anything in my life.'

****

It was after midnight when Hal Nelson finished his shift and found he couldn't get into his locker. He checked he had the right key. It was. It crossed his mind it had been tampered with, but this wasn't school or a public changing room. Yet his padlock wouldn't open. He studied it closer. The metal around the keyhole was scratched. It looked like someone had tried to unlock it with a metal pick and slipped a few times. It didn't make sense. He was a police officer in the RAF and his locker was in the middle of the station. A thief couldn't wander into the changing room and interfere with his locker. He wasn't sure what the answer was. If the lock had been compromised, it was by someone who worked there. No one had an axe to grind with him. He had no enemies. But then he thought about Naomi. He had thought about little else all night. Their encounter earlier that afternoon had been a steamy one. Mind-blowing. The endorphins in his bloodstream were so powerful he thought he was going to pass out at one point. There was no way her husband could know unless she'd told him. Ernest Metcalfe was a revered officer and a mysterious character. Hal had never warmed to him.

There had been an incident on shift earlier. He'd heard the gossip that Ernest Metcalfe had bombed the flight sergeant's desk with the water cooler, soaking Alf and anyone nearby. Someone else had said Alf was struck on the head by a computer keyboard and hid beneath his desk while Metcalfe threw stuff at him. It sounded like it had been exaggerated as most things on the base were. Something must have happened. There was no smoke without fire, and he had wondered what had caused the ruckus in the first place. No one on shift had any idea what had sparked it off, but it was well known Sergeant Metcalfe had anger issues. Word had it he had come back from Afghanistan damaged and unstable. There was talk of him being invalided out of the air force but his superiors wouldn't have it. They held Metcalfe in very high esteem. Very high esteem indeed. Whatever happened in Afghanistan, Metcalfe was lauded by the brass, but the entire episode was top secret. Rumours were rife. An officer in HR had said the records and interviews in his file had been redacted to the point where they were blank. Metcalfe was a hero, so the fact he'd bombed the flight sergeant's desk and destroyed air force computers was being played down. Nothing was being done about it. A lid had been put on all witnesses and Flight Sergeant Alf Rogers had been summoned to a meeting and his post was covered. Rumours were that Alf didn't come back to finish his shift. He sensed the brass had taken control of the incident. Damage limitation. The question was, did it have anything to do with his locker being interfered with?

Hal's instincts told him Ernest Metcalfe had something to do with his locker. Was it guilt or was he being paranoid? Did he think that Metcalfe could be responsible because he was fucking his wife? There was no way he could know about him and Naomi. No way. Only they knew. They had promised silence to each other no matter what happened. They promised to deny everything if accused of an affair. Neither wanted their affair made public. There was too much to lose. Yet he was torn in two. He had fallen in love with Naomi Metcalfe and he couldn't help himself. There was nothing he could do about his feelings for her. They were real and powerful. He would leave his wife and children and the air force if she asked him to. His feelings were that powerful. No doubt about it. His emotions were in turmoil. He wasn't sure if she felt the same. Their relationship was intense but did she love him? She said she did. Asking her to give up her family to be with him was something he could never do. She loved her three daughters more than life itself. That would have to be her decision.

He pushed the key into the lock again and wiggled it left and right. After the fourth attempt, it opened. He removed it from the clasp and opened the locker door. His belongings were intact. He reached for his phone and it was off. That was impossible. He never turned it off unless he was flying. He switched it on and waited for it to load. The wallpaper appeared, and he checked his messages. His inbox was empty. Completely empty. There were no messages, unread or otherwise. The entire history had been wiped. He scrolled through the phone in a panic. No Facebook, no Instagram, no Twitter. All the apps he'd installed were gone. His phone had been wiped clean except for his phone and Messenger. All the messages from Naomi were gone. Everything was gone. It was as if his phone had reset.

Chapter 12

The Next Day

Bishop Hansen was irate. Lately, his job had become all about reining in the priests who had strayed across the lines. Controlling wayward priests was harder than one would expect. His authority was being undermined at every opportunity. The police were no help. In fact, they were unsympathetic to anything he said. Father Derek Corbin was missing. Lately, he was acting in a rebellious manner, demanding to be formally dismissed from his duties and compensated financially. Bishop Hansen wasn't prepared to do either of those things. It would be acknowledging the fact that Derek had been a predatory priest all his career, which spanned four decades and included countless complaints and cover-ups. The previous administration was prone to brushing everything under the carpet to the point of there being no more room and no more carpets. They'd brushed so much shit under so many carpets that there was no way of knowing where it began and where it ended. The bishop was under immense pressure from his superiors, the public, and the press. Public opinion of his response to the scandal surrounding Father Patrick Creegan was dire. He had set up an enquiry, which had done little to nothing to quell the furore. They went through the motions to no avail. No one believed a word he said. The press reported the bishop and his legal department had manufactured another whitewash, which resulted in absolutely no one being removed from service or prosecuted, Derek Corbin included. It was deemed to be yet another shambolic cover-up akin to what his predecessors had done for decades. Different face, same bullshit coming out of the mouth. Different dog, but it was still infested with fleas. The investigation following Father Patrick Creegan and his cohorts had been covered internationally by television, radio and newspapers with a fervent determination to name and shame the culprits who had been involved in the systemic abuse of teenagers and younger victims. Little wonder the public was vitriolic in its response to the enquiry. It was a disgusting horror show of the betrayal of the most vulnerable.

The detective at the centre of investigating Father Patrick Creegan, DI Alan Williams, had been incredibly critical of the enquiry and its findings. His was the face of the doubters and the distrusters. The people who didn't believe the Church would take any meaningful action. He had used the media to voice his opinions of the cover-up and encouraged historical victims of abuse at the hands of the Church, to seek compensation and take out private prosecutions against the perpetrators. His campaign to expose anyone involved in the systematic abuse of teenagers had brought yet more accusations to the fore. Dozens of names previously unheard of had been exposed by the local and national press. Three men in their late sixties had been arrested, prosecuted, and jailed as a result of DI Williams and his campaign yet he still would not be silenced. The man was on a mission and was becoming a massive pain in the bishop's arse, which amused Derek Corbin and the priests like him no end. Bishop Hansen knew what Derek Corbin was up to, and he wasn't playing his game. He would not compensate an employee financially for being a paedophile. He would rather see them miserable and bored to tears until they drank themselves to death. It would be easier to pay the perverts to disappear, but there were so many it could break the Church financially. Congregations were dwindling, and the screws were on budgets and finances in general.

It was fair to say the press hounded him day in and day out and the public were accusatory to the point of being convinced every member of the cloth was a paedophile. Every single one of them. He had tried to contain the outrage with a campaign of local events to help the poor and unfortunates across the diocese, but no one gave a shit anymore. Too much damage had been done by too many. He was the boy with his finger in the dike while hole after hole appeared; the rain was pissing down and the water was rising fast. It felt like he was drowning beneath a deluge of historic abuse. No one had any sympathy for him. Not even God.

'What the hell is Corbin playing at? I don't understand why he hasn't been in touch,' the bishop said, shaking his head in despair. 'Is this the first time he hasn't come back to the vicarage?'

'Yes. He usually comes back pissed but he comes back.'

'He comes back pissed, but he drives?'

'Yes. He doesn't care. That's the problem. We ask him if he's been drinking and he says yes and becomes abusive. Yesterday, he told me to fuck off and pulled his trousers down to show us his backside. He is becoming completely unmanageable but he comes back. But last night, he didn't come back. He said he was going fishing and we can't lock him up in his room. What are we supposed to do?'

'Call the police,' the bishop said. 'Before he does any more damage. The man is a liability.'

'We have. They don't care. He's a grown man.'

'What about his car?' the bishop asked.

'What about it?'

'Does it have a tracker?'

'Yes. All the new pool cars have them.'

'Report it stolen.'

'Isn't that dishonest?'

'It isn't dishonest. His car belongs to the Church. And it's missing along with him.'

'I'm not comfortable lying to the police.'

'They're used to being lied to. Everyone lies to the police. Report the car stolen and do it now. I want to know where Father Corbin is and I want to know today!'

Chapter 13

Florence Mills rang the doorbell and waited. It was embarrassing standing outside the door. Whenever she visited, the neighbours ignored her and threw dirty looks in her direction. Everyone knew who lived there, and they frowned on his visitors. Not that he had many. In the last two weeks, dogshit had been pushed through the letter box and someone actually pissed through it. She wasn't sure how that was done. The flap was stiff, and the spring was powerful. It would break your finger if it got trapped. Placing your penis in the gap was a brave thing to do. The hallway still smelt of urine.

There was no answer. He hadn't mentioned that he was going out. She looked at the handle and realised the doorframe was cracked around the lock. The damage looked to be recent. She pushed the door tentatively and it opened with a creak. The light was on in the hall, which was unusual in the daytime. He was as tight as a duck's arse with his money.

'Hello, Dad,' she shouted, stepping in. 'It's Florence.' There was no reply. 'Hello, Dad. Are you home?'

She felt a sense of unease as she closed the door behind her. Something felt wrong. Her nerves were tingling as she listened for a reply. There were long splinters of wood on the carpet. Maybe her father had been tinkering with the frame although she doubted it. He could have locked himself out and had to break in. That was unlikely. DIY wasn't his strong point. Being a lying bastard was his strong point. If he wasn't her father, she wouldn't have anything to do with him. Her siblings, two brothers and a sister, hadn't spoken to him for years. When the scandal was exposed, her sister had finally spoken out. At first, Florence thought she'd jumped on the bandwagon after being silent all her life. She said their father had abused her for over ten years. It was difficult to believe what she was saying until it was all over the news. Paedophile priests. There were dozens of them, all intertwined like a rat's nest, sharing victims like passing watched videos on to friends. They were the scum of the Earth but he was her father, nonetheless.

Florence walked down the hallway into the kitchen. It was neat and tidy as it always was. 'Cleanliness is next to godliness,' he used to say. 'Brush your teeth, wash behind your ears, and put on clean knickers in case you get run over by a bus.' She could hear his voice in her head. There had been no sign of any deviancy throughout her childhood. He had appeared to be the doting widower, caring for his children and his parishioners. It was after her mother died, he converted to Catholicism. With hindsight, he was probably running from an awkward accusation but she loved him as any daughter would. Her heart was broken by the scandal which engulfed the Church and her father. She hadn't believed the accusations against him until her sister cracked and told of her abuse. How could she not have known? The guilt was crippling. Part of her wished it had been her not her younger sister, but the thought of taking her place even for a second turned her stomach and twisted her mind. She wished she could take the pain away for her but it wasn't hers to carry. Her sister had come to her before she went to the police. They had spent the night drinking wine and crying, shouting at each other and comforting each other. Florence couldn't take it in. Even then she made excuses for him until the third documentary on the subject was aired and there was a public backlash so vitriolic that it couldn't be ignored. When he was removed from his parish and forced into early retirement, she had to believe them. It had sickened her. To think the man she adored and respected was a horrible child molester, ruining young lives, including her younger sister, was too much to deal with. So, she didn't deal with it. She pretended it hadn't happened and she visited him and cared for him and she would continue to do so until he died. He would have to face God and explain himself to him. Maybe he would understand. Florence didn't.

She moved into the living room and looked around. His laptop was where it always was and he had been playing his board game. It was a war game based on World War 1. He'd explained it to her once but she had no idea what he was talking about. She walked back into the hallway and peered into his bedroom. She didn't want to go in there. It felt tainted and off limits now she knew who he really was. That was a contradiction in itself. Her father was a paedophile, and she was a grown woman in her forties. She shook off the thought and looked around. His shoes were cleaned and polished on the rack where they always were. He only had two pairs of shoes and both of them were in place. His slippers were missing, which meant he had been wearing them when he left the flat. He didn't wear his slippers outside of the house, not even for a minute. Outside was clean shoes, inside was slippers and the two things didn't cross. If he had gone outside in his slippers, then he'd gone unconsciously or unwillingly. Florence took out her phone and called the hospital.

Chapter 14

Naomi was getting ready to take the girls to school. She was creeping around like a frightened mouse. Good. Maybe a little fear in her heart might make her think twice before she strayed again. Slut. She looked at her phone and frowned. He smiled inside. Her home screen would look alien to her. He had factory reset it. She would no longer be able to contact Hal-fucking-Nelson unless she actively sought him out and reinstalled the apps she used to speak to the slimy bastard. It was a simple test of her resolve. Infidelity was a terrible thing for the injured party to cope with but he was dealing with it. She would have to deal with her own demons. He had fixed her phone while she was asleep. She would be confused by what had happened to her phone and it would cross her mind he had interfered with it but she would be too frightened to ask. Confused and frightened was where she deserved to be. Slut.

'Is there something wrong?' Ernie asked, gesturing to her phone. Are you looking to see if the slimy bastard has messaged you? She blushed and shook her head. Fucking slut. 'You look baffled.'

'I'm just checking the time,' she lied. Fucking liar. Slut. 'Come on girls or we'll be late,' she shouted up the stairs. The thunder of shoes on the stairs could be heard. The girls streamed past in a blur of chatter. They kissed Ernie on the cheek and filed out to the car. Naomi followed them in silence.

'Aren't you forgetting something?' Ernie asked. Naomi looked confused. Frightened and confused. He pointed to his lips. She blushed again. 'Let's make an effort, shall we?' Naomi walked up to him and kissed him quickly on the lips. Ernie grabbed the back of her head and held her there. He pushed his tongue between her lips and kissed her hard. Naomi almost gagged. 'That's better.' He smiled and slapped her behind. 'Hurry up back. I'll be wanting a repeat performance of yesterday when you get home. Let's keep the fires burning, shall we?' Naomi nodded; her stomach twisted into knots. 'See you shortly,' he said, kissing her cheek. She hurried out of the door and slammed it behind her. He watched as she unlocked the car and climbed inside. She wiped her eyes. The tears of the guilty. Crying because you were caught out. Slut. Ernie checked the time. It took twenty-five minutes to the school and back. He would give her a five-minute window either way. Don't push me any further. That would be a huge mistake. Slut.

He checked his watch again. His commanding officer had called earlier and insisted on coming to the house to speak to him about the incident with Flight Sergeant Rogers. With hindsight, he shouldn't have thrown anything at a superior officer. It couldn't be taken back, and the truth was Ernie wasn't worried about the incident. He should be but he wasn't. His ability to feel worried or concerned for himself was stifled. Muted to the point where he felt numb. There was no fear. He recognised that wasn't normal but what was normal, anyway? Feeling frightened or worried wasn't an emotion he was familiar with. He had never been controlled by it at any stage in his life, but when he was younger it had been there in the background. He remembered it vaguely in the misty parts of his mind. Especially as a younger man when he was spotty and awkward and lacked confidence but that was a lifetime ago. He had lost it somewhere, or more likely suppressed it for his own protection. Whatever the reason, he felt no concern about the visit from his superior. It wasn't his priority. He had plans to make and decisions to take. There was an imminent threat to his family unit, and it needed to be equalised. The sad thing was the threat came from within. It would take all his cunning to keep his opponents from knowing he was aware of their betrayal. Stealth and psychology would win this war. If he had to revert to violence, it would be swift and brutal. He would annihilate the enemy to restore the balance.

A knock on the door disturbed his thoughts. The first strike had been made. Strike first and strike hard. That was what his dad had always taught him. Hit them first and hit them hard, especially when they're not expecting it. Hal-fucking-Nelson had a few surprises in store. He opened the door.

'Good morning, Ernie,' Mick Milligan said. His silver hair was swept back from a ruddy face. A warm smile put him at ease. Mick had been his commanding officer since he joined the RAF Police after university. They had been to the Gulf and Afghanistan together. Their relationship was built on mutual respect yet the line between their ranks was seldom crossed. 'You've got the garden looking nice.'

'Thank you,' Ernie said. 'Come in. You haven't come here to compliment me on my roses.' He stepped back and let the aging officer in. 'I'm sorry you have to be involved. Do you want coffee?'

'No.' Mick shook his head. 'I'll be peeing all day. Old age is creeping up on me, Ernie. I ache all over. I'm thinking of retiring next year. It would be a few years early on a reduced pension, but it's time to put away the airplanes and medals and do nothing but read and drink brandy in the sunshine.'

'Good for you,' Ernie said. He gestured to the dining table rather than the settee. 'Take a seat.' Mick sat down and looked around the room. Photographs of the girls were dotted about. 'The girls are growing up. They look like their mother.'

'They're innocent. Unfortunately, their mother isn't.'

'I sense there's more to that comment?' Mick asked.

'Their mother has been fucking Corporal Nelson,' Ernie said matter-of-factly, sitting down. Mick looked shocked by his bluntness. 'I suspected something was going on but didn't have proof until yesterday.' Mick nodded and sighed. He looked genuinely concerned. 'I pretended to go to the base yesterday, and he was here within half an hour. I watched him walk into my house and I watched her closing the bedroom curtains. My bedroom curtains,' he muttered. 'He left two hours later. We both know what they were doing for two hours. I have pictures of him arriving and leaving with the timestamps on my phone if you need to see them?'

'No need,' Mick said, nodding. 'I believe you.'

'I'm struggling to deal with her behaviour. She brought another man into my home. Into my bed,' Ernie said, shrugging. 'She has had little interest in a physical relationship with me yet she fucked another man in my bed.' Ernie shrugged and shook his head. His eyes looked distant as he thought about his next words. Mick waited patiently for him to finish. 'I lost my marbles for a while.'

'That was the trigger for your outburst last night?'

'Yes, sir,' Ernie said. 'I wasn't thinking straight. Alf pushed the wrong buttons and I lost control for a few minutes. I took it out on him. It's not an excuse and I know it's a disciplinary incident but it's the truth. If I'm charged, I won't challenge it. I hold my hands up. It was shock.'

'Okay, thank you for your honesty,' Mick said. 'You only found out yesterday?'

'Yes.'

'Have you confronted either of them?'

'No.'

'Do you intend on confronting them?'

'No.'

'What do you intend to do?'

'I don't intend to do anything,' Ernie said. 'Don't worry. I'm not going to accuse Nelson of anything, nor will I attack him. If my wife felt the need to turn to another man, I've been doing something wrong.'

'That's a very Christian way to look at it,' Mick said.

'I'm trying to balance things out in my mind. I have a part to play in this. You know what this job is like. It can take over your life completely. Add three stroppy daughters into the mix and I've probably been neglecting Naomi and taking her for granted. I have to change my behaviour to make sure she doesn't feel the need to stray.' Bitch. Slut. Cheating whore. Till death us do part. Slag. Tramp. Judas, bitch. 'I'm taking responsibility for my part of this breakdown. I have to.'

'You're calmer than I would have been,' Mick said.

'I threw the water cooler at my flight sergeant,' Ernie reminded him. 'Calm is not what I am right now.'

'True.' Mick laughed. His face was lined with deep wrinkles. Liver spots covered his scalp and forehead. 'I'm not comfortable with any of this. There's something wrong with a man who betrays a fellow officer, his wife, and rank and jeopardises his honour and two families in the process. Sergeant Nelson will be on my shit list from here on in. He's a disgrace.'

'I don't want him to know that I know, sir.'

'He won't. If that's the way you want to play it, that's fine but you can't throw water coolers at the flight sergeant or anyone else for that matter,' Mick said, shaking his head. 'Are we clear?'

'Yes, sir.' Ernie nodded that he understood. There would be no more water coolers being tossed at people. Things had gone beyond lashing out in anger. Now was the time for the strategic destruction of the enemy. The annihilation of any threat to his family unit.

Chapter 15

Alan and Kim walked up the path to the Trigg property in Morawelon. He could see the old electronic factory, MEM, where his sister once worked. Behind it, across the sea he could see Church Bay in the distance. To his left was the harbour. There was an Irish ferry cruising into the inner harbour, white foam in its wake. Storm clouds were brewing in the far distance. Lightning flashes lit up the point where the sea met the sky on the horizon. At the front of the house, a uniformed unit was on duty in an interceptor. The officers waved a greeting. They looked like they were losing the will to live. It was boring work, but the marked police car was a deterrent to even the most determined criminals. The family would be safe for now.

As they approached, the sketch artist was leaving. He was in his early twenties and dressed like a teenage skateboarder – baseball cap on sideways. Under his arm was a leather art folder instead of a board. Patchy bum fluff covered his chin. His greasy hair was memorable as were the myriad of blackheads on his face. Alan wasn't a big fan of his. Professionals should dress as such, not look like an adolescent on the way to sign on.

'How did it go?' Alan asked.

'So, so,' the artist said.

'Can we have a look or do you need to colour them in at home?' Alan said. Kim squeezed his elbow and tried not to laugh.

The artist took out his impressions. Three men wearing dark hoodies and baseball caps. Two of them had the lower part of their face covered with a scarf or bandana. The third was a side profile. Alan looked at the drawings. They looked like baddies in a Marvel comic. 'That could be the Backstreet Boys or Bros,' he muttered. 'We could put a BOLO out for a nineties boyband on the island.'

'Who?' the artist asked, frowning. 'Before my time, bro.'

'Don't tell me you haven't heard of the Backstreet Boys,' Alan repeated. 'Or Bros. They had an album cover that looked just like that.' He pointed to the sketches. 'He could be the drummer. No one remembers the drummer. These sketches are so vague, they could be anyone. They're beyond useless, bro.' Alan emphasised the word bro, as an indicator he didn't like it. 'Were there any logos on the caps?'

'The boys can't remember any.'

'That's a total waste of time,' Alan said, shaking his head.

'I can only draw what the subjects say they saw,' the artist said, offended. 'They're just kids. I drew what they told me they saw.' He protested.

'You may as well have drawn Big Bird.' Alan grimaced, unimpressed.

'I can do Big Bird. I can draw anything, portraits of cartoon characters, or serial killers. Hannibal Lecter, Michael Myers, or famous evil people if you like but it defeats the object, doesn't it?'

Alan shrugged. In his mind, he couldn't justify the money they'd spent. 'I can only draw what they've seen. I'm not a mind reader nor am I there to influence their memories.'

'You should ask for details and make a decision if it is drawable before you set out to draw Tony Hawk.'

'Who?' the artist asked, shrugging. 'Another boy band?'

'A famous skateboarder.' Alan sighed. He was getting older, and everyone else was younger. The artist was from a different time zone. 'It's better to draw nothing than to draw that,' Alan said, pointing again.

'I drew what they said they saw.'

'You're missing the point. I could draw that,' Alan said. 'I would add a big yellow sun and a house. Maybe a tree and a dog too. It's a total waste of time and money. You've drawn three characters from *Grand Theft Auto* and charged us five-hundred quid.'

'*Grand Theft Auto*? Funny,' the artist said, walking away in a hurry. 'You should be on the telly.' He slammed the gate behind him. 'You're about as funny as a kick in the bollocks,' he added for good measure. 'And the bill will actually be five-fifty plus VAT. How funny is that?'

'Fucking hilarious,' Alan muttered. His tolerance level was at an all-time low.

'I don't think he likes you,' Kim said, knocking on the door.

'He might not be a *GTA* fan,' Alan said, shaking his head. 'My lads loved it. He has nailed all the bit-characters there, fair play to him but that doesn't help us.'

'Maybe you were a bit harsh to him,' Kim said, shaking her head. 'He's only young and we're short on sketch artists.'

'It's not his age that's the problem. The problem is, he's an artist, and he's embraced being the arty type. You can tell from the way he dresses. Arty people are always way too sensitive.'

'Arty people?' Kim asked, frowning.

'Yes. Jimmy Goldberg in school, for instance. He was a brilliant artist. Best painter and sketcher in the school.' Alan shrugged. 'Always crying. He wet his pants in history because Mr Jeffries explained what hung, drawn, and quartered was.' Alan shrugged again. 'He had to spend an hour in the matron's office while they dried out his pants. Way too sensitive. It's what arty people do. Good at drawing, crap at everything else.'

'That's quite a sweeping statement,' Kim said, knocking again. She smiled and shook her head at his logic.

'Look at Van Gough,' Alan said. 'Arty person. He's the quintessential tortured artist. He cut his own ear off. Oversensitive, you see.'

'He sounds like he had mental health issues?'

'Nope. He was pissed off because no one bought his paintings when he was alive. Cutting his ear off was an act of attention seeking. Probably looking for sympathy. Oversensitive. One-hundred per cent.'

'You should be an agony uncle,' Kim said. 'Fifty-years ago, you would have been on the television.'

'Fifty-years ago?' Alan said, frowning. 'It's as relevant today as it ever was. Too sensitive.'

'I'll take your word for it,' Kim said, shaking her head. 'Although, if the stereotype police are listening, you're going to prison.'

The door opened and Tom Trigg opened the door. He looked worried. He called his mum. His mother came to the door and invited them in. Morris Trigg was sitting in his armchair in his boxer shorts and a dressing gown, sipping a mug of tea. The smell of bacon and eggs was in the air. There was an empty plate on the table next to him. It reminded Alan he hadn't eaten since yesterday lunchtime. Morris burped.

'You're so embarrassing. Go and get some clothes on,' Brenda hissed. Morris reluctantly got out of the chair and went upstairs. 'The sketch artist has just left. He drew some pictures, but I'm not sure they will be any good for you. I hope so but the boys didn't see much,' she said, fussing. 'Would you like a cup of tea or coffee?'

'No. We're fine,' Alan said. 'We just need a quick chat with the twins.' The twins were sitting on the settee like two bookends. 'How are you boys feeling today?'

They shrugged but didn't speak.

'I bet this is all very disturbing for you?' Alan said. The boys looked at each other and nodded. 'Are you frightened?'

'He wet the bed last night,' Tom said. Philip punched him in the arm. 'Well, you did, pissy-pants.'

'Shut your face!' Philip said angrily. 'Mum, tell him not to call me pissy-pants.'

'Don't call your brother that,' Brenda said, frowning. 'He couldn't help it.'

'Dad called him pissy-pants this morning,' Tom complained.

'Your dad shouldn't be calling him that,' Brenda said. She walked to the bottom of the stairs. 'Don't you call our Philip pissy-pants, Trigg,' she shouted upstairs. There was no reply. 'There's no need for that.'

'Don't worry, Philip. It's nothing to be ashamed of,' Alan said. He smiled. 'What you witnessed in the woods was unnatural and incomprehensible. Your brain can't process the information because it's too bizarre. It's normal to be disturbed by an experience like that.' Philip nodded, embarrassed but encouraged. 'What happens in our minds when we sleep is beyond our control, so if you have an accident, you know the reason why, don't you?' Philip nodded again but couldn't lift his eyes from his feet. 'We need you to help us put together what happened after you saw what you saw.' Alan paused. 'I need you to focus for a few minutes and try to remember everything you possibly can about what happened when you turned around to leave the clearing.' The twins looked confused. 'You have gone over what you saw in the clearing a dozen times, but I want to focus on what happened when you decided you had seen enough and left,' Alan said in a calming voice. The twins looked thoughtful. 'Let's start with who made the decision to leave?'

'He did.' Philip pointed to his brother. 'Tom said we needed to get out of there,' Philip said. 'So, we crept away on our stomachs. Like soldiers in the jungle.'

'Okay, good,' Alan said, nodding. 'Tell me how far you crawled like soldiers in the jungle.' The boys looked flummoxed. 'Was it from here to the telly or from here to the end of the garden?' The boys exchanged glances. 'There is no right or wrong answer. What's your best guess?'

'I don't think it was very far. To the telly,' Tom said. 'We crawled under the bush until we were clear of the thorns, then we stood up and ran but Phil was hopping a bit.' Philip nodded in agreement.

'Did you run on tiptoe quietly or did you just run full speed?'

'Full speed,' Tom said. 'We were scared. But Philip was limping so not as fast as normal. He's slower than me, anyway.'

'I'm not slower.'

'Yes, you are. I always win our races.'

'You don't win them all, liar, liar, arse is on fire,' Philip said angrily.

'Philip Trigg!' Brenda said, embarrassed. 'The police officers will arrest you and put you in prison for using that language.'

'No, they won't,' Philip muttered. He looked at Alan unsure if he would arrest him or not. 'Arse isn't a bad swear word, anyway. Dad taught me that saying, anyway.'

'Why does that not surprise me?' Brenda said. She shouted up the stairs again. 'Your son is swearing in front of the detectives down here, not that you're arsed.' The twins sniggered. 'Don't laugh, you two. It isn't funny,' Brenda giggled. She couldn't contain herself. 'Sorry,' she said to Alan. 'I'll put a pound in the swear box when you've gone.'

'Swear box?' Tom said, frowning.

'I believe you,' Alan said. 'Thousands wouldn't.' He turned back to the boys. 'Okay. When you were running away, can you remember if you made much noise?' Alan asked. The boys were confused again. 'You know, crunching leaves and snapping twigs on the ground. Did you speak, maybe egging each other on?'

'I suppose there was noise,' Philip said. 'Tom kept asking me if I was okay but we whispered.'

'Why are you asking this?' Tom asked. He frowned. 'Do you think the bad men heard us?'

'No,' Alan lied. 'I need to be clear in my mind the sequence of events and how they happened.' He smiled. The boys seemed to relax a little. 'When you came out of the woods, you were near the barrier on the old road which leads to Trearddur Bay?' The boys nodded. 'Then where did you go?'

'We crossed the main road and climbed over the fence into Penrhos Woods,' Tom said. 'We stayed off the paths and ran through the trees to Penrhos beach. No one saw us. We saw a woman walking her dogs, but we ducked behind a wall and waited for her to pass. She didn't see us. We practice hiding all the time.'

'Very clever,' Alan said. 'Why were you hiding? Did you think you were being followed?'

'No, but we were being careful,' Tom said. 'Dad says the paedos are in the woods, so we always hide when we're there.'

'Jesus, Mary, and Joseph,' Brenda muttered, crossing her chest. 'That man will have them demented. Paedos in the woods?'

'They're everywhere, Mum,' Philip said, nodding knowingly. 'Dad says trust no one. You can't tell who the paedos are.'

'Always best to be on the safe side,' Alan said, hiding a smile. 'What you did is good. Very clever. Then what did you do?'

'We reached Penrhos and checked out the car park. There was only one car there. We ran all the way across the beach to Ffordd Beibio without stopping,' Tom said. 'We were puffed then, so we had a rest. Then we cut through the estate to here.'

Alan nodded. He looked at Kim. She was smiling at the boys. 'No one in a car could have followed you home that way,' Kim said. 'Well done.'

'Do you know who they threw into the fire?' Philip asked.

'Not yet,' Alan said. 'Best not to think about it. Sometimes bad people have arguments with other bad people and they kill each other. We think that's probably what has happened.'

'Not a serial killer?' Tom asked.

'No. They usually work alone,' Alan said, smiling.

'Fred and Rose West didn't,' Philip said, shaking his head. 'I saw a documentary on Netflix. They buried their daughter under the patio.'

'They did,' Alan said. 'Thankfully, couples like that are a rare occurrence. We think this may be criminals attacking each other, not another Fred and Rose.'

'Like a vendetta?' Philip asked. Alan nodded, smiling again. 'Or a hit.'

'Yes. Just like that,' Alan agreed. 'It could be either of those things. We don't know yet.'

'It's probably an OCG straightening things out,' Tom said, looking serious. Philip agreed. 'We watch *Line of Duty* on a Sunday night when Mum's at work,' he explained. Brenda rolled her eyes and shook her head.

'I thought the twins were in bed before nine o'clock on Sunday night?' she shouted upstairs. 'Bloody liar,' she added.

'If you watch that, then you have a good idea about how these things work,' Alan said, ignoring Brenda. 'Best not to dwell on it. You might want to look for an explanation of what you saw, but the reality is, there isn't one. It's much more complicated than we can understand. The truth is, there is no explanation for why people are cruel to each other. Don't get yourselves wrapped up in looking for reasons, okay?'

'Okay.' The boys nodded. Alan and Kim stood up and thanked Brenda. Morris had come down and was lurking in the kitchen. Alan had a sneaking suspicion there was a reason Morris Trigg was evasive when they were there. He was polite enough but either suspicious of police officers or frightened by them. That usually meant the individual was up to no good or had a history of criminality. He made a mental note to check him out. They said their goodbyes and walked back to their vehicle. The wind blew in from the sea, cutting through their clothes. They climbed in unaware of the eyes watching them from the industrial units next to the abandoned electronics factory. Their presence and the marked interceptor outside the house were all that was needed to identify where the witnesses lived.

•

Chapter 16

Hal Nelson kissed his wife, Maisy and his two children as they left for the school run. They had been married for ten years, tying the knot before Noah was born. He was conceived on their honeymoon. Their love was total back then, and he couldn't imagine wanting another woman. Maisy was all he'd needed. He found it sad and confusing how his feelings had changed. Maisy had been his childhood sweetheart, but the fire had burnt out many years ago. He hadn't noticed the passion dying. It just happened. Life pisses on the fires of passion. Work, kids, mortgages, extended family, in-laws, niggling arguments about nothing. Becoming familiar. Familiarity breeds contempt. It was true in his case. Maisy wanted to be dressed in designer gear from head to toe, and she treated the kids like a Barbie and Ken doll set. Armani for this and Hugo Boss that. It was exhausting listening to her ever-growing wish list. Maisy began getting on his nerves, moaning all the time about what she couldn't afford to do and why didn't he get a better paid job, and the sexual attraction faded. Realising that the shine had become tarnished over the years was a sad fact of life. It all takes a toll. One day he suddenly realised there was nothing there. He loved her like he loved his sister, but he didn't want to fuck his sister. After years of abstinence and avoiding each other apart from the odd five-minute fumble, he became accustomed to it. Then he got chatting to Naomi, and the hormones began to circulate once again. Desire coursed through his veins, and it felt magical. He couldn't get enough of her, yet he knew it was all superficial at first. Lust. Longing. Yearning. Hunger. They were powerful emotions. Urges. Irresistible itches that needed to be scratched. But it had become so much more than that. Now she was everything. There wasn't a moment when he wasn't thinking about being with her again. It was exciting and it was painful. Guilt was prickling his soul. Passion and pain. Isn't that what living is all about? Feeling the passion made him able to accommodate the pain. The payoff was worth it, but he could see no happy ending in sight. Someone would get hurt along the way. His mother used to say, 'it will all end in tears', and he knew what she meant now.

Hal drove to the base and was stopped at the gate, which never happened. The barrier remained down. His number plate wasn't triggering the entry code. It had been recognised but the barrier remained down. The guard on the barrier waved hello apologetically and frowned. He tapped at the keyboard trying to find out what was wrong. They had seen each other every morning for three years.

'What's the problem?' Hal asked, winding down the window.

'Bear with me a second, Hal,' the guard shouted. He looked baffled as he checked the computer. He was reading the screen with a frown on his face. 'You need to report directly to HR,' the guard said.

'What?' Hal asked. 'Who authorised that?'

'Group Captain McCormack,' the guard said, shrugging. 'The Wicked Witch of the West,' he mouthed.

'What does she want, for fuck's sake,' Hal muttered. He drove through the base until he reached the admin buildings. HR was the last place he wanted to be right now. They were interfering busybodies with fuck all to do except dissect everything to the finest molecule. He parked in the visitor car park and headed for reception. The officer on the desk looked like she was straight out of university. Her uniform was recently out of the packet and still had creases in it. She told him to take a seat without actually looking at him, which was a skill only a receptionist can master. His nerves were on edge. They couldn't know about him and Naomi and it was nothing to do with them. He was worrying unnecessarily. No one could possibly know. Only two people knew. Him and Naomi.

He waited forty-five minutes before being called into one of the interview rooms. Master Clerk Lowry Bracknall was sitting at the desk. Her rank was an administrative one but equivalent to the rank of sergeant major. He had only dealt with her a few times, and she was a ballbreaker with an attitude. Her wife was a stunner, which rankled with some of the more misogynistic rank and file. Bracknall had a file of notes in front of her, a laptop and a tablet. Hal was becoming increasingly curious and concerned as to what this was all about. He couldn't help but feel guilty of something.

'Take a seat, Corporal Nelson,' Bracknall began. 'I need to ask you some awkward questions, which may lead to an investigation.

Flight Sergeant Norris will be taking notes.' The flight sergeant nodded without speaking. She looked at him as if he was something she'd stood in with her best Jimmy Choos on. 'I have to offer you the option of having a witness if you feel you need one?'

'I don't know if I want a witness as I'm not psychic.'

'I don't think that attitude is helpful,' Bracknell said, looking over her glasses.

'I'm not giving you attitude. I don't know why I'm here. I don't know what you want to talk to me about yet,' Hal said. 'Do you think I need a witness?'

'That's up to you, but if we begin and you feel like you want one, we can stop until we find one. Is that acceptable?' she asked, taking off her glasses.

'Whatever,' Hal said, shrugging. 'I haven't done anything wrong so, can we start with what the hell am I doing here when I should be starting my shift?'

'Yes. Let's do that.' Bracknall put on her spectacles and looked over her laptop at him. 'I'll get straight to the issue at hand. There's no point in beating around the bush. You sent a rather inappropriate message to the Air Commodore, Pauline Verwood, last night.'

'Who did?'

'You did.'

'I didn't send any message to the Air Commodore.'

'There's no point in denying it. I have it here.'

'Bullshit.'

'It's a fact.'

'No, it isn't because it didn't happen,' Hal insisted, shaking his head. He folded his arms.

'She made a formal complaint to HR first thing this morning hence we need to investigate it immediately.' Bracknall paused, but Hal just shook his head. 'Do you recall sending the message?'

'No. Because I didn't send it.'

'Were you intoxicated last night?'

'I was working, Einstein. How could I be intoxicated?' Hal asked, incredulous. 'I worked a full shift last night, which I would assume you have checked before you waste my time and yours but you clearly haven't done your homework.' He looked at the two officers. They both blushed. 'You haven't checked, have you?' Hal snorted with disgust. 'You're a joke, Bracknall. I don't recall sending any messages to the Air Commodore because I haven't sent any messages to her. I have no idea what you're talking about,' Hal said, folding his arms again.

'Is this your Facebook account?' Bracknall asked, turning the laptop to face him. He looked at the profile and felt his blood boiling.

'Yes. That's my profile, but I didn't send a message to her or anyone else last night. I was at my desk and as you well know, no social media devices or apps are allowed on shift. Someone's hacked my Facebook.'

'We will need to go through your messages, which will require you to surrender your laptop and mobile phone, so we can verify that,' Bracknall said. 'I've printed off the consent forms here for you to sign. Once we've checked your messaging accounts, we can let you have them back if we decide there is no case to answer.'

'I'm not giving you permission to do jack shit.' The female officers glanced at each other. 'This isn't going as you planned, is it?' Hal asked angrily. 'Cagney and Lacey would be spinning in their graves watching you two perform.' Hal took a deep breath. 'What am I supposed to have sent to her?' he asked.

'That's confidential, I'm afraid.' Bracknall removed her glasses and stared at him. 'But it was highly inappropriate.'

'I'm assuming the content was sexual?'

'Very. And violent. She's considering calling the police.'

'I didn't send her any message so, with respect, she can call whoever she likes,' Hal said. He stood up and pushed his chair under the desk. 'Let's get something straight.' Bracknall frowned at his impertinence. 'Facebook gets hacked all the time. I haven't sent any messages to the Air Commodore, inappropriate or otherwise. I was at my desk from six o'clock until after midnight and my phone was locked in my locker, where it should be. I have no access to social media from my work computer. So, I couldn't have sent any messages. It really isn't rocket science. Basic police work would tell you to look for opportunity, which I didn't have. Means, which I didn't have access to and motive, which I don't have.'

'We will need to verify that by checking your devices.' Bracknell looked embarrassed. 'We can sort this out quickly and without any fuss.'

'Not while I have a hole in my backside.'

'I beg your pardon.'

'You heard me. You're not getting my phone or laptop. Absolutely not in a million years.' Hal shook his head and glared at her. His temper was flaring. 'If you do your research properly, you will find that there is no fucking chance of you getting a warrant for my personal devices unless there's an espionage investigation, in which case MI5 and MI6 would be all over the base like a plague of locusts and they would be asking me the questions with police officers on the door, not you two jokers. You're an admin officer, not Detective Inspector Vera Stanhope, so if there's nothing else you want to accuse me of, then I suggest you and Sergeant Norris fuck off back to your desks and analyse something important, like who takes a shit more often, officers or aircrew. You could do a nice little bar chart and send it to everyone on the base to justify you being here. Or do another line graph. Your line graphs are a personal favourite of mine.' Hal looked at the female officers. Both looked appalled by his behaviour yet remained silent. 'Am I going to be marched to the cells under armed escort?' Bracknall stared at him blankly. 'I gather we're done here?'

'I'm going to take this up with your commanding officer,' Bracknall said angrily. 'Your insolence is astounding,' she added. 'Absolutely astounding.'

'As is your incompetence,' Hal said. 'Put it in an email and copy me into it please,' Hal said. 'If there's anything else, you know where I'll be. At my desk where I was last night.'

Hal stormed out and got into his car. He slammed the door and took a deep breath. Bracknall was glaring at him through the window. Fuck her. Stupid bitch. He started the engine and reversed across the car park too quickly. The dashboard clock said he was nearly an hour late for his shift. He would make it up and stay a little later. His boss was a good friend and would understand the situation. HR were notorious for making mountains out of molehills. He weaved his way across the base, speeding where he knew the CCTV couldn't see him.

The police station was on the edge of the airfield and he could see a trio of jets queueing up on the runway to take off. Their engines were deafening, making his chest vibrate as they taxied to the main runway. He felt the vibration through the steering wheel. It ran through his fingers and wrists, up to his elbows. The vibration increased, and it was difficult to grip the wheel. He looked at the speedo. Forty miles per hour. Well over the base limit, but not enough to cause the violent tremor.

The vibration became a wobble. His knuckles were white now.

The wobble became a violent tug. Then the vehicle lurched to the left, ripping the wheel from his hands. He stamped on the brakes and he heard the sound of metal on concrete. Sparks flew over the bonnet. He ploughed into the back of a silver Mercedes. Steam hissed from the bonnet. The vehicle he had hit was crumpled badly. It was a new silver Mercedes and it took him a few minutes to recognise it. The Mercedes belonged to the Air Commodore.

He looked towards the building where her office was located and he could see her looking out of the window, her hands covering her mouth in horror. Pauline Verwood wasn't a happy woman.

Chapter 17

Father Frank Gamble listened to the ringing, then it clicked to voicemail, just as it had done for the last few days. Father Derek wasn't answering his phone. *He must be on a bender*, Frank thought. He liked a drink and when the pressure was on, he drank more. The bishop was smothering them to the point of suffocation. They literally couldn't move without the pious prick looking over their shoulder. It was becoming oppressive. There was nowhere to hide anymore. Their faces had been all over the television, the news, documentaries, and plastered all over social media. The world and his dog wanted to beat them to smithereens. There was no tolerance of paedophiles even if it was an affliction they were born with. It wasn't as if they'd chosen to be attracted to teenagers. They had no choice in the colour of their eyes, their hair, or skin. No choice in the name they were given or the language they would learn to speak or how tall they would become. Nor could they choose their sexuality. Frank wished he could get an erection watching women twerk on the television or seeing them fornicate on porn channels, but it wasn't his preference. He had been cursed with a sexual attraction that society would not condone, even for a second. Nor would society turn a blind eye anymore as it had once.

He was a marked man, and he was tired of being vilified.

Frank had shaved his hair to a number one and grown a full beard, but the disguise didn't fool everyone. He was asked to leave a local junior football game when one of the officials recognised him. The linesman made a song and dance of asking him to leave the touchline where he was spectating, and some of the parents became very aggressive. One of the mothers spat in his face and kicked him hard in the thigh. She was aiming for his testicles but he managed to twist his body enough for her to miss. It was a painful miss but better than what she had in mind. One of the fathers grabbed him painfully by the wrist and frogmarched him to the car park. When they were behind a van, he punched him hard in the stomach, winding him. Frank had vomited and felt like he was going to choke to death. He hadn't ventured out much since then.

There was no one to talk to but the other priests involved in the scandals. They were dwindling in numbers too. Some of them had just up and left without saying where to and faded into obscurity, probably living somewhere remote under an alias. Some of them had died from illness or plain old age, and some had simply vanished. That was concerning. No one truly vanishes. They leave without saying goodbye or someone takes them away forcefully, murders them and makes sure they cannot be found. Frank was beginning to feel isolated. Isolated and frightened. He was in his mid-sixties and arthritis was creeping through his bones. He could no longer take a cork from a bottle of wine without wincing at the pain. His hands were gnarled and painful. He couldn't defend himself anymore.

Maybe God had removed his health in retaliation for his betrayal of his oaths. Not that he believed in God anymore. He wasn't sure he ever had. If he did exist, then he gifted him with his attraction to teenagers. Fuck him.

Frank tried again but there was no answer. He left a quick message for Father Derek and hung up. A draught touched his skin. He stood up and walked into the kitchen. The back door was open. He was sure he had closed it earlier, but his memory was going the same way as his grip. It was cold. He crossed the kitchen and closed the door, turning the key in the lock. The small bones in his hand screamed at him and pain flared up his arm. Even the simplest things were becoming painful. He turned around and saw a man in a balaclava. He held a large funnel in his hand. In the other, he had a large bucket containing grey powder. He put them onto the kitchen table and took a cylindrical piece of metal from a sheath on his hip. A flick of the wrist extended the telescopic baton to its full length. The metal was dull grey. It looked heavy and deadly.

'Hello, Father Frank,' the man said. 'It's been a long time.'

Chapter 18

Pamela Stone walked into the operations room at Holyhead police station. Her ginger curls were swept into a ponytail. Alan gestured for her to come into his office. Her assistant, Rob Wilkinson, made his way to the coffee machine and chatted to some of the detectives he had worked with. Rob was a Liverpool FC fan and loved to wind up the Man United supporters. Kim made her way from her desk and joined Rob fetching drinks for the meeting. Detective Sergeant Richard Lewis entered operations in a fluster. He was running late. The collar on his dark jacket was sticking up on one side and there was shaving foam behind his left ear. There were more whiskers on his jacket than his chin, but nothing could wipe the smile from his face. His smile was infectious. He'd left home in a hurry but he was there in the nick of time. He weaved his way through the desks with his laptop bag on his shoulder. Alan waved him over. Kim and Rob grabbed their drinks, said their hellos to Richard, and took a seat. Kim closed the door and drowned out the chatter from the operations room, then she straightened Richard's collar. He blushed and thanked her with a nod and a smile. The Major Investigation Team was building up steam on the investigation and more detectives were arriving every hour, drafted from across the North Wales force.

There was some formidable talent in the team.

'Thanks for coming in, Pamela, although I get nervous when you come here to talk to us.'

'Why would I make you nervous?' Pamela asked.

'You have either found something incredible or something really crap that will send the investigation into a tailspin,' Alan said, sitting down. 'I have a fifty-fifty chance of being happy.'

'I don't think that's accurate,' Pamela said, white teeth showing. Mischief twinkled in her eyes. 'Some things are better explained in person, especially to you.'

'What does that mean?' Alan asked, frowning.

'You get narky if I give you bad news over the phone.'

'That's not true.'

'It is very true,' Kim agreed with Pamela.

'One-hundred per cent accurate,' Richard agreed.

'You two are fired,' Alan said.

'Great. I always wanted to work with horses,' Kim said. 'I'll get my coat on the way out.'

'I always wanted to be a farmer,' Richard said. 'I might start a lawn mowing business. Can you give me a lift home?' he asked Kim.

'When you've finished,' Alan said. 'I'm not having you two doing things you enjoy. You will stay here and be miserable with me.' He turned to Pamela. 'Seriously, you never come here with results unless they're really good or really crap.' He sipped his coffee and waited. 'Which is it?'

'It's a bit of both.'

'Come on. Spill the beans. The suspense is killing me,' Alan said, slurping his coffee.

'I'll begin at the beginning. We have cause of death, which is no surprise,' Pamela said, nodding. 'There were fragments of lung tissue remaining. It's badly damaged by both smoke and fire, indicating they were alive when they were thrown into the pit. Obviously, they both burnt to death.'

'Amazing. I don't know how they do it,' Alan said, feigning surprise. He looked at Richard and shook his head. 'How do they do that?'

'It's amazing,' Richard said. 'She gets it every time.'

'Will you two pack it in, please,' Kim said. 'I want to hear what they've found.'

'The fun police are here,' Alan said. He sipped his coffee and ignored Kim's glare. 'Kim wants to know what else have you found?'

'The most baffling things are the two rucksacks,' Pamela said. 'One of the Trigg boys mentioned seeing them on the floor next to the van.'

'Tom said that,' Alan said, nodding.

'If the bags were next to the van when the twins saw them, they must have been tossed into the pit after the boys had gone and the flames had died down somewhat. The exteriors of both bags are melted and shrunk, like a crisp packet in an oven but we managed to cut some of the contents from the remains.'

'Tell me you have an ID and I'll love you forever,' Alan said.

'We have two,' Pamela said, smiling. 'One from each rucksack.' Rob handed out photographs of the remains to the detectives. 'The first image shows partial remains of a bank card, which was melted to a Maltese driving licence and an EU health card issued in Valletta. The bank card is from the Bank of Valletta, obviously Maltese too.'

'Maltese?' Kim said.

'Yes. The second is an EU identity card and a Mastercard cash passport both issued in Bugibba. The names on the cards are Arturo Troisi and Ganni James. Both names are common to the indigenous residents of Malta but all the other details were burnt away.'

'That's great news,' Alan said. 'Kim, get those details to the team. I want to know why they were here, where they were staying, and where they last spent money. Probably backpackers heading for the Irish ferry?'

'Possible. Although Anglesey may have been their destination. That's for you to fathom,' Pamela said. 'There's one problem, hence us coming here to discuss it with you.' Pamela handed out photographs of the recovered skull and the dental work which remained.

'I don't like the sound of that. What is the problem?' Alan asked. He looked at the photographs and frowned.

'We can't extract any DNA from the bones or teeth we recovered, but I can age the victims roughly. Both victims were over fifty at least, probably older. I can tell from the deterioration and thinning of the calcium in the bones. One of the victims had a metal hip. The serial number on the steel joint is registered to a hospital in Gobowen.'

'Gobowen is in Shropshire, right?' Alan asked.

'Yes. There's a specialist orthopaedic hospital there,' Pamela explained.

'So, we can get a name of who the joint was fitted to?' Alan asked.

'Their computerised records only go back to ninety-eight, which means your victim has his hip replaced prior to that. It's rare a hip is replaced on a patient under forty. If you do the maths, the victim could be late sixties, probably older.'

'And not from Bugibba,' Richard added.

'Exactly,' Pamela said, nodding. 'When I add to that the veneers we recovered were of the type manufactured and fitted in Turkey. They're the type commonly used twenty-years ago. I can't marry the rucksacks to the victim's remains with any certainty. There are no dates of birth on the identification we recovered but there were tweezers, a nailfile, and scissors and hair gel in one rucksack and beard oil in the other. Beard oil is something of a new grooming product in the UK although it's been around elsewhere. Some of the clothing remnants appear to be the type worn by cyclists, more akin to younger men. The type of men of an age that might go cycling-backpacking across Europe.'

'So, the rucksacks might not belong to the victims?' Richard asked.

'I'm saying the victims are a mystery as yet,' Pamela said. 'I wouldn't hang the entire investigation on tracing the owners of those documents we've recovered. I know budgets are tight and I don't want you wasting time on them.'

'Okay. Thank you. You're right. We could spend thousands of pounds needlessly. Let's find out how they got into the country, airline or ferries, when they got here and where they've been. If they're not the victims, let's rule them out quickly.' Alan stood up.

'I think the hip joint is telling,' Pamela said. 'If we get anything else, I'll pass it over as we get the results in.'

'Thanks for coming over. I'll call you later for an update.'

Chapter 19

Bob Dewhurst and April Byfelt were driving up the hill away from Porth Dafarch following the report of a missing vehicle. Its tracker had put it in the Trearddur Bay area and a passing interceptor had spotted it during a chase but couldn't stop to investigate. Bob was annoyed that they were given the shout.

'I don't know why you took this shout,' Bob moaned. 'Missing vehicles means paperwork, paperwork, and more paperwork.'

'It's computerised now,' April said.

'It's paperwork without using a pen and I cannot be bothered doing it.'

'It was this, or a peeping Tom in Bodedern,' April said, grinning. 'I know how much you love the sexually deviant side of human nature, so here we are looking for a vehicle.'

'Another peeping Tom in Bodedern?' Bob said, shaking his head. 'I think there is a competition going on. There's a prize for who can make the most unnecessary phone calls to the police in a week,' Bob scoffed. 'The last time it was a tourist looking for his aunt's house on London Road but he went to the wrong London Road. He should have been in Holyhead. The poor bugger was in the back of an interceptor for an hour explaining himself.'

'Hence, I took the missing vehicle shout.'

'It's just a ball ache. Anything to do with insurance companies is a pain. It's not stolen, so who reported it missing?' Bob asked.

'Michael Hughes, asset manager. He's employed by the Church to look after properties and vehicles,' April said, checking her tablet. 'This vehicle is leased by the diocese, and the named driver is Father Derek Corbin. He said he was going fishing. He is getting on and was expected back at the vicarage in Benllech the day before yesterday, but he hasn't shown up and they're getting very worried as to his whereabouts.'

'The day before yesterday?' Bob asked. 'Why the delay?'

'I don't know,' April said. 'The name rings a bell with me.'

'Father Derek Corbin?' Bob asked, frowning. 'Isn't he one of the DI's favourite paedos?'

'The name rings a bell,' April said. 'There are a lot of them on his list, to be fair. It's a very long list.'

'That's his age,' Bob said. 'Your tolerance level lowers as you get older. He's getting close to retirement and his temper is shorter than it used to be.'

'That makes sense. You're old and have zero tolerance and a bad temper,' April said, nodding.

'Bugger off.'

'See what I mean. That's your age showing.'

'I tolerate you, don't I,' Bob muttered, trying not to smile. 'Anyway, Corbin was definitely on the DI's hit list.'

'His hit list is massive. I can't be expected to remember them all.' She shrugged. 'Paedo or not, he's missing and his car is right there,' she said, pointing. They pulled in behind a blue Ford Ka. It was parked with two wheels on the grass verge. They got out and checked around it. 'It's locked and there's no sign of any damage.' She checked the tablet again. 'Michael Hughes said he was going fishing,' she said, gesturing to the stile, which led onto the grange and the cliffs on the coast. 'Mackerel Rock is over there.'

'It is a five-hundred metre walk from here and he's hardly likely to have been fishing for three days.'

'Granted, but we need to check,' April said.

'Let's alert the lifeboat that he may have gone into the water the day before yesterday. They can keep an eye out. If he is in the sea and went down around here, he's due to come up soon over Rhoscolyn way. Probably today.' Bob set off to climb the stile. 'I'll have a look to see if anyone is fishing there today, although it's a complete waste of my time and public funding. And that's on you.'

'Stop moaning. People fish there all the time, don't they?' April said. 'If he left his tackle, it will be long gone by now.'

'Someone would have reported abandoned tackle,' Bob said, disappearing behind the dry-stone wall. 'Abandoned tackle is not a good sign,' he shouted. The wind took his voice away.

'Neither is an abandoned vehicle by the coast,' April shouted back, but Bob didn't reply.

Chapter 20

Maisy Nelson pulled into the car park at Tesco, Holyhead. It was quiet at that time of day and she could get close to the main doors on the top floor. The coffee shop was just inside the entrance and she always called in there before she did her shop. They had decent WIFI and the bacon butties were good. It was a little piece of escapism from the norm of being a wife and mother. Apart from the gym, she didn't really do much outside of the house. She had some friends on the base but not many and people were posted here, there and everywhere at short notice, so friends came and went quickly. It was best not to get too close to anyone. One day they were sipping wine on your patio, the next they were being shipped halfway across the planet. She parked her car and went inside. There was no queue. She ordered a large latte and a bacon sandwich. The cashier told her to take a seat and she would bring her food over. Tesco was the nearest thing to a day out she had. Covid had shut down what little social activity there was and it hadn't recovered since. Maisy was born and bred in Chelsea and she missed the social whirl of her youth where everyone was judged by how much their outfit cost and how big their lips were. It may have been superficial, but it was exciting. Now they lived on Anglesey. It was beautiful but so boring. Yes, the sea was lovely and yes, the mountains were lovely but the highlight of her week was walking around Tesco. Bangor was the nearest city and despite holding the record for the longest high street in the UK, the shopping was limited. In fact, the shopping was Debenhams. The rest were charity shops, betting shops, and cafés. Not that she had designer brand money to spend, anyway. Hal earned peanuts in comparison to what he could have earned in the city. He had wanted to be away from London as soon as he was old enough to join the RAF. Maisy longed to be back there.

Maisy sat down and took out her phone. She had two messages, which was two more than she normally had. She opened her inbox. One was from Jamillia, a casual acquaintance from the gym. She was of Jamaican origin and strikingly beautiful. Her husband was one of the highest-ranking black officers on the base. He was a gym goer and looked like he was carved from jet. They were friendly enough, but she'd never had a text from her before. She opened it with interest, excited it might be an invite to a cheese and wine evening or something social that would get her out of the house. She opened the text message, hoping it was something to look forward to.

Maisy. Your husband sent me several unacceptable text messages last night to my work phone. They were very suggestive. I'm guessing he was drunk. I don't want to cause any problems between you but please tell him never to message me again. If I showed them to my husband, he would kill him.

Maisy read the message three times and felt her stomach tighten with anger. Anger and embarrassment. How could he message another woman? Another married woman. They were rarely intimate anymore but that was his fault. He paid her no attention and made no effort. She thought about ringing him but wasn't sure what to say. Her sandwich arrived and she thanked the waitress and smiled but her appetite was gone. She looked at the second message. It was from her mother. She hadn't heard from her mother for over a year. They had never been close and she didn't like Hal. She didn't have time for the kids and forgot their birthdays and Christmas. They had never had a present from her. Her mother was a drunk and a man-eater. She prowled wine bars on the Kings Road in search of younger men. She bounced from one man to the next, dependent on who was buying her jewellery and alcohol. Hal called her the Merry-Widow. She opened the message and nearly spat her coffee out.

I had a message from your husband last night asking me if I wanted an affair. Apparently, I'm still sexy despite my age and he can feel the chemistry between us. Have you had an argument or has he finally lost his marbles? You really should take better care of your men. Love Mum x

The messages had the ring of truth to them. Why would two people she knew, one of them her mother, send her messages claiming the same thing? Hal had been distant lately. It had crossed her mind something was amiss but she put it down to his work. They were expecting the Red Arrows squadron for a month or two, which always caused a fuss on the base. Photographers, press, and fans of the squadron would encamp around the perimeter fences and cause a security nightmare. Many of them would climb over to get closer to the planes. Hal had been wittering on about it for weeks. She thought that was what was bothering him when clearly he was thinking about other women.

'Hi there,' a voice said, disturbing her thoughts. She looked up into the eyes of Ernie Metcalfe. He was vaguely familiar to her but she couldn't remember his name. He was one of dozens of men she'd met at base barbeques. The introductions were always quick and forgettable. Sergeant-so-and-so. Corporal-this-and-that. Captain-thingy-bob. Flight-something-whatever-his-name-was. She couldn't remember them for more than a few seconds. 'How is Hal?' Ernie asked, feigning concern. Maisy looked confused. 'Sorry. I'm Flight Sergeant Alf Rogers. I work with your husband.' He held out his hand. Maisy shook it. Her eyes were dilated and watery. 'How is Hal feeling?'

'I don't know what you mean?' Maisy said, shaking her head.

'He called in sick yesterday afternoon.' Ernie lied. 'I was just wondering if he is all right?'

'Yes. He's gone to work today. He's fine, thank you.' Maisy felt sick. Hal had gone into work early yesterday. At least, he said he was going into work to do a double for the overtime. What the fuck was going on?

'Excuse me, can I squeeze past you there please?' a voice asked. An elderly couple were struggling to pass.

Ernie moved out of the way for them. They walked behind him and he stepped towards Maisy. He nudged the table hard with his leg and dropped his coffee. It hit the table and splashed all over Maisy's arms and face. Her jacket was covered in froth. Maisy's cup toppled from its saucer and her drink spilled all over the table and her legs.

'Oh, for fuck's sake!' Maisy snapped. She stood up and glared at Ernie. 'Look at the state of me.'

'I'm so sorry,' Ernie said, grabbing napkins and handing them to her. 'That couple nudged me and I lost balance. I can't apologise enough.' He went to the condiment station and grabbed more napkins. The waitress came over. 'Can you replace both drinks, please, and I'll pay for them,' Ernie said. 'Why don't you use the sink in the ladies to dab your jacket and make sure it doesn't stain. I'll wipe the table dry.' He began cleaning up frantically. 'I'm so sorry.'

'I don't believe this,' Maisy said, wiping her jeans with a tissue. 'Not one drink, but two. That just about sums up my luck.'

'I'm so sorry,' Ernie said. 'I've ordered you another coffee.' Maisy walked away without speaking. She was pissed off and didn't hide it. Her stare could turn a man to stone. If Medusa had descendants, she was one of them. She disappeared into the toilets. 'Sour faced bitch. No wonder your husband is fucking my wife,' Ernie muttered beneath his breath. He reached over and looked into her handbag. No one was sitting at the nearby tables. He did what he needed to do and threw the soaking napkins into the bin. The waitress bought two lattes over, one in a cup and one in Styrofoam. Ernie paid for them and tipped her for her troubles. He sipped his latte and waited for Maisy to return.

'I'm so very sorry,' he repeated. 'Here is another coffee and if you need anything dry-cleaned, tell Hal to let me know how much it costs and I'll reimburse you.'

'There's no need,' Maisy said. 'Thank you for replacing my coffee.'

'Honestly. If there's anything I can do?'

'No. Thank you.' Maisy couldn't maintain eye contact with him. Ernie was well aware he was annoying her.

'I feel like I've annoyed you,' Ernie said. He looked at her in the eyes but she couldn't hold his stare. 'Are you annoyed with me?'

'No,' Maisy said. Her face reddened, and she sipped her latte. Ernie didn't budge. 'I'm not annoyed.'

'You should tell your face that,' Ernie said, grinning.

'I beg your pardon,' Maisy said, confused.

'If you're not annoyed, you should tell your face that,' Ernie repeated. His smile disappeared, and his expression became blank. 'You face doesn't know you're not annoyed.' Ernie pointed to her face. 'Your face tells me that you're fucked off because I knocked over a couple of drinks.' He shrugged. 'It's not the end of the world, darling,' Ernie said, shaking his head. 'Smile. You might crack your face.'

'I'll smile when there's something to smile about,' Maisy said as calmly as she could. The man was scaring her. 'I'll tell Hal you were asking about him and thanks again for replacing my drink.'

'Oh, that's no problem. Nice to see you again,' Ernie said, walking away with a quick wave and his takeaway coffee. 'Give my regards to Hal.'

Maisy didn't reply. She couldn't find any words. Alf whatever-his-name-was, went down the travelator and was gone from her view and she couldn't be more relieved. What a strange man he was. She thought about following him and asking him about Hal not being in on a double shift yesterday, but there was no way she wanted a conversation with the man. He was a weirdo. Anyway, Hal had told her he was going in early and told work he wasn't going in. He was obviously lying to her and there could only be one reason why he would lie about where he was and that was because he was with another woman. Maisy felt lost and lonely. She wished she could talk to her mum, but she was crazy and Hal had messaged her too. How low could a man sink? To proposition his wife's mother was beyond betrayal. It reeked of desperation and a lack of respect and any sense of consideration for the damage he had caused by approaching her in the first place. Her mother had a warped moral compass. Maybe he saw her as vulnerable and likely to jump into bed with him without much argument. She needed to talk to someone. The only friend she had on the base was Caroline Greenman. She was a nurse in Bangor and had gone to the convent school in Holyhead when she was a child. Maisy scrolled to her number and dialled. She picked up her coffee and moved to an empty table where no one could overhear her conversation. It rang a dozen times. She was about to hang up when Caroline answered.

'I was just thinking about you,' Caroline said. 'How are you?'

'Pissed off,' Maisy said. 'You will not believe what's happened this morning. I don't believe it myself.'

'Is it anything to do with Hal sexting people?'

'For fuck's sake,' Maisy said, sighing. 'How do you know?'

'I've just been to the gym and Jamillia Squire was showing everyone in the changing room the text messages Hal sent to her last night.'

'Oh no.'

'Oh, yes. Was he drunk?'

'He was at work, allegedly, but one of his work colleagues has just asked me if he's feeling better. Apparently, he called in sick yesterday,' Maisy said, her voice breaking. 'I can't believe Jamillia was showing people in the gym.'

'The whole island will know by now,' Caroline said. 'I didn't know you guys were struggling.'

'Neither did I,' Maisy said. 'What did his messages say?'

'You don't want to know,' Caroline said. 'The man has a screw loose if you ask me.' Caroline went quiet. 'You do know it wasn't just Jamillia, don't you?'

'No. Please don't tell me he messaged someone else.'

'He messaged Pauline Verwood,' Caroline said. 'She's the Air Commodore, which to me and you, means she's so far up the ladder we can't even see her.'

'I don't want to hear this.'

'She has put a formal complaint into HR. Between me and you, Hal is right in the shit. What was he thinking?'

'God knows,' Maisy said. 'He messaged my mum.'

'What?' Caroline asked, astounded. 'He didn't sext her?'

'He did,' Maisy said. 'I won't be able to go into the gym ever again. It's the only place I go. He's crossed the line. I feel like taking the kids and fucking off back to London.'

'I don't know what to say to you,' Caroline said. 'Have you spoken to him?'

'Not yet.'

'He may have an explanation.'

'Like what?'

'I don't know,' Caroline said. 'Dementia?'

'I'm going to kill him,' Maisy said. 'I can't think straight.'

'Where are you?'

'Tesco café,' Maisy said.

'I'll meet you at the Black Seal,' Caroline said. 'We can have a large gin and put things into perspective.'

'Okay. I'll be an hour,' Maisy said.

Chapter 21

Hal Nelson watched the truck pull his vehicle away from the rear of the Mercedes. The boot of the Merc was folded like a concertina and the doors wouldn't open. It looked like a write-off. Some of his colleagues from the base police force were taking statements. There wasn't much he could say. He had driven into a stationary vehicle. Hal felt drained of energy. The morning had been a disaster and gone from bad to worse. His encounter with HR was as baffling as it was concerning. Of all the cars on the base he could have hit, it was this one. Not only did it belong to Pauline Verwood, a senior officer, it belonged to a senior officer who was convinced he was a massive pervert who had sent her lewd messages the previous night. Whichever way he played this, he would look like a complete arsehole.

The mechanic pointed to the passenger side front wheel and beckoned Hal over. He sucked in air between his teeth and shook his head frowning, as only a mechanic can. His expression said, this will be fucking expensive, mate.

'That's the problem right there,' he said. 'You had a blowout. The tyre literally exploded. There's a screw in the tyre, so it would have been a slow burn, deflating as the tyre got hot then, bang, a massive blowout.'

'A screw in the tyre caused all this?'

'Don't underestimate a screw in the tyre, pal.' The mechanic shook his head again. 'A screw in the tyre is a real bugger up the back. It would explain what you experienced before the crash. The vibration and pulling the steering wheel from your hands. There was nothing you could have done about it.' He took a closer look. Hal followed him. He shook his head and walked around the vehicle, checking each tyre with interest. 'This is very strange. Very strange indeed. Have you been doing any building at home?'

'Building?' Hal asked, confused.

'Yes. Carpentry or something with wood?'

'No,' Hal said.

'Have you been on a construction site recently?'

'No.' Hal didn't have the energy to enquire why he was asking stupid questions. He could see people nosing through the windows. The Commodore's staff were obviously aware of the accident outside their office. Pauline Verwood was clearly fuming. She had come out of her building with a look of horror on her face. The look she gave Hal would have withered the strongest man. It was pure hatred and contempt. Believing he had sent her a disgusting message the night before hadn't helped. She clearly thought the accident wasn't an accident. He felt helpless. There was nothing he could say that wouldn't make him appear to be guilty and making ridiculous excuses for his inappropriate behaviour. He wanted the ground to open up and swallow him. 'I haven't been on any building sites and I don't do DIY.'

'In which case, I don't understand the screws, I'm afraid,' the mechanic said, shaking his head again. Deep lines furrowed his brow, a confused expression on his face.

'Surely, a screw in the tyre is a good thing from an insurance point of view?' Hal said.

'A screw in the tyre is a good thing?' the mechanic asked, baffled. 'How does that work?'

'Because it means it was an accident.' Hal shrugged and raised his hands in question. 'Look. I'm late and all I need to know is that it's clear to everyone that this was an accident?' Hal asked. All he needed was the mechanic to say was, 'yes' and he could go to work and carry on as normal. This was a coincidence. A terrible coincidence. The insurance companies would fix everything, and he would avoid the Air Commodore for the rest of his life. Pauline Verwood could hate him forever. It didn't matter. He would never have to work directly with her, and he could avoid her socially.

'I can't say this was an accident. You have screws in every tyre, pal,' the mechanic said, shaking his head. 'The thing with screws is they keep the air inside the tyre until the rubber gets hot. Then the tyre explodes.'

'I don't understand what you're saying,' Hal said, sighing.

'This looks deliberate to me. It was just a matter of time until one of them blew. You could have been doing seventy on the motorway, in which case we would be scraping you off the seats.

Unless you've been building something at home or visited a building site, this wasn't an accident. Someone has got it in for you.' The mechanic shrugged. 'Have you got a family, pal?'

'Yes,' Hal said. 'Wife and two kids.'

'The kids wouldn't do this, thinking it was a joke?'

'Of course not.'

'They could have been in the back of this when one of those tyres blew,' he said, lowering his voice. 'You need to get onto the police, pal.'

'I am the police,' Hal said.

'I mean the real police,' the mechanic said. 'Not you Mickey Mouse RAF officers. You can't do fuck all off this base.' He shook his head again and frowned. 'Get the police involved. You could have been killed.'

Hal took a deep breath and closed his eyes. This was karma paying him back for being a cheating bastard. It had to be something to do with Ernie Metcalfe. His phone being wiped, the lewd messages being sent to senior base personnel. Who else could be responsible? Why would anyone else bother?

'I'm going to take it to whichever garage your insurance company specifies. I'll call you when I know which one. In the meantime, you need to tell the police, pal.' He winked. 'And get yourself to the hospital. You look like you have whiplash to me. Could be a few grand in it for you. Every cloud has a silver lining.'

'I've got enough to deal with without fraud thrown in,' Hal said. 'Take it to the garage and forget you ever met me.'

'Suit yourself,' the mechanic said, using a winch to drag his vehicle onto a low-loader. 'There's no helping some people. You need to watch your back, pal.'

'I will,' Hal said, walking away. He went into the building where the Air Commodore worked and left his insurance details with her secretary. That was a frosty conversation if ever there was one. The secretary eyed him like he was a sex offender, waiting for the chance to pounce on her. It was clear the offending message had been shown to members of her staff. All the evidence in the world wasn't going to clear his reputation. Shit sticks. He could feel the anger bubbling away beneath the surface. Ernie Metcalfe must be responsible, but if he was, how could he challenge him without waving a flag saying he had been fucking his wife? He needed to speak to Naomi. Quickly.

Chapter 22

Father Frank was in agony. All his transgressions were being paid for in full today. Today was the day he was going to die. He looked at the bucket. There were a few inches of cement left. He had been forced to drink the rest. The lye in the cement was acidic and it was burning the flesh it touched. His stomach felt like it was on fire. The liquid was beginning to harden in his stomach, forming a swelling, solid mass. It burnt the flesh in his mouth and throat and the weight was beginning to rupture the delicate tissue around it. His attacker had told him it would be painful and that he would enjoy watching him suffer. Frank had refused to drink it at first, but the alternative was having his genitals cut off with garden shears. Frank would rather die with his bits and pieces attached to him. He had asked his attacker why he wanted him to drink cement and he explained it would kill him very painfully and stop his body from resurfacing when he threw him into the sea. The weight of the cement trapped in his abdominal cavity would hold him to the seabed until he eventually rotted away and was devoured by the bottom feeders.

Frank didn't care what came after death, but he wanted his time on Earth to end now, this second. The pain was excruciating. He couldn't cope with it. Every nerve ending was on fire and the pain burnt from his fingertips to his toes. Even his teeth hurt. There was no escape from the torment. He wondered if the suffering would continue after his heart had stopped beating. His misery was beyond torture, beyond anguish. It was a living hell.

'You look like you're struggling, Father Frank,' the man said, watching him. He was eating a bag of salt and vinegar crisps and drinking a glass of water from the tap. The same tap he had used to mix the cement. He took out his phone and began filming again. Frank could hardly breathe. 'Come on,' the man said. 'Let's get the rest of this cement drunk. I don't want you snuffing it before we're done. My dad would be spinning in his grave if he thought I was going to fuck this up.' Father Frank opened his eyes and tears ran freely from them.

'I can't take any more,' Frank said, his voice a whisper. 'Just kill me and be done with it.'

'No way, paedo,' the man said. 'You're going to suffer until the last breath.'

The man tipped the bucket to Frank's lips and poured the grey sludge into his mouth. Frank couldn't swallow any more of it and it ran down his chin onto his chest.

'Why?' Frank whispered.

'You know why, paedo. You knew my old dad. You killed him. You and your scumbag mates. You make me puke. He'll be watching this with a smile on his face, you dirty old bastard. I hope he is. If there is a God, he is watching. I would give anything to tell him what happened to you.' The man put the bucket down next to the baton on the table. He picked up the rose pruners and clicked them open and closed menacingly. 'It's time to cut your cock and bollocks off,' the man said matter-of-factly. 'I've been looking forward to this. This will be an Internet sensation.'

'But you said…'

'Yes. I said if you drank the cement, I wouldn't cut your nuts off but I lied,' the man said, grinning. 'You lied to my dad, and you lied to dozens of other kids. Not nice, is it?'

'Please just kill me.' Frank shook his head in submission. His expression pleaded for mercy. It begged for an end to the pain.

'It's a terrible thing being in pain and having no control over when it begins or ends, isn't it?' The man switched on his camera and zoomed in on Frank's face. He filmed him sobbing for the pain to end. 'Seeing you suffer is like watching the most riveting film ever made. I don't want to blink and miss a single moment. When I upload this, the world is going to see what should happen to paedophiles like you. They need to realise we're coming for them all. Us and people like us. And when they do realise what's going to happen, not a single one of you will sleep tight in your beds ever again.'

Chapter 23

Naomi felt her phone vibrating. She'd put it on silent to be on the safe side. Something had happened to it overnight, and she suspected her husband had something to do with it. Ernie was behaving in a strange manner and she was frightened. Frightened that he knew she'd cheated, and frightened of what he was going to do about it. She was convinced he suspected something. There had been a paradigm shift in his behaviour towards her. He had forced her to have sex several times in the last twenty-four hours, and the sex was different. He was animalistic and rough. She had scratches and bite marks all over her. It was as if he was trying to hurt her purposely. There was no other explanation for what he was doing, yet he hadn't actually accused her of anything. Not knowing one way or the other was torment.

He told her he would slit her throat if he found out she was sleeping with someone else. He had never said anything like that before so, why say it now that she was, unless he knew? It was too much of a coincidence.

'I will slit your throat if I catch you fucking another man,' he had said. He never called it fucking. Not ever.

She looked at the screen. The number calling was withheld. She was wary of answering the call, but she was hoping Hal would try to contact her. She needed to talk to him even if it was dangerous. She had no idea who was calling. Her phonebook had been wiped, which was another indication that Ernie was on to them but the question she kept on asking was how could he know?

'Hello,' she answered.

'Can you talk?' Hal asked. He sounded stressed.

'Oh my God,' Naomi said, her voice breaking. 'I'm so glad you called. I've been going demented. Everything has fallen to pieces.'

'What's happened?' Hal asked.

'I think he knows about us.'

'Ernie?'

'Yes Ernie. Who else would I be talking about?' Naomi snapped. Hal didn't bite at the remark, but he noted her short temper. 'Ernie has gone strange on me. He's behaving weirdly. I don't know what he's thinking at all. It's been an absolute nightmare.'

'Where is he?' Hal asked.

'He's gone out for a while. He said he had to go and see someone. I don't know who,' Naomi said. She felt tears forming in her eyes. 'I've been so frightened. I think he knows about us.'

'What makes you think that?'

'The way he's behaving. He's clearly on edge but pretending not to be. I haven't seen him like this since he came back from tour. I didn't know what to say or do. He said so many weird things.'

'Has he mentioned my name?'

'No. He hasn't actually said he knows about you, but I can't explain his behaviour any other way. What else can it be?'

'I think you're right,' Hal said, sighing. 'There's been a lot of weird stuff happening to me too. I think he got a hold of my phone.'

'When?'

'Yesterday. My locker was tampered with while I was working and some people have had abusive messages from me, which I didn't send.'

'What people?' Naomi asked, confused.

'Pauline Verwood. The Air Commodore for one. She's put in a complaint,' Hal said. 'HR called me into the office this morning and grilled me about messages sent to her on Facebook Messenger. Apparently, they're of a sexual nature.'

'That's how you first messaged me,' Naomi muttered.

'What?'

'You sent your first message to me on Messenger.'

'What has that got to do with anything?'

'I'm just saying. She's very attractive, and that's how you approached me.'

'I don't see the relevance of how attractive she is. Are we still talking about your husband losing his marbles, or are you asking me if I've sent her a flirtatious message?'

'Well, you sent me one,' Naomi said, feeling strangely jealous.

'Don't go off on one,' Hal said. 'I haven't sent any messages to anyone.'

'But they were definitely from your phone?' Naomi asked.

'Yes. They appear to be. That's the point. I think he has tried to drop me in the shit and then reset my phone.'

'That would explain a lot. All my apps have been wiped from mine. That can't be a coincidence,' Naomi said.

'It's not a coincidence. It can't be.'

'He's behaving irrationally. I can see his brain ticking over but he hasn't confronted me. The things he's been saying are just off the wall.'

'Like what?'

'He's been talking about our future bringing up the girls and how important it is' – Naomi paused – 'He went on and on about how much it was going to cost for college and university and weddings and how he would have to work until his retirement and how much his parents do for us.' Naomi paused to think. 'He said he would cut my throat and make me disappear if he finds out I've been sleeping with another man.' She paused again. 'But he didn't say it so nicely.'

'He threatened your life?' Hal asked, astounded. 'The man is a nutcase. He had a meltdown and threw a watercooler at the flight sergeant last night.'

'Oh my God,' Naomi said, shocked. 'He didn't say anything about that to me. I wondered what was going on when he came home early.'

'And someone has put screws in my tyres,' Hal said. 'I'll give you two guesses who that was.'

'Why would he do that?'

'Because he's fucking nuts.' Naomi didn't reply. 'Why did he say he was home early?'

'He said he's taking some leave. I've been beside myself because I haven't been able to call you. I feel like he knows and he's watching me, waiting to catch me out.' The line went quiet. 'How could he know about us, Hal?'

'I don't know,' Hal replied. 'Could he have seen any messages on your phone?'

'God no,' Naomi said, shaking her head. 'I deleted all that rude stuff we were saying yesterday. It made me blush just writing it. I wouldn't leave anything like that on my phone.'

'Wait a minute, Naomi,' Hal interrupted her. 'What rude stuff?'

'The stuff we were messaging after you left here and went to work,' she said. 'It was way too rude to leave on my phone. Did you delete it from your phone?'

'What time was this text conversation?'

'I don't know,' Naomi said. 'Early evening, I suppose. Don't you remember what you were saying?' she asked, blushing. 'It made me very embarrassed. I haven't texted like that before.'

'Naomi. I didn't send you any rude text messages,' Hal said, sighing.

'What do you mean you haven't sent me messages?'

'My phone has to go into my locker when I start a shift,' Hal said. 'We're not allowed to have a mobile phone at our workstation. I didn't send you any messages.'

'Oh fuck,' Naomi said. 'Do you think…'

'Ernie was using my phone,' Hal said. 'It would explain everything. What exactly did you say to him?'

'It was rude,' Naomi said.

'What did you say exactly?'

'All sorts of rude stuff. Your texts were asking me what I liked the most and what had turned me on and what made me orgasm. I was a bit coy at first.'

'At first?'

'Yes. But I got into it and it was very rude,' Naomi mumbled. 'Almost pornographic.' She went quiet.

'You've gone quiet. What are you thinking?'

'I mentioned doing the anal thing,' Naomi said, lowering her voice as if someone could hear her. She paused and sighed. He could hear her sobbing, but didn't speak. 'It explains everything.'

'What do you mean?'

'When he took me upstairs. It was awful. He has never tried to do that before.'

'What do you mean?'

'I don't know how to say this. He's been demanding things we have never done before. Things that me and you did.' She took a deep breath. 'Oh my God, I practically told him what we've been doing, and it was him on the other end, not you. How could I be so stupid?'

'You weren't to know,' Hal said.

'He knows everything. I was texting him thinking it was you.' Naomi broke down. She was almost hysterical. Hal listened and it was heartbreaking.

'Tell me what happened when he left work and arrived home yesterday,' Hal said. Naomi gathered herself a little.

'He came home early from work last night all romantic with wine and a takeaway, and he practically forced himself on me. He basically dragged me to the bedroom, and he wanted the type of sex I mentioned in the text messages,' Naomi said, sniffling. She spared him the gory details. 'He wanted sex today as well. We never do it two days on the trot. It can be months. I avoid it. But he was different. I didn't know how to say no to him.' The line remained quiet. 'It's been an absolute nightmare. Just being near him is making me feel sick. I don't think I can do this.'

'Do what?' Hal asked.

'Be normal when nothing is normal anymore.'

'We have to stay quiet,' Hal said. 'He's playing games with us but he hasn't confronted either of us.'

'Why do you think that is?'

'Because he doesn't want anyone else to know, and he thinks he can cause trouble for me and make me think it's not worth the trouble. Then he can rescue your relationship.'

'But he can't,' Naomi said, crying. 'It's too late for that. I never intended this to be anything more than what it was. Just two people sharing intimacy with someone. I was flattered by the attention and excited by the secrecy. I didn't think it would go this far. My feelings towards Ernie have changed completely. I can't pretend this hasn't happened.'

'What are you saying?' Hal asked.

'I don't know,' Naomi said. 'But I know that I can't let him go on playing this game, pretending we're fine. Does he think forcing me into the bedroom is going to fix everything that's broken?'

'I have no idea what he's thinking.'

'It's gone too far to go back,' Naomi said. 'There is no going back. I'm going to face up to what we've done.'

'Wait a minute. Are you thinking of confronting him with this?' Hal asked. His voice was full of caution.

'What else can I do?'

'Slow down a bit. We need to tread carefully. Ernie Metcalfe is not a well-balanced individual. Everyone on the base knows he's a ticking time bomb. He goes off at the slightest thing. He might be your husband and still in love with you, but that doesn't mean he's not a danger to us. He put screws in my fucking tyres. I could have had the kids in the car when it blew.'

'You can't know that was him,' Naomi said. 'Surely, it could have been an accident.'

'Like sending messages from my phone was an accident?' Hal said. 'He's being very devious and devious is dangerous.'

'I've never thought of Ernie as dangerous,' Naomi said, her voice drifting slightly. 'Not until yesterday. It was as if a switch has been flicked inside him and a different Ernie was turned on.'

'Whatever you choose to do, I'll be behind you,' Hal said. 'But we need to be careful.'

'I think it might be too late to be careful,' Naomi said. 'We clearly weren't careful enough.'

'I need to think about our next step. We can't just rush into anything.'

'We need to have a plan. What are we going to do?'

'Maisy and the kids are my concern. They are innocent in all this. I don't want them hurt.' Hal sounded distant. 'You know how it works on this base. The kids at school can be cruel. If this gets out, we'll be the talk of the base for months. I don't want my kids vilified for what I've done.'

'And what about my children, Hal?' Naomi asked, annoyed. 'Do you think I want them to know what I've been doing behind their father's back?' She paused to calm down. 'They absolutely idolise their father and they're not stupid. The eldest is becoming sexually aware. They would never forgive me. And as for his parents, they would never talk to me again in ten lifetimes. I appreciate Maisy and your children are your priority, but they weren't top of your mind when you were fucking me, were they?'

'There's no need for that,' Hal said, surprised by her tone.

'The truth hurts, doesn't it,' Naomi said. 'You can't back out and take your ball home now. You're in this up to your neck, wife and kids or not.'

'I'm not dodging the blame. I'm saying there is no need for what you said,' Hal protested.

'I think there's every need for it. It's true,' Naomi said.

'Naomi, I'm not saying my concerns are more important than yours,' Hal said. 'I'm thinking aloud.'

'Maybe you shouldn't,' Naomi said. Fear was taking control of her emotions. Her barriers were coming back down. 'We're both as much to blame in this.'

'I know that and I'm not pointing the blame at you. I don't understand how he suspected us in the first place,' Hal said.

'I don't think that matters one iota. It's inconvenient my husband has found out and not your wife, but it was really just a matter of time before one of them did. Now, they will both know and so will everyone else. We need to try to limit the damage as much as we can,' Naomi said, sniffling. 'The cat is out of the bag and we need to deal with it.'

'How do you propose we do that?' Hal asked, his head in his hands. He couldn't see any easy way out of the situation. 'I'm open to ideas because I haven't got any of my own.'

'That's helpful,' Naomi said. She took a deep breath. Her heart was banging like a drum in her chest. Ernie would be back soon and he would look into her eyes, into her head, into her soul, and he would know that she'd spoken to Harold Nelson. He would know. 'I think we both need wiggle room. Time to think what's best for our families.'

'Don't be hasty. Let's think this through.'

'We should have thought it through before we got into bed with each other. That was the time for thinking, not now.'

'What we have is special. This isn't just a fling,' Hal said. 'I'm in love with you, Naomi. I can't walk away and not see you again.'

'Are you prepared to leave Maisy and your children and set up home with me and mine and deal with all the fallout that would cause?' Naomi challenged him, sarcasm in her voice. Hal didn't answer. 'I didn't think so. If you want me then I come with baggage and conditions and three children. You need to be careful before you start bandying the love word around. We're not a couple of love-struck teenagers. We have lives to protect or destroy.'

'I'm not sure you're thinking straight,' Hal said.

'I'm thinking as straight as I can at the moment.'

'We can't start to think about setting up home, kids or otherwise. One step at a time,' Hal said.

'We don't have the luxury of taking our time with this. There is no transition time to be had. My husband knows we've been fucking and your wife will know soon, if she doesn't already know. Those are the unfortunate facts we are facing. What happens next is anyone's guess, but it's not going to be pleasant.'

'What are you saying?'

'I'm saying we end it now. Delete my number and this call from your phone log and I'll do the same. Don't try to contact me under any circumstances no matter what happens.' She waited for a response but there was none. 'I mean it. Do not try to get in touch with me. I'm going to play along with him and keep him from flipping his lid until he's ready to confront me and by then, we may be able to discuss the situation like adults, not crazy people.'

'What about us?'

'What about us?' Naomi asked. 'I have nowhere to go and three daughters to think about. Ernie will throw me out and I'm not going anywhere without my children. We would be out on the street and I'm not going to take them to a refuge or worse. I have no money of my own, no family to turn to and no options. My children need their father in their life.'

'What about me?'

'You were my only other option but you've shown your true colours.'

'That's not fair.'

'Fair?' Naomi said. 'We've betrayed our partners and disgraced ourselves and our kids. That's hardly fair on them, is it? Nothing about it is fair. You're more concerned about how this will affect Maisy, so I clearly can't count on you,' Naomi said, coldly. 'This is for the best in the long run. We both have too much to lose and with hindsight, this was a huge mistake. I don't know what we were thinking.'

'Naomi. Listen to me for a moment.'

'No, Hal,' Naomi said. 'That's how I got myself into this terrible mess in the first place. Do as I ask and leave me alone for your sake and the sake of your family. If you have any feelings for me, you'll do that. I don't want to see you again. Not ever.'

Chapter 24

Father Frank Gamble was terrified. Not terrified of death, terrified of what life he had left. He wanted an end to the pain. His attacker was holding pruning shears and intended to cut off his genitals with them. The world was warping into a bizarre nightmare. He could feel his insides dissolving and the cement hardening. His breathing had become shallow and laboured, and he knew he was close to death. He wanted to take the final step and be away from the torture.

'Undo your trousers,' his attacker ordered. Father Frank shook his head. His hands were in his lap, fastened together with cable ties. He could see the silver blades of the shears glinting. They were curved and sharp and frightening. The thought of them anywhere near his testicles made him want to scream in terror. 'Don't make this difficult, you dirty old bastard. It's time to pay your dues. You weren't slow in getting your tackle out to abuse the youngsters like my dad. Now it's time to answer for it. I'm not going to ask you again. Undo your trousers or I'll make it worse.'

'No,' Father Frank muttered. His attacker moved towards him, focused on removing his clothing and then his bits and pieces. The man bent low and reached for the priest's waist. Father Frank glanced around for help. He focused on the table. Maybe God hadn't deserted him just yet. He grabbed the metal baton from the table and raised it above his head. He brought it down with every last ounce of energy he could muster. It struck his attacker on the back of his head and cracked his skull like an egg. The man toppled forward, a surprised expression on his face. He fell in a heap at the priest's feet. Father Frank raised the baton again and hit the attacker as hard as he could. He felt his attacker's spine snap at the base of his neck. He staggered to his feet and grabbed his mobile, and then collapsed onto his back. The pain was unbearable. He made the emergency call, his voice a whisper, and then the world went black.

Chapter 25

Kim knocked on the door of Alan's office and opened it before he could speak. He was on the telephone, looking surprised at something. His eyebrows were raised, his eyes wide. Kim waited for him to beckon her into a seat but he didn't. She listened to a one-sided conversation before he hung up. Alan shrugged and dropped his pen onto the desk with a clatter.

'Well, I never get surprised anymore but today, I am surprised,' he said. 'Just when you think something is put to bed, it jumps right back up and bites you on the arse.'

'That obviously means something to you but for those of us living outside of your head, we haven't got a fucking clue what you're talking about,' Kim said, putting a coffee in front of him. She sat down and sipped her own. 'What are you so surprised about?'

'That phone call. Have a guess who that was,' he said, shaking his head and drinking his coffee.

'I don't know.'

'Guess.'

'Ryan Giggs asking you to play for Wales?' Kim said, shrugging.

'Giggs has been suspended from duty accused of assaulting his ex-missus and her sister, so it can't be him,' Alan said, frowning.

'Who's in charge then?' Kim asked.

'I have no idea,' Alan said, frowning. 'Why do you need to know that?'

'Just asking,' Kim said.

'If you're not going to take this seriously, just ask me who it was on the phone. Don't make a silly guess. You'll just embarrass yourself.'

'You told me to guess, and you're my boss,' Kim said. 'Who was it?'

'Seeing as though you asked nicely, it was DS Michaels from Caernarfon,' Alan said. 'DS Michaels doesn't share information unless she has a gun to her head and then she won't share anything useful. She shares all the useless shitty bits. Her department is tighter than a lady duck's whoopsie.' He slurped his coffee. 'I'm not going to ask you to guess what she was calling about because you will never get the answer right.'

'Okay. I won't guess. Just tell me.'

'Caernarfon CID had a call from a lady called Florence Mills, who lives near Trefor on the other side of Caernarfon,' Alan said. 'Florence Mills is married to George Mills, who is an ex-copper, which isn't significant except to explain her surname,' he said. Kim looked baffled, but was used to his confused mind-mapping. He often went around the houses to get to the point. 'Her maiden name is Blackstone.'

'Okay,' Kim said.

'Blackstone. Does that ring a bell?'

'Blackstone, Blackstone, Blackstone…' Kim said, thinking aloud. 'It does ring a bell but it's not coming to me. Don't tell me.' She held up her hand to stop him speaking. 'Rupert Blackstone,' she said, grinning. 'He's on your hit list.' Alan nodded. 'Your very long list of paedophiles you want to lock-up.'

'You're nearly right,' Alan said. 'He was on my hit list,' Alan added.

'Was?' Kim asked. 'Is he dead?'

'From the information DS Michaels has just shared with me, we can only assume so,' Alan said, typing on his computer keyboard. 'Detective Superintendent Michaels has kindly sent me a link to a video, which has been uploaded to a paedophile hunting group called the Justice Asylum.' Alan shrugged. 'The name means nothing to me. Have you heard of them?'

'I can't say I have,' Kim said, shaking her head. 'Richard is the expert at following online stuff. I haven't heard him mention them.'

'The DS reckons they were set up in the aftermath of the Father Patrick Creegan case,' Alan explained. 'Apparently, they were making a lot of noise and empty threats at first, but there have been several violent incidents over the past six months or so, all of them on her patch. Caernarfon, Trevor, Abersoch, and as far south as Harlech and Barmouth.' He sat back and folded his arms. 'The incidents seem to have been escalating in their frequency and ferocity.'

'What has Rupert Blackstone got to do with this group?' Kim asked.

'It's all on the video. She warned me that this isn't pleasant. Let's take a look, shall we,' Alan said, turning his screen so they could both see it. The website looked professional and active. They could see pictures and posts being uploaded as they watched. Most of them were images of local men recently convicted of sex crimes from across North Wales. The general reaction of the members was to promise to beat the crap out of them the next time they were spotted. If everyone did what they said they were going to do, the local glazing companies would be busy. Alan clicked on the video he wanted and pressed play.

The camera focused on an elderly man in a chair. Alan recognised him as Father Rupert Blackstone. A priest who had avoided any serious repercussions for his loathsome behaviour over decades. Blackstone had managed to avoid photographs and videos somehow, and the evidence against him was verbal and uncorroborated. He had been careful to attack victims alone and not part of the wider group, hence there were no witnesses. Alan despised him and had tried to move mountains to find enough evidence to convict him. He had failed to meet the threshold for prosecution. The CPS tossed his case into the no further action bin.

Blackstone looked beaten and battered. He was clearly distressed and terrified. Blood ran from his nose and his eyes were blue and purple and so swollen they were almost closed. His lips were quivering in fear and pain. Alan almost had sympathy for him.

Almost, but not quite. Two men came into shot, wearing balaclavas and surgical gloves. One of them was holding an orange bucket from a popular DIY superstore. It appeared to contain a grey liquid with a thicker viscosity than water.

'What the hell is that?' Kim asked, tilting her head. The men grabbed Blackstone by the hair and chin and tilted his head back, forcing his mouth open. The audio was missing, but it was obvious the men were shouting at the priest. The priest was struggling as much as his bindings would allow. One of them punched Blackstone in the genitals and his resistance faltered. They forced his head back and opened his mouth, and poured the grey sludge into him. 'Is it cement?'

'I think so,' Alan said, nodding. They watched for a few more seconds. He stopped the video. 'DS Michaels said the video shows Blackstone being forced to ingest cement over a ten-minute period before they removed his clothing and castrated him with an electric freezer knife.' He paused, looking at the screen. 'I have no desire to watch that as much as I detest the bastard, I don't need to see it. The video has been shared thousands of times and has over half a million likes already. The live castration of a paedophile priest. It will trend worldwide. This is big, and it's only going to get bigger.'

'When did this take place?' Kim asked.

'We know it was uploaded three days ago.'

'And his daughter contacted the police because he was missing?'

'She reported him missing the day before and she'd seen him two days before that, so there's a forty-eight-hour window. There were signs of a break in at his bungalow in Trevor. She checked the hospital and then called the police. A mis-per file was opened but later that night, she was sent an anonymous text message with a link to the video. Someone deemed it reasonable to send the video of Blackstone being tortured and castrated to his daughter.'

'That's sick,' Kim said.

'It's cruel,' Alan agreed. 'It's not her fault her father was a paedophile. Obviously, she was very distressed when she saw it and she made a triple nine call but the operator told her it wasn't an emergency, so she turned up at Caernarfon nick in a state. DS Michaels has let us know because she thinks it's likely to be linked to the Father Creegan case.'

'No shit, Sherlock,' Kim said. 'I can see why she reached the giddy heights of superintendent. Has she seen any other content on the website relating to Creegan?'

'She has,' Alan said. 'She said she would send me the link to another video, which has been removed by the host operators, but they've recovered it from the dark web,' Alan explained. He showed Kim the link, and they watched another silent video. This time it showed an elderly man fishing. He was attacked by a well-built male and kicked into the sea. The footage finished when he disappeared beneath the waves for the final time. 'Unless I'm very much mistaken, that's Father Derek Corbin,' Alan said, rubbing his eyes. 'I'm one-hundred and ten per cent certain it is.'

'Another one of the names on your hit list,' Kim said, nodding.

'Another one indeed,' Alan said.

'What's DS Michaels doing with the case?' Kim asked.

'They're passing the videos onto the Internet experts in Liverpool to see if they can trace where the videos are being uploaded from and by who,' Alan said.

'It looks like we have a group of vigilantes on the warpath,' Kim said. She could see Alan's brain ticking over. 'What are you thinking?'

'I'm thinking DS Michaels wants this to be related to our case because it's going to be a shitshow. Vigilantes attacking abusers would be a national sport if the public had their way. Fox hunting, no but cutting the bollocks of a paedophile priest gets half a million likes. I don't want it to be our case. It's connected historically, but this is a new case on her patch. She can run with it for now, but I have a feeling it will come our way. For now, I want to concentrate on our investigation and find out who was in that firepit,' Alan said. 'Have we had the info on the Maltese men yet?'

'Richard is on that. I'll go and ask him,' Kim said, leaving the office. Alan pulled up a word document on his laptop. It was a list of names. He typed the word *Deceased* next to two of them. There were eighteen still breathing.

Chapter 26

Maisy finished her coffee. She managed to drink it rather than wearing it. The idiot who had knocked her drink over was a real oddball. He said his name was Alf or something similar. Whatever it was, he was a stupid man and rude. And he was very discourteous telling her that her face didn't know she wasn't annoyed. Cheeky bastard. No one would get away with that kind of cheek in Chelsea. He would be bashed about the head and thrown in the gutter where he belonged. His entire manner had been odd. Concerning even. She couldn't stop thinking about him, and that wasn't good because his face was making her blood boil. The blank expression on his face and piercing eyes belonged to a simpleton. She didn't want to give him a second thought, but she couldn't help herself. He had disturbed her.

Maisy took the travelator down to the supermarket and got a shopping trolley that worked. It was the third attempt when she found one with wheels, which went in a straight line. She rushed up and down the aisles filling the trolley with the essentials they needed for a week or so. All the time, she was planning what to say to Hal. It was difficult to fathom what he was doing. Was he planning to leave her and live the life of a single man, or was he having some kind of crisis?

The thought of being left alone with two children filled her with dread, but she wasn't going to allow him to roam around shagging everything in sight. Her stomach was tied in knots. She reached the checkout and piled her items onto the conveyor belt. The cashier chatted shit in a local accent. Maisy couldn't understand most of it. Every sentence ended in, ye. She nodded and smiled as if she was interested but her head was in another place. Tell your face you're not annoyed, she thought. Cheeky bastard.

'That's a hundred and ninety-five pounds exactly,' the cashier said. 'Twenty-five per cent off on the wine saves you a fortune. The more you drink, the more you save, ye?'

Maisy reached into her handbag for her purse. It wasn't there. She searched again, blushing this time. It still wasn't there. The people in the queue behind her were growing impatient.

'I'm sorry,' Maisy said. She emptied her bag but the purse wasn't there. 'I must have left my purse upstairs in the café. I bought a coffee and bacon butty before I came down here.'

'Push your trolley against the wall there,' the cashier said. 'Go up and ask if it's been handed in, Doll. Don't worry. It will be behind the counter if it has.'

'I will,' Maisy said. She was cringing with embarrassment as she pushed her trolley to the side. 'I'm so sorry. I won't be long,' she added, running away towards the main doors.

Maisy ran up to the first floor and waited patiently while the cashier served the line of people with coffee. She asked if her purse had been found and it hadn't. Maisy checked all around the table where she'd been sitting, and then checked the toilets. She couldn't remember if she'd taken her bag in there but she was pretty sure she hadn't. Someone must have taken her purse when she was in the toilets. It was that simple. She stormed out of the café in a rage and reached for her mobile. That wasn't there either. But she'd used it to call Caroline in the café. She searched again as she marched towards her car. Her phone still wasn't there yet she checked a third time. She began to cry, angrier and more frustrated than she'd been for decades. In fact, she couldn't remember being so angry. It started to rain as she reached the car. She felt for her keys to open it and realised they were gone too. Maisy turned around in a circle, wondering what to do. She stared at her vehicle. The car looked lopsided. She stood in front of it and shouted at the sky. Her passenger side wheels had been slashed, the rubber ripped open with a knife or something sharp. She leant against the vehicle and balled her hands into fists. Tears mingled with raindrops as her anger boiled over into pure despair. She had no purse, no debit card, no money, no car keys, and no phone to get help. This was Hal's fault. She didn't know how, but it was. Harold Nelson could go and fuck himself. She was done.

Chapter 27

DS Richard Lewis put the phone down and crossed out another phone number on his list. His initial enquiries indicated that Arturo Troisi and Ganni James were Maltese priests, cycling across Europe to raise money for orphanages on their island. He had found out more about them from social media than from their employers, but the event was not being advertised. The posts about them were muted. There were no images of them or their cycles or the people they met along the way. A search into their private lives was equally vague. They appeared to be employed by an Italian tranche of the Catholic Church based on Malta, but the details were murky and either disorganised or disguised. He feared it was the latter. Gut instinct. Richard had spent hours trying to find out exactly where the Maltese men had been since leaving Malta and where they were heading to. He pieced it together like a jigsaw of the map of Europe. It appeared that they'd hopped from country to country using a network of catholic diocese and other priests for accommodation and to top-up supplies along the way. There appeared to be long gaps in their progress. Longer than it would take to travel and much more. They appeared to have spent several weeks in Rome, but he couldn't find anyone to confirm where they'd stayed or where they'd gone after that. They were mentioned by a local page in Milan, but there were no photographs of them. There were no photographs of them anywhere. Kim approached his desk and sat down next to him. She carried the scent of Poison today. He liked that perfume. Especially on her.

'The boss wants to know where the Maltese men are,' Kim said. 'He's growing impatient,' she added.

'Alan is never impatient,' Richard said. 'He drinks too much whisky to be impatient. It lowers the blood pressure and keeps you calm. It should be available on the NHS. There would be less stressed people around.'

'There would be fewer people around,' Kim said, shaking her head. 'Lots more dead people.'

'Everything in moderation,' Richard said.

'That's the voice of someone who knows his whisky. I'll take your word for it,' Kim said.

'You should try it.'

'It tastes minging,' Kim added.

'You're a heathen,' Richard said. 'Beautiful, but a heathen. A heathen but beautiful. A beautiful heathen.'

'And you're boring me,' Kim said, smiling. 'Have you got any information about the Maltese men, or not?'

'I am searching, and I feel my questions are unwanted and not appreciated. I have discovered that Malta is more catholic than the Vatican and slightly more secretive,' Richard said.

'What has the Vatican got to do with it?' Kim asked.

'Arturo Troisi and Ganni James are priests, but their records are very sketchy. I have no home addresses or dates of birth, and no one will confirm exactly who they're employed by. I know they're on an Italian payroll, but the Maltese banks are independents and won't give out any information whatsoever. It's like talking to a brick wall.'

'You're kidding me,' Kim said, moving closer to see the screen. 'They're catholic priests. Alan will have a swearing episode when he finds out.'

'I thought the same thing. The word, fuck, will be banded about the office willy-nilly. Not his favourite topic at all,' Richard agreed. 'I've confirmed they're cycling across Europe for charity, or I should say, they appear to be,' Richard said.

'What do you mean?'

'There's no pomp and ceremony and photographs of them arriving or leaving anywhere or running total of how much money they've raised,' Richard said. 'It's all a bit subdued to be credible.'

'Why would anyone fake a charity bike ride?'

'Unfettered access across borders, an excuse for being somewhere without looking suspicious.' Richard shrugged. 'The lord moves in mysterious ways, apparently.'

'He is also a shadow to hide behind,' Kim said.

'Exactly. Both men are in their late forties according to their travel documents, but their employment records don't confirm that. Their employment details are redacted. Names only.'

'No dates of birth?' Kim asked.

'Nope. And when I ask why, I'm fobbed off, hung up on or suddenly they can't understand English. I've traced them here and there, travelling through Italy, where they spent a few weeks in Rome, then Switzerland, France, and eventually here. From what I can tell there are no hotels involved. They have been staying with other priests or wider connections, which is making their whereabouts difficult to confirm. All I have are social media posts made by their hosts and when I ask them a question, I'm blanked or blocked. As usual, no one wants to talk to the police,' Richard said, shaking his head. 'I can't imagine why there's so much secrecy around this charity ride but that's what I've been up against.'

'Do you know where they are now?' Kim asked.

'No,' Richard said. 'They don't have mobile phones. Apparently having no contact with social media is part of their challenge. The last place that will confirm their route is a vicarage in Shrewsbury. The lady I spoke to said they were heading through North Wales to Holyhead. They planned to tour Anglesey and complete the island's coastal route as part of their fundraising. Then they were heading to Dublin, where they were planning to fly to New York.'

'What were they going to New York for?' Kim asked.

'I haven't had the chance to ask them because I can't find them,' Richard said. 'Have you been listening to what I've been saying?'

'Sort of half listening,' Kim said. 'You do waffle on.'

'I waffle?'

'Yes. What's the shortened version of what you've said?'

'Basically, I don't know if they're alive or dead.'

'So, we can't rule them out of the investigation?'

'I'm afraid not,' Richard said.

'Why didn't you just say that in the beginning?'

'I have no idea.'

Chapter 28

Hal arrived home in his courtesy car. It was a tiny Fiat that would have been at home on a Scalextric track. He was later than he usually would have been. His head was spinning. He had driven to the beach at Rhosneigr and walked as far as he could before the cold beat him back. The time had ticked by and it was dark and wet and miserable, which was how his soul felt at that moment. He had lost Naomi, the one thing that felt right. There was no way to be with her, and no way he could live without her. If you play with fire, you get your fingers burnt. He had played with fire, and now it was raging and threatening to engulf everything he had. He had no answers. No solutions. He had gone over the waterfall in a barrel and there was no way of knowing what would happen when he hit the bottom.

Maisy was already home, sitting in her friend's car on the drive. Her friend was Caroline Greenman. She was a pretty woman with a very low opinion of the male species and she wasn't afraid to speak her mind. If Maisy felt she needed some back-up, Caroline was the best candidate. Hal knew what was coming. There would be a torrent of abuse, which he would have to deflect and have an explanation for yet he had no credible excuses, only speculation.

Today was supposed to be Tesco shopping day, but there was no sign of her car. He checked his phone in case she had rang him. No missed calls. Maisy would have been to the gym and Tesco, and he was in no doubt she would have been told the rumours about him texting the Air Commodore. The gossip mill would be churning out inaccurate shite at full pelt. Pauline Verwood was a social media icon to thousands of empowered females who looked up to her and her success in the RAF. Maisy followed her online. Maisy followed everyone who had a modicum of success, nice make-up, and expensive clothes and flashy motor cars. She followed them because she envied them. She envied their ability to pay five-hundred pounds for a pair of trainers and not blink at the price. Hal couldn't afford for her to do that, and she resented it. She didn't outright say she did but she did. He could see it in her eyes when she looked at their overdraft. She wished she'd married a wealthy entrepreneur with biceps to match his bank balance. Someone made in Essex with abs and tattoos. The disappointment wept from every pore of her body and it made him feel like a failure when he was far from it. Maisy just didn't appreciate mediocrity. He was a low-ranking police officer in the RAF. His mother was proud of him, but Maisy wasn't. Pride doesn't buy Prada, currency does. Was that part of his affair with Naomi Metcalfe? Probably. He couldn't be certain. Maisy was impressed by labels and price tags, but he couldn't blame Maisy for his betrayal. He had managed that all by himself. Maisy would have heard some of what had happened, but he didn't know if Ernie

Metcalfe had told anyone what he knew about Hal and his wife; he was about to find out.

Maisy and her friend Caroline got out of her vehicle and walked towards him, arms folded across the chest, lips curling down at the corners. As she neared, he could see her face was like thunder and she'd been crying. She looked like she'd been crying for a week. It was obvious she'd been told the news but how much did she know was the question.

'Where the fuck have you been?' Maisy shouted.

'Nice to see you too,' Hal said, climbing out of his car.

'Don't try to be funny,' Maisy said, shaking her head. 'Not today. Not after what you've done.'

'And what have I done?' Hal asked.

'I've been told,' Maisy said. 'You bastard.'

'Whatever you've been told is bullshit.'

'So, Jamillia Squire and Pauline Verwood are making it up, are they?' Maisy shouted. She picked up a potted laburnum and hurled it at him. He ducked and it hit the hire car.

'That's a hire car!' Hal protested. 'There's a huge excess on that.' Her words sank in. 'Jamillia who?' he asked, frowning.

'Jamillia Squire,' Maisy said.

'I don't know her.'

'Yes, you do,' Caroline interrupted.

'Her husband is Bradley Squire, and he will snap you in half when he finds out you've been propositioning his wife.'

'Captain Bradley Squire?' Hal asked, confused.

'Yes. I see him in the gym all the time and he's built like a brick shithouse.'

'I know who he is. What has he got to do with this?'

'Don't pretend you don't know what I'm talking about. You sexted his wife last night,' Maisy said, her eyes bulging from her face.

'I haven't sexted Jamillia Squire or anyone else,' Hal said, glad Naomi hadn't been mentioned. 'I don't even know the woman. If I was going to sext someone, I would try to avoid Bradley Squire's wife. I don't have a death wish.'

'What does that mean?'

'It means it didn't happen.'

'You would say that. And what about my mother?' she ranted. 'I suppose she's lying too.'

'Your mother,' Hal asked, sucking in air between his teeth. 'Please tell me what your mother has to do with this?'

'Don't you make a joke out of this, you bastard. How dare you?' Maisy screamed at the top of her voice. 'How fucking, dare you?' She picked up another terracotta pot and tossed it, but it fell well short of the mark and smashed on the bonnet of the hire car.

'Not the hire car,' Hal shouted.

'Fuck off!' Maisy snapped. 'I don't give a toss about your stupid car. Is my mother lying, is she?'

'Your mother?' Hal sighed. He walked to the front door and sat on the step, his head in his hands.

'Yes, my fucking mother!' Maisy shouted. 'That's the lowest of the low. How could you do that to me?'

'Do you seriously believe I've texted your mother?' he asked, pleading. Maisy looked at him as if he was something she'd stood in. 'Think about this clearly. Stop being angry for one minute and think about this calmly.' Hal said, shrugging. 'The simple truth is I can't stand your mother. I wouldn't fuck your mother for a gold clock. In fact, I would rather try to fuck Bradley Squire than your mother and you're right, he would snap me in half but I would take my chances over propositioning your mother.' Hal smiled sadly. 'I would rather cut my knob off with a rusty spoon than go anywhere near your mother with it.' Maisy looked set to burst but he could see her thinking about what he was saying. 'I may not be much, Maisy, but I'm not stupid enough to send text messages to your mother and the Air Commodore and Mrs Squire or anyone else for that matter. You're saying that I messaged three women at random on the same night when I was working, and my phone was in my locker.'

'That's what you say,' Maisy said. 'No one checks if you have your phone on. You've told me that yourself.'

'I have told you that. No one checks but that doesn't mean I can sit at my desk texting people.' He paused and held up his hands. 'Forget the details for one minute. You say I sexted your mother. A woman twice your age who I cannot stand the sight of. If I wanted an affair, your mother is not a candidate in this lifetime or any other. Do you really think I would do that?'

'I've seen the messages sent from your profile on Jamillia's phone,' Caroline said. 'How do you explain that?'

'I'm not denying the messages were sent, I'm telling you I didn't send them.'

'How do you explain it then?' Maisy said, her anger subsiding.

'I can't be sure, but I think my phone was either hacked or taken from my locker while I was working.'

'You have your phone,' Caroline said. 'I saw you looking at in the car.'

'I do have it and it's been wiped completely. Whoever took it, put it back so I wouldn't know what they'd done with it until it was too late. I still have my phone therefore I sent the messages from it,' Hal said. The two women looked at each other. They didn't believe him. 'I know this is difficult to understand, but I think someone has got it in for me. They're setting me up to look like a sex pest.' He paused. 'And it's worked. You two believe it, don't you?' Caroline and Maisy exchanged glances again. 'Today has been a really shit day. I was called into HR this morning and accused of sending messages to Pauline Verwood and then I had a blowout in the car.' He gestured to the hire car but left out who's car he hit. 'The breakdown mechanic said there were screws in my tyres. He thinks it was done on purpose.'

'Why would anyone do that to you?' Caroline asked, suspiciously.

'Your guess is as good as mine,' Hal said. He looked at Maisy. 'Come on, Maisy. Do you think I would message your mum for sex?'

'I don't know what to think,' Maisy said.

'Where's the car?' Hal asked her.

'It's a long story.'

'I'm here all night,' Hal joked. The women didn't laugh.

'I had my purse stolen from Tesco. They took my purse, my keys, and my phone.'

'While you were in the supermarket,' Hal asked, confused and annoyed. 'Why didn't you ring me and tell me?' Hal asked, looking concerned.

'Because they took my phone, genius,' Maisy said. She folded her arms defensively.

'You should have used a landline.'

'I don't know your number. Do you know my number in your head?'

'No,' Hal said. 'I don't know any.'

'I didn't realise what had happened until I got to the checkout with a trolley full of shopping,' Maisy said. 'When I looked for my purse, it wasn't there. I emptied my bag onto the counter to be sure. I could have died I was so embarrassed.' She glared at Hal. 'I went upstairs and asked if it had been handed in. Of course, it hadn't. Then when I got to the car, the tyres were slashed.'

'Someone slashed your tyres?' Hal repeated angrily. 'That can't be a coincidence. It has to be whoever stole your purse.'

'There's no fooling you, Sherlock,' Maisy snapped.

'I'm trying to make sense of all this,' Hal said. 'Did you have your bag all the time you were there?'

'No. One of your workmates spilled his coffee over me in the café, and I had to go and use the toilets to clean my coat and jeans. I left my bag on the chair.'

'One of my workmates?'

'Yes.'

'What was his name?'

'I can't remember. Al or Ads or something shit. I don't listen to anyone you work with. They're all such knobheads.'

'What did he look like?' Hal asked, ignoring the jibe.

'A twat in sunglasses and a baseball cap,' Maisy said. 'Standard issue for you lot. You all think you're *Top Gun* on that base. They're not even proper policemen,' Maisy added, talking to Caroline.

'I can't believe someone went into your handbag and no one saw anything?' Hal asked, ignoring her cutting remarks again. It started to rain, and they all looked up at the moody sky. A gust of wind from the sea spurred them into action. 'It's very cold and I could do with a drink. Let's go inside and talk about this, shall we?'

Caroline and Maisy looked at each other and mutually agreed it was for the best. They were cold too. Hal reached for the key and opened the door. The sound of water running met him and he stopped in the doorway, confused. He reached inside and switched on the lights as he entered and stepped into two inches of water. Maisy followed behind him, horrified. Caroline waited a few seconds before risking it. They moved slowly down the hallway to the kitchen. Hal put the light on and looked inside. The kitchen was awash with water, pouring from the overflowing sink. Both taps were turned on fully. Water poured through the ceiling around the light fitting. It ran down the walls noisily. Hal knew it was from the bathroom upstairs. He also knew it was no accident. The plaster was sagging in the middle of the ceiling, ready to collapse at any minute. Every cupboard had been opened, and the contents strewn across the kitchen surfaces. Jars and bottles were smashed, and every item of crockery had been tossed against the walls and shattered into pieces. There wasn't a single cup or plate intact. The fridge had been opened and tipped over backwards and was now full of water like a novelty bathtub. A tub of Lurpak floated in it next to a Jiff lemon, three onions, and some cheese slices. It was a surreal image etched into his mind. He had seen enough.

Hal splashed his way along the hallway. The staircase had become a waterfall and looked spectacular in a bizarre way. The water glinted from each rise and fall. Every picture had been ripped from the walls and smashed. When he reached the living room, he cried tears of anger and frustration. The carnage was difficult to absorb. His eighty-five-inch television was still fixed to the wall, but it had the coffee table embedded through it. Water ran down the walls saturating everything. The settee had been slashed and the stuffing tossed in every direction. The destruction was total and it was devastating to see. It was overwhelming.

'Turn off the taps down here,' Hal said, turning to the women. 'I'll go upstairs and stop the water.'

Hal ran up the stairs and went into the bathroom. The bath was overflowing; the shower was on and pointing at the floor, and the sink had been blocked with a towel and the taps turned on fully. He turned everything off and ran into the ensuite in the bedroom, which was above the living room. The toilet bowl had been cracked into three pieces and the ballcock ripped off so the cistern was constantly overflowing. There was no way to fix it quickly. Hal ran downstairs and opened the cupboard under the kitchen sink. He turned the water supply off at the stop-tap. The trio stood in the kitchen in silence for long minutes. The sound of dripping and water running through the ceilings was deafening.

'I'll phone the police,' Hal said quietly. 'Whoever took your keys did this. There must be CCTV at the supermarket. I want the bastard arrested.'

'Everything is ruined,' Maisy said. She hugged Caroline and Hal felt the weight of guilt crushing him. He knew who was responsible. His first instinct was to tell the police but he couldn't do that. He couldn't tell Maisy who had stolen his phone. He couldn't tell her who had stolen hers because if he did, he would have to explain why he had done those things. Ernie Metcalfe was the culprit. Hal was absolutely certain it was him.

'It will dry out,' Hals said.

'I don't care if it burns to the ground.' Maisy sniffled. 'I hate it here,' she said. 'I hate Anglesey, I hate the RAF, and I hate you,' she added, wiping her nose with her sleeve. 'I'm going home. Fuck this, fuck the RAF, and fuck you. You can text whoever you like. Have whoever you want. I want a divorce.'

'You're upset,' Hal said, calling the police.

'What have you done, Hal?' Caroline asked. He looked at her, his eyes full of anger. 'Don't look at me like that,' she said, smiling sourly. 'You have upset someone you shouldn't have, and you know it. Whoever sent those messages did this to your home. You have pissed someone off, big style,' she added. 'And if this is what they're capable of, you're in big trouble.'

'I'm going to pack some things for me and the children and we'll stay at Caroline's tonight.' Maisy looked at her friend, and Caroline nodded her agreement. 'I need to be away from this and away from you.'

Chapter 29

Ernie pulled into Stermat car park in Valley and parked in front of the Chinese takeaway. He picked up a used pair of gloves from the passenger seat. They were soaking wet and ripped. His blood had saturated the left glove. A three-inch wound to the palm of his hand had bled profusely but was slowing down. He took the gloves and the hat he'd worn and put them into a plastic carrier bag and tied the neck into a knot. The car park was quiet. He looked across the road at the Valley Hotel. It was quiet there too. He opened the glove box and took a new pair of latex gloves from the box he'd bought through lockdown. His covid routine had been thorough, but it kept him and his family free of the virus. They wore latex gloves everywhere they went to. He put on a different baseball cap and sunglasses and opened the door. He took the bag with him. The skip at the side of the Chinese was unlocked. He lifted the lid and tossed the bag inside. The smell of decaying food and rancid grease hit him momentarily. It vanished as soon as he closed the lid. Ernie looked around. No one was taking any notice of him. He locked the car and walked into the hardware store, grabbing a basket.

Stermat was an Aladdin's cave of tools and household goods. It was the size of a small warehouse and crammed ceiling to floor with things everyone needed, without even realising they needed them. Stuff that made you wonder how you had lived so long without it. Ernie used it all the time. He would go in for a tube of superglue and leave with a basket overflowing with tools and accessories that would cost him twenty times the price of the tube of glue. It was impossible not to spend more than you planned to. He went to the tool aisle and put a moulded steel claw hammer and a three-metre length of rope into the basket. He carried a long-handled wood axe. Four rolls of duct tape, three tubes of No Nails, a pack of six-inch nails, a hack saw and spare blades, an electric circular saw, and a paint-stripping heat gun. A packet of thick cable zip ties went in as an afterthought. He queued up and paid for them before putting them into the boot of the car, then he returned for four sleeping bags. One for Naomi and one each for the girls. The cheap nylon ones were ideal, they were more flammable and would burn the hottest.

He toyed with the idea of using large plastic tarpaulins, but they had a limited effect. Burying bodies very deep was the best method. Six feet at least, then fill the hole half full and place a dead sheep in there. That way the dogs and ground penetrating radar would be tricked that they'd sensed a dead animal, not a human. If the situation deteriorated, he could always come back. Last but not least, he picked up a carbon-handled spade and a steel blade pickaxe. They would dig through the toughest ground. Ernie was happy with his purchases. He tossed the receipt into the litter bin outside and put the sleeping bags and tools into the boot. His stomach rumbled, and he realised he was hungry. He hadn't eaten for days. His appetite vanished when he was stressed. A neon sign flashed in the kebab shop window. Donner meat and chips and a coke. That would do the trick and give him the energy he needed. It was time to up the ante.

Chapter 30

Alan and Kim arrived at Ysbyty Gwynedd and they followed the one-way system through one packed car park to the next. After fifteen minutes stalking lane after lane, they eventually found a parking space. Alan was not happy at being pulled away from the operations room at Holyhead. The investigation was at a crucial phase, poised to respond as the forensic results trickled in. Detective Superintendent Michaels had called and insisted on sharing some complicated news in person. She was already at the hospital, so she suggested he meet her there.

'You know Carla Michaels and I go back a long way,' Alan said, moaning. 'She's a bossy bugger at times. You can't give her an inch or she'll take a mile.'

'Is she good at her job?' Kim asked, knowing the answer. Alan shrugged and nodded reluctantly. 'That's all that should matter.'

'And she's very good looking,' Alan added. 'Not that I'm saying she was promoted for anything other than her ability as a detective.'

'Sounds to me like you might be a tad envious of Superintendent Michaels?'

'How very dare you,' Alan chuckled.

'Why couldn't she say what she needed to say on the phone?'

'Somethings need to be said face to face,' Alan said.

'What do you think she wants to say?'

'She's knee deep into investigating these paedophile hunters from the Justice Asylum and it's a lose-lose situation.'

'How so?'

'Because the public love them. Every time the face of a convicted paedo appears online, they grow in stature. They're doing what the public think we should be doing.' Alan paused to think. 'No one wants to see these modern-day folk heroes charged. They think they should be given a medal and she's well aware of that. Her popularity will be besmudged if she has to charge them. So, it's better to spread the pain by merging the investigations.'

'What do you think?'

'I think she wants to dump all the shitty bits of the investigation into the Justice Asylum website over to our team, and then she can clear up the simple stuff, like the assaults and look good when it comes to performance review time. League tables on performance are the in thing at the moment. League tables and budgets. Good old-fashioned police work takes a back seat.'

'It's called progress,' Kim said. 'Making the force efficient means more coppers on the streets.'

'Bollocks,' Alan said. 'It's absolute bollocks, but her figures are the best in Wales, not because she's an outstanding detective, it's because she's sharp and savvy at which cases she manages. She won't touch anything complicated and someone up the ladder is making sure she gets the cases she wants.'

'Really?' Kim asked. 'You seriously believe the chain of command is feeding her with only solvable cases?'

'Probably not,' Alan conceded. 'Do I sound bitter?'

'Bitter and twisted,' Kim said, nodding.

'I probably am,' Alan agreed. 'Clear-up rates are the hot topic nowadays and some people actually give a shit about the league tables. Carla Michaels is one of them.'

'And you don't?'

'Not while she's above me in the league,' Alan said, smirking. 'I might do if I was top.'

'Surely, she's not that shallow.'

'Paddling pool depth at best.' Alan mulled it over in his mind. 'I might go so far as to say, puddle depth.' He nodded. 'Small puddle depth.'

He turned off the engine and climbed out of his BMW. Kim pulled on her new padded jacket and covered her hair with the hood. Alan noticed the motif on the left sleeve. He didn't recognise the name, but he had three sons and knew a motif on the left sleeve made it an expensive coat.

'Nice coat,' he said.

'About time you invested in a new one,' she said, gesturing to the worn elbow of his wax jacket. 'That's seen some action. It should retire with distinction and spend the rest of its days at the back of a wardrobe.'

'I might treat myself for my birthday,' Alan said. 'How much was that one?'

'I'm not going to tell you or you'll go on about it for months,' Kim said. 'Aren't you going to lock it?' Kim asked as he walked away from the vehicle.

'No. I'm hoping it's not here when we get back,' he said. 'I need an upgrade and a new coat.'

'Is it insured?' she joked.

'As far as I can remember, it is,' Alan said. He fastened his wax jacket to the neck and took his beanie hat out of the pocket. His thinning hair did nothing to insulate his head. 'We're closer to Caernarfon than the hospital,' he moaned. They were in the last overflow car park. 'We're four car parks away from reception. Imagine if one of us was really sick,' he said. 'We would be dead before we got halfway there.'

'I would have dropped you off at the door, then parked,' Kim said.

'I would have dropped you off at the door and gone home,' Alan said. 'No point in two of us waiting around.'

'Such a charmer,' Kim said.

'They're very good here. They would have phoned me when you were well enough to pick up,' Alan said, nodding. He smiled at his own ingenuity. 'That would save me at least a fiver for parking and the wear and tear on my old knees. I feel like I'm climbing Snowdon.'

'Stop whining,' Kim said. They walked on in silence for a while. 'What are the chances of him surviving?'

'Father Gamble?'

'He's why we're here,' she said.

'I don't think he's got much chance, do you?'

'You're hoping he doesn't make it, aren't you?'

'I have no preference to be honest,' Alan said, thoughtfully. 'It sounds like he's suffered a terrible ordeal.' He paused to catch his breath. The car park was on an incline, climbing towards the hospital. 'Being made to drink cement would be very painful, which is a suitable end for the dirty old bastard but if he survives, I don't think he's going to be in good shape, which will mean he has to endure more pain and suffering, which is poetic justice in my mind, so either way suits me.' Alan glanced at her and caught her pensive expression. 'It's one less predator to worry about. Are you feeling sorry for him?'

'No. Not sorry. But I have sympathy for his condition. He must be suffering a great deal. I can't help but think that no matter what he's done in the past, he's an old man,' Kim said.

'He's an old paedophile and there's a difference,' Alan said.

'I'm sure you have an explanation in your head?'

'I do. Old age brings reverence and respect from society. We tend to protect our elderly. Not always but mostly we look up to them and care for them. It affords respect. Frank Gamble deserves no one's respect. He's damaged dozens of people for the rest of their lives. They will carry their scars into their old age too.' Alan was getting annoyed. Sympathy for paedophiles was way beyond the level of his comprehension. 'He has never shown any remorse or any sign that he will change,' Alan argued. 'He was chased away from a kids' football match not long ago. The terms of his release stipulate that he doesn't go anywhere near schools or playgrounds or sporting facilities where children frequent yet he still persists. Age hasn't dulled the sickness inside him. He's a monster. Don't let the grey hair and wrinkles fool you.'

'I'm well aware of who he is and what he is,' Kim said, shaking her head. 'I don't like to see anyone suffering needlessly. It goes against the grain for me. If he has to die, I hope it's quickly.'

'Fuck him,' Alan said, turning up his collars. 'I hope it takes weeks and I hope it hurts like buggery.'

They walked the rest of the way in silence. Partly because they fundamentally disagreed on the topic and partly because Alan was out of breath. His left knee was paining him. He'd twisted it years ago at the bar in the Black Seal, when it was called the Waterfront. He'd been sitting on a stool when a fight had broken out and he was in the way of the pugilists. He was supposed to take Naproxen to ease the pain, but it made his stomach burn when he drank whisky. He enjoyed his Scotch, so stopped taking the tablets and lived with the painful knee.

They reached the reception and were directed to a surgical ward on the first floor. DS Michaels was on her phone in the corridor when they stepped out of the lift. She saw them and ended the call.

'Hello Alan,' she said, smiling thinly. There was no warmth in the greeting. Michaels saw everyone as competition. She was wearing a tight pinstriped suit that hugged her curves. Alan had to admit to himself she looked good for her age. Her eyes absorbed Kim in a few seconds. 'You must be Kim Davies. I've heard good things about you,' she added. 'A pleasure to meet you.'

'Nice to meet you, superintendent,' Kim said, blushing.

'Some people say DS Michaels is on the other bus,' Alan whispered into Kim's ear loud enough for Michaels to hear. 'You understand. She probably bats for the other team.'

'Some things never change. Your wit is still as sharp as your dress sense.'

'I think I've touched a nerve,' Alan said, smiling. 'How are you, Carla?'

'Fuck off, Alan,' Michaels said, smiling. 'For your benefit, Kim, DS Michaels is working at the moment and her sexuality is totally asexual at work. Contrary to what your antique DI is suggesting, when she isn't at work, she likes cock. Not that it's any of his business,' Michaels said, shaking her head. 'You should have been buried in the eighties, where you belong. You're a fucking dinosaur.'

'Thank you. I'll take that as a compliment. That's the niceties out of the way,' Alan said, smiling. 'All jokes aside, why are we here?'

'Typical Alan. Don't beat around the bush,' Michaels said. 'Okay. If I need to be specific, Father Frank Gamble is the reason you're here.'

'What happened to Gamble is a new crime on your patch. What makes you think that involves us?' Alan asked.

'As you know, he's one of Creegan's cohorts.' Alan didn't respond, although that was true. 'And because of all the media coverage you've courted on the subject, Creegan and his legacy are your cross to bear. You exposed a ring of paedophiles bigger than any before in the UK. There may have been bigger in America, but here, you're the man. Your name will always be associated with busting them.'

'I haven't courted the press for my own benefit. I've used the press to raise awareness and encourage victims to come forward,' Alan protested. 'I don't do it to get my picture in the paper.'

'I don't care why you've done it,' Michaels said. 'The fact is, you're the paedophile hunter and always will be. The public want to see you on the news standing with your foot on a priest's throat. They don't want me in charge of it.'

'The paedophile hunter?' Alan half smiled. He looked at Kim and nodded. Kim rolled her eyes skyward. 'I guess if the cap fits, wear it. Enough massaging my ego, superintendent, let's just get to the point,' Alan said.

'Okay, to summarise. Gamble made a triple nine call from his house in Bangor. He was incoherent and nearly dead, in and out of consciousness, but he told the paramedics he was attacked by a man in a balaclava and forced to drink cement. The attacker was going to castrate him but he managed to grab a baton and disable him.'

'We know that. If someone attacked Gamble in Bangor,' Alan leant forward to emphasise his words. 'Then it was in Bangor. Bangor is your patch. He's your cross to bear, as you put it. This is nothing to do with Creegan.'

'Oh, come on. You know it is.'

'It's fallout from the case, granted. I'll give you that, but it's a new crime. This is the work of online vigilantes using a website you're investigating. All the associated attacks have been on the mainland, not Anglesey. The link is tenuous at best.'

'The ACC will make that decision. Let's not argue over the semantics. We all do as we're told in the end.' Michaels cleared her throat. 'The facts are his attacker made him drink cement from a bucket and was about to cut off his goolies with a pair of rose pruners but Gamble hit the man with a steel baton belonging to the attacker.'

'He made him drink cement. Like Blackstone,' Kim agreed, nodding. 'Is he still alive?'

'Barely,' Michaels said. 'The surgeons are trying to remove the cement but apparently his throat, duodenum, and stomach are a bloody mess, burnt by the lye. They may have to remove the entire intestinal tract. Most of the damage is irreparable.'

'What about his attacker?'

'They thought he was dead, but he's in surgery,' Michaels said. 'Fractured skull and broken neck. If he survives, he'll be paralysed from the shoulders down.'

'Do we know who he is?' Alan asked.

'Not yet. We're running his prints now,' Michaels said. 'His mobile phone was found at the scene but it's locked. We're working on that too. There's no sign of a getaway vehicle, which makes me think there was an accomplice waiting outside.' She paused. 'The question is, Alan, did you watch the Blackstone video until the end?'

'No,' Alan said. 'We watched a few minutes of him being forced to drink cement and decided not to watch the castration. Netflix is about my limit. Why, what did we miss?'

Michaels took out her tablet and brought up the video. She forwarded it to the timeline she wanted. Alan smiled at Kim, who looked anxious about watching it. She was a sensitive soul and it would disturb her. She pretended to be made from asbestos but wasn't.

'Take a look at the table in the background,' Michaels said, pointing. In the foreground, the priest was flapping in the chair like a dying fish, his mouth wide open, gasping for air. Blood pooled on the floor between his feet where his genitals had fallen, ripped and torn by the electric freezer knife. It reminded him of the giblets his mother used to take from the Christmas turkey and turn into soup. On the table behind him was a blue plastic tarpaulin and some elastic bungee cords. They were red and yellow. 'I checked your murder book details online. According to your witnesses, your victims were wrapped in something similar, weren't they?'

'Not similar,' Kim said. 'The same.'

'I thought as much,' Michaels said. 'Look, if we have a bunch of vigilantes targeting the remaining men implicated in the Father Creegan case, are they anything to do with the double murder you're investigating?' She shrugged. 'Look at the tarpaulins and bungees. This video would suggest it is, in which case, we're going to end up sharing this one and pooling our resources.'

'It does suggest the cases are linked,' Kim agreed, looking at Alan. Alan shrugged, defeated. 'The blue tarpaulins and bungee cords are the same as what the Trigg twins described.'

'They are exactly the same,' Alan agreed.

'Did you just agree with me?' Michaels asked.

'It doesn't mean we're best mates or anything,' he said. 'Can we take a still from that video without a mutilated priest in the foreground and show it to the twins?' Alan said. 'They're ten. I don't want to traumatise them any more than they are already. If they identify them as the same as the ones they saw, we can assume one of the victims in the firepit is Father Rupert Blackstone.' He paused and rubbed the grey stubble on his chin. He needed a shave. 'If the men in that pit are affiliates of Father Patrick Creegan, then I will feel a whole lot better about it. It takes the pressure off.'

'I don't follow,' Michaels said, frowning. 'How does it take the pressure off?'

'Simple. They're not innocent victims,' Alan said. He shrugged. 'They're career paedophiles and if it's them in the firepit, I will feel better about it.'

'I see, although I'm not sure admitting that's how you view it is constructive or press worthy,' Michaels said. 'The ACC won't want to hear that.'

'I'm hardly likely to say it in front of him, am I?' Alan countered. 'So, he won't know. Unless you're going to tell him.'

'Of course not.'

'The ACC would agree with me if he could, but we can't all be politically correct all the time. Thanks for the advice,' Alan said, under his breath, 'I wasn't planning on adding it to a press release, I am thinking aloud.'

'Maybe keep your thoughts in your head?' Kim said, grimacing.

'How many more are there?' Michaels asked.

'That's like asking how long is a piece of string?'

'Give me a ballpark figure,' Michaels said.

'Once the investigation got going, we had upwards of fifty names implicated in taking part or covering it up. Once we narrowed it down, dozens in the wider investigation.'

'Dozens?'

'You have to remember, the investigation was focused on Creegan and who he came into contact with over a thirty-year career,' Alan explained. 'People came and went. Many of them found the area didn't suit them and moved away. Some of them went abroad and never returned. Across the UK eighteen priests were investigated with a view to prosecution but were released through lack of evidence.'

'But they weren't absolved of any involvement?'

'No. They were guilty. The lack of evidence being witness statements. Witnesses from thirty-years ago,' Alan said. 'They were captured on film. Some of the footage is so old and poor quality, we know they were present but can't identify specific victims.'

'No victims, no crime,' Michaels said. 'No wonder there was such a backlash.'

'Exactly. It doesn't mean they didn't do it,' Alan said. 'The entire investigating team were convinced that everyone we put forward to the CPS was guilty.' He shrugged. 'The Church made all the right noises and said they would ensure those investigated were kept in check. They said they would be policed by the diocese but that turned out to be bollocks. We know they've been shuffling them from one place to another. The bishop claims he only moves them when they've been identified by someone. Whatever the reason, we don't know where they are because they were not convicted.'

'They're clearly in danger of being attacked,' Michaels said.

'Yes. Isn't that brilliant?' Alan said. Michaels looked confused. 'If you're right, we need to trace the remaining eighteen priests and account for their whereabouts,' Alan said. Michaels nodded her agreement. 'Most of them are in the care of the diocese under the watchful eye of the bishop, so it shouldn't take too long to trace them.'

'What is he like?'

'He's a typical mouthpiece for the Church, promises much and delivers fuck all,' Alan said. 'Anyway, eighteen were never convicted. The videos of Corbin and Blackstone indicate they're dead and Gamble is in surgery, so the answer to your question is fifteen unaccounted for.'

'Fifteen?' Michaels asked, frowning. 'That's a lot.'

'There are three down that we know of but all the other men accused and not charged are still out there.'

'That's worrying,' Michaels said.

'I don't see them all in imminent danger,' Alan said, shaking his head. 'I suppose it all depends on where the Justice Asylum are getting their information. If they have access to the wider investigation, then we have no chance of protecting them all,' Alan said. 'If they cast their net wider to the men implicated but not actually employed by the Church, we could have upwards of fifty.'

'Fifty?' Michaels said, shocked.

'It could be that many.'

'I see. Were the names of those under investigation made available to the public?'

'Not officially,' Alan said. 'Unofficially, who knows? We all know names get leaked.'

'That's concerning. If they're all targets, we could potentially have dozens of victims?' Michaels said, astounded.

'We can only hope so,' Alan said.

'What?'

'I've got my fingers crossed,' Alan said, shaking his head.

'What?'

'The more the merrier in this case,' Alan said. 'Let's hope the Justice Asylum get to them before we do.' Alan turned and walked towards the toilets. 'Excuse me for a minute. I need to spend a penny.'

Kim and Michaels watched him walk away. Michaels looked at Kim for an explanation but she just shrugged.

'Did he really just say that?' Michaels asked. 'He actually wants them to be attacked?'

'I think it would make his day, to be honest,' Kim said. 'You should hear him when he's in a bad mood.'

Chapter 31

Tom and Philip came out of school and were approached by a group of older boys and girls. The twins were the talk of the playground as the news of the murders spread. They recognised most of them as living near them in Morawelon and they always walked home as a group. There were a few who didn't normally walk home that way, who were tagging along to hear the gossip. The others lived across town in various places on the way home. It was a mile or so from school to their house, depending on which route they took and that varied. The weather had a lot to do with which way they chose. In winter, they took the shortest most sheltered way, whereas summer could involve walking the long way, along the Newry Beach to Land's End. If it wasn't sunny, they usually cut through town and walked over the metal footbridge to the station. They would cut through the cafeteria area and exit through the ticket hall and walk past the taxi rank, which halved the distance. When they reached the road, they would stick their heads into the Edinburgh Castle pool room to see if their dad was in there, hustling people for a pound a frame. He was a decent player and had lots of plastic trophies which did their mum's head in as they collected dust. The last stretch was past Lidl, up Richmond Hill. Their entourage would become smaller as they went across town. By the time they reached their street, there would only be them and Barry Wallis left. He lived in the next street with his nan.

It was a long walk with a sore ankle, and Philip wasn't looking forward to it. He was going to ask his dad to pick them up, but he was in a bad mood because their sister Nia had a love-bite on her neck. Nia said it was a twister done by her friend as a joke, but dad said he wasn't born yesterday and if she came home pregnant, he would pack her bags and drop her off at the station. Nia said she wanted to leave anyway, which didn't go down well, so Philip decided not to ask for a lift.

'Hey, twins,' one of the older kids shouted them. 'Is it true you saw the murder in Tinto woods?'

'Yes,' Tom said, blushing. 'We can't talk about it.'

'Why not? Everyone else is.'

'We're witnesses. So, we can't.'

'Don't be stupid. Everyone knows about it,' the boy said. 'Tell us what happened.'

'We can't say anything,' Philip said. 'The police have told us we have to keep quiet until they've carried out their investigations.'

'I heard you saw the killers?'

'We did but we can't say anything about it.'

'How many were there?'

'We can't say,' Philip said.

'I heard you saw them toss someone into a fire?'

'We did but we can't say anything.'

'Who was killed?'

'We don't know.'

'Who were the killers?'

'We don't know. Look, there's no point in asking us stuff. We can't say anything,' Tom insisted.

'No way,' the boy said. 'We won't tell anyone, will we?' he asked the group.

'No.'

'You can trust us.'

'We won't say a word.'

'We can't say nothing,' Tom said. 'We're witnesses.'

'It's not a secret, dick-head,' a big lad called Franny said. Tom and Philip were scared of him. He was big and ginger and a bit nutty. Rumours said he had thrown a brick off the bridge at Valley and smashed the window of a lorry driving along the expressway and it nearly crashed, and he didn't even run when the police came. He stayed there and lied to the police. There were other people there, so that was true, although their stories differed. Another rumour said he had fingered Mrs Tomkins, the art teacher at County school, in the storage cupboard where they keep the paints but everyone reckoned he made that up himself. Mrs Tomkins was well fit. It was unlikely she would let Franny in her knickers but he was scary, so no one said anything. 'Do you think you're in the secret service or secret squirrels more like? The whole town is talking about it. How do you think we know it was you who saw it, dick-head?'

'Don't call me a dick-head,' Tom said. Franny was ten stone heavier than him and his brother combined. He grabbed Philip by the arm and crossed the road. Philip hobbled as quickly as he could. 'Come on. We'll walk on our own. Ignore him.'

'What are you doing over there?' Franny goaded them. 'Don't call me a dick-head,' Franny mimicked him in a squeaky voice. 'Don't call me a dick-head or I'll cry like a girl. Don't call me a dick-head or I'll wet my little pink knickers. Or what will you do, Trigg?' The twins ignored him. 'Nothing is what you'll do, little faggots.'

'He's such an arsehole,' Philip said, limping.

'What did your sister just say?' Franny shouted. The group laughed. 'Philippa has got a sore leg. Poor little Philippa. Pair of faggots,' Franny scoffed. 'Come on, tell us what you saw, girls. What were you doing in the woods, anyway, playing dollies?' The twins walked on, embarrassed but quiet. 'The Trigg sisters don't want to be seen walking with us.'

Franny tossed a bottle across the road and it exploded close to the twins. They jumped away from the cloud of glass shards.

'We just wanted to hear what you saw. You little knobheads. Only a grass would do whatever the police say,' he added, tossing a stone at them. A police car slowed down and stopped next to the group. Bob Dewhurst climbed out of the passenger seat.

'Alister Francis, get over here,' he said, beckoning Franny. 'Do you know what throwing a glass bottle at someone is called?'

'Target practice,' Franny said. The group laughed.

'Very smart,' Bob said. 'It's called assault. Get over here now while I explain it to you, moron.'

'Moron. Is that a breed of pig, Sergeant Dewhurst?' Some of the group distanced themselves from Franny. They were stunned into silence by his jibe. Calling a sergeant a pig wasn't the brightest thing to do. 'I didn't throw a bottle,' Franny said, smirking. The crowd stopped. Some of the kids horrified that the police had stopped them and some of them were frightened because of what Franny had said. 'Did anyone see me throwing a bottle?'

'No.'

'Nope.'

'I didn't see anything.'

'I did,' Trudie Baxter said, raising her hand as if she was in school.

'You saw him toss a bottle at the twins?' Bob asked.

'Yes. The twins said they couldn't say anything about the murders because they're witnesses and Franny said they were faggots and Tom was a grass and threw a bottle.' The group watched open-mouthed. 'I'll give a statement if you like.'

'Fucking grass, Trudie Baxter,' Franny said, shaking his head.

'Shut up, Franny,' Trudie said. 'No one cares what you think.'

'Don't they?' Franny said, angrily. 'I'll tell everyone you felt Carl Bolting's cock in the cinema.'

'I wouldn't be able to find yours, fatty,' Trudie fired back.

'That's enough,' Bob shouted. 'Come here, Alister,' he said. Franny shuffled over to the police car. 'Get in the back of the car,'

Bob said gruffly. Franny got in reluctantly and stuck two fingers up to the twins through the glass. 'The rest of you bugger off home and if I hear anyone has been bothering the twins, you'll have me to answer to.' The kids nodded that they understood. 'Get going,' Bob said, clapping his hands. 'Go home and have your tea and behave yourselves.' He looked at the twins. 'Are you okay?'

'Yes, thanks.'

'How's your ankle?' Bob asked.

'A bit sore,' Philip said, blushing.

'Get yourselves home,' Bob said. 'Don't hang about anywhere. Go straight home.'

The twins headed across the car park to cut down an alleyway, which led to Williams Street. They didn't see the white van parked behind the market hall in the Conservative club car park. Neither did Bob Dewhurst.

'What do you think?' the van driver asked.

'There are too many people around when they walk from school,' the passenger said. 'We'll have to go to Plan B.'

'Plan B is never good.'

'No. Plan B is the last resort. He said no witnesses and we need to deliver that, even if they're young.'

'*Suffer the children unto me,*' the driver said. 'And so they shall.'

****

Hal watched Maisy and the children leaving in Caroline's car. His son was teary and waved through the rear window, smearing the glass. It was gut wrenching. He waited until he couldn't see the lights before walking into the kitchen, his feet splashing in the water. His heart sank. The room was in tatters. The house was in tatters. His marriage was in tatters. His career was in tatters, and he knew who was to blame. Ernie Metcalfe. He felt his blood boiling, anger simmering in every sinew of his being. There would be time for recompense, but it wasn't now. He needed to take stock of the situation with a clear head. Maisy was gone but that wasn't why his heart was broken. It broke his heart watching his kids climbing into the car. It broke his heart hearing Naomi saying she didn't want to hear from him again. It broke his heart when she ended the call. Naomi was the real reason for all this chaos. He loved her and it was that simple. They had been cautious because of Maisy and his family, and now they were gone. One of the hurdles stopping them from being together was no longer there.

Hal stooped and looked in the cupboard next to where the fridge used to live. At the back was a bottle of Kraken spiced rum. He reached in and took it out, twisting the top off.

'You missed this, Ernie,' Hal said, drinking it straight from the bottle. It burnt and made his eyes water. He trudged out of the kitchen and went upstairs. His bed was the right way up, which was a bonus. He sat on the edge and swigged the rum and thought about what to do next. How could he salvage anything from this disaster?

Pauline Verwood was going to try to get him dismissed from the service. She was renowned for being tenacious. Like a dog with a bone, and she wanted him buried. He needed to speak to her face to face to explain his situation. He might even tell her the truth. He had made a mistake by falling in love with a married woman and her husband had found out. His wrath was the reason for whatever had happened since. He was understandably pissed off and he had set out to cause Hal as much damage as he could. She might see it for what it was if he told her the truth. The car crash was a genuine accident. No one would have questioned that had the messages not been sent the night before. The Air Commodore was obviously a rational, intelligent person. If he could appeal to her and explain, maybe he could salvage his career. If he could salvage his career, he may be able to offer Naomi an alternative life to the one she had. Maybe they could be together. Ernest Metcalfe would be angry. Angrier than he was already but he would have to accept what was going to happen and take it like a man. Hal swigged the rum and let the warm glow spread through him, comforting him. Making him believe there was sunshine after the rain. He steeled himself for what needed to be done. Ernie Metcalfe was just another man, and he wasn't scared of him. The moon shone brightly through the window, its silver glow making him feel safe.

Chapter 32

DS Carla Michaels was waiting for the phone to ring. The techs had the mobile phone that Father Frank Gamble's attacker had taken to the priest's home. Luckily, it wasn't an iPhone, and they could hack into it, eventually. It was a decent Samsung, so not a burner phone. That meant two things. First, there would be history stored on the phone and the sim card. Photographs, emails, text messages, voicemails, social media apps, and all the information they could yield, which was massive. The second thing was it meant the owner was not a forensically educated criminal, or he was stupid, possibly both. He had taken his own phone to an execution, which was a schoolboy error. His second schoolboy error was leaving his baton within reach of his victim.

The GPS would give them the route he had taken there, proof of his whereabouts at the time the triple nine call was made and information on the build up to the crime. The attacker probably staked out the property in the days or weeks before, and the GPS would confirm that. The evidence gleaned from the mobile would put him away for a long stretch. On top of that, the CSI team had recovered fingerprints and DNA from items the attacker had come into contact with, including a crisp packet and a glass. The attacker was clearly low IQ or so arrogant, he didn't care. She was looking out of the hospital window towards the Ogwen Valley when her phone rang.

'DS Michaels,' she answered.

'Afternoon, boss,' her DI said. 'We've cracked the phone.'

'Brilliant,' she said, smiling. 'Tell me it's his own phone.'

'It is,' the DI confirmed.

'So, we have an ID?'

'Howard Shields,' the DI said. 'Twenty-eight-years old from Abersoch. There's a shedload of information in his phone. He's married with two kids and he works as a car salesman for a dealership near Caernarfon. He's a regular contributor to the Justice Asylum website and one of the founders by the look of it. There's also a lot of homophobic shit on his profiles and he's a member of the EDL and a bunch of far-right anti-Muslim groups.'

'He sounds like a real diamond,' Michaels said. 'Get someone over to his home. I want to speak to his wife before this kicks off online. I don't want her finding out from Facebook that her husband was about to execute a priest.'

'I've sent what we have so far to your laptop, but there's plenty to put him in the frame for organising some of the recent attacks. He took video of parts of the attack on Gamble too.'

'Perfect,' Michaels said. 'Call me if we get anything else.'

****

Pauline Verwood was the highest-ranking female on the base at RAF

Valley and that role carried the weight of responsibility. Some of her male counterparts were wary of her. Most of them respected her but some feared her authority, others resented her for reaching heights they couldn't scale. The fact she was female should not matter yet it did. Many deemed her rank as positive discrimination on behalf of the service. The token female high-ranking officer, which each base required. Alongside the correct number of different religions, a mixture of ethnicities, and abilities and the impression of a genuine sense of fairness. It was a difficult balance to find. The air force was as scrutinised as every other career and the subject of gender and ethnicity diversity through the ranks was a hot topic. Pauline felt the pressure of expectation. The expectation of success from her family, friends, supporters, and admirers and the expectation of failure from the sceptics, haters, and misogynists.

Personal relationships were virtually impossible, which suited her. Her position protected her. The lower rank and file dared not approach her on a personal level. Her rank acted as a barrier between her and the idiots who didn't respect her as an individual and only saw the woman as a possible sexual conquest. Those who failed to see the rank and only saw the female were few and far between. There were some who deemed her part of the weaker sex and as such, only really useful for her ability to have sex. It was highly unlikely she would choose to be with someone with that mentality. Not on a consensual basis. The enlisted men and women on the base wouldn't approach her in any flirtatious manner. She shut down any approaches from social media and the wider public forums.

Sometimes she felt the loneliness of being a single, professional woman but mostly she embraced it. She had no time for a husband or wife and wasn't quite sure which she would prefer. Children were something she had considered and ruled out of her life. She had no maternal instincts. Her career encompassed her hopes and aspirations.

She was shocked by the messages she'd received from a low-ranking police officer. They were offensive and threatening. She was shocked and angered. Corporal Harold Nelson had crossed the line and broken every rule in the book. The language and tone used in the messages he sent to her were straight from a seventies porn magazine. She doubted the women of any era actually found that kind of approach attractive. *"I'd love to tie you up and smash your back doors in…"*

That was just one of the gems, which stuck in her mind. It was disturbing at best and endearing never. There was only one way to deal with it and that was officially. She had used the correct channels and complained to HR first. He had been interviewed and denied everything. His resulting behaviour had been unexpected. Nelson had driven his vehicle into the rear of her new Mercedes and claimed it was an accident. That was a monumental mistake on his behalf. A jilted narcissist turned to violence when questioned by authority, was a potential danger to society. She intended to prosecute him through the service and through civilian avenues as well. Her afternoon had been spent sending emails to everyone above her, her solicitor, her union representative, the camp commander, and the highest-ranking female in the RAF. The first female Air Vice-Marshall, Elaine Bell. She was going to force the pursuit of the issue as serious sexual harassment and criminal damage. Until Nelson was drummed out of the service or he resigned, she wasn't going to let it lie.

Pauline turned on the taps to run her bath. She undressed and folded her uniform onto a chair, dropping her underwear into the laundry basket. Her attention was taken by her reflection in a full-length mirror. She was pushing forty but looked trim. Her breasts were still defying gravity, although the telltale signs of stretching were beginning to show on the skin below her collarbone. Her hips and thighs were full and toned from using her jogging machine and multi-gym and frequent treks in Snowdonia. She was feeling pale. A respray of St. Tropez was due if she was to maintain her lightly tanned appearance. It was her evening ritual. Her bath plank was already set up with her Kindle, candles, and a glass of Chardonnay. She would lie in the hot water for an hour, topping up with hot water until her fingers and toes were wrinkled. Then she would towel dry, moisturise her skin, and dress in her pyjamas and fluffy dressing gown while she ate her evening meal. It was a well-needed switch off. A few hours away from the workload which came with her position. Once she'd put her crockery into the dishwasher, she would read and reply to her social media contacts and messages for a few hours. There weren't enough hours in the day. She barely watched television. There was always too much to do. She couldn't remember the last time she watched a film. Her bath was her oasis from the stress and strains of the day.

A cold breeze touched her skin and goosebumps appeared on her arms. She felt the chill on her shoulders. She grabbed a towel and wrapped it around her. Pauline wondered if she'd left the door open by mistake but knew she hadn't. She was security savvy. In fact, because of an episode when she was a teenager, she was OCD about security. All the doors and windows were closed and locked all the time, without fail. They always were. If one of them had been opened, someone had broken in.

Pauline felt vulnerable. She stepped into her underwear and trousers and pulled on her housecoat. The water running was the only noise she could hear. She turned the taps off and walked to the top of the stairs, peering over the banister at the hallway below. There was no sign of an intruder, and it was silent. Deathly quiet. She went into her bedroom and opened her bedside drawer. A tin of pepper spray and a stainless-steel knuckle duster lay side by side. They were given to her by her ex-girlfriend while she was stationed in Saudi Arabia for a three-month exchange. She had taken them out of the drawer twice. Both were false alarms. The spray fit into the palm of her left hand and the steel knuckles slipped over the fingers of her right. It felt cold and heavy and lethal. It would rip flesh and shatter bones and give her enough time to escape and raise the alarm. She walked to the top of the stairs and listened. It was quiet. Pauline released the air in her lungs and took a deep breath. It had been an eventful day. Maybe she had overreacted. She sighed and tried to relax. A heavy blow to the back of her skull sent blinding lights through her brain. The pain was mind numbing. Her knees folded and she toppled forward and tumbled down the stairs. She hit the fourth step with her face, smashing her teeth. The taste of blood filled her senses as she somersaulted again. She hit the granite tiles at the bottom of the staircase with a sickening thud. Consciousness faded and her vision narrowed. She saw a figure walking down the stairs towards her, a steel hammer in his hand and then she felt the blackness engulf her.

Chapter 33

Clive Roland pulled off the road onto a small car park. Car park was probably an overstatement of what it was. It was a patch of gravel big enough to park two vehicles side by side. Drystone walls separated it from the chapel grounds and miles of undulating wilderness. The chapel was surrounded by rolling fields which climbed gently to the lower slopes of the Snowden range. The peak of Tryfan loomed in the distance, snow on the upper slopes. To the north was Bethesda and south was the road to Betws-y-coed. A heavy goods vehicle thundered past making the ground vibrate. He waited until it had gone before opening the door and climbing out. The cold hit him like a wall of ice. Cool air rolled down the mountains into the valleys where it remained. A shiver ran down his spine, which was nothing to do with the cold. It was something else. He hadn't slept well the night before. Faces from the past had visited him. Faces he hadn't seen for decades. His parents, his younger brother, his sister. All the people he cared about who were gone. Not dead, just gone.

His appointment was already there. He could see him looking at the headstones in the graveyard. The man was listed as Mr Jones. He was wearing a dark overcoat, dark gloves, and a dark scarf, which covered the lower half of his face. His hair was cropped to his scalp. This was only the fourth viewing he had done here in as many years. It was a property which became a millstone for the practice. No one cared if it sold. Builders avoided it because of the regulations involved. Converting redundant chapels and churches was vogue in the eighties before building regulations tightened and the cost of touching listed buildings became ridiculously prohibitive. Developers made a killing in the eighties but it was a different kettle of fish nowadays. Legislation had strangled the regeneration and renovation boom yet people whinged about the lack of housing. Not in my backyard was the catchphrase of the moment. Build as many housing estates as we need but don't build them near me. People wanted it all ways as long as it suited them. It was difficult to be excited about trying to make a sale when it was virtually impossible to wean a profit from the site. His mood reflected the weather. Dull.

'Hello,' Clive said, waving. It started raining. He could hear the babbling brook, which ran beside the graveyard at the rear of the property. It sounded louder than usual. The rainwater from the previous days was swelling the streams on the lower slopes. The sky was slate grey and moody. Apt for showing a potential buyer around a redundant chapel and graveyard. 'You must be Mr Jones. You found it okay?'

'It would be hard not to find it,' the client said, looking around. There wasn't another building for miles. 'There's nothing here but mountains and sheep.'

'You'd be surprised,' Clive said. 'The satnav announces your arrival about four miles up the road. I've lost count of the number of clients who haven't made it.'

'I think satnavs are great if they're combined with a modicum of common sense. Something sadly lacking nowadays,' Mr Jones said. 'Have you done a lot of viewings here?'

'Not a lot. No.'

'Are there any interested parties at the moment?' Mr Jones asked, still looking at the headstones. He appeared disinterested in Clive's arrival.

'No.' Clive lowered his voice as he walked through the gate, which was hanging by a single hinge. Grass and weeds made it difficult to open fully. It was knee deep except for on the graves. Rust had blistered the wrought iron, and the metal groaned its resistance to being moved. 'Between me and you, there is no one interested at all.'

'We're sharing secrets already,' Mr Jones said, turning towards him. Clive felt himself being scrutinised. It made him feel awkward.

'I'm not supposed to give you that information but there is hardly a queue of buyers waiting to snap it up,' Clive explained. 'We don't have a bidding war on our hands so, if you're interested, a decent offer would probably steal it, to be honest.' Mr Jones seemed to be oblivious to his conversation. He wandered between the gravestones, reading the inscriptions. 'I see you are getting to know the locals,' he added, gesturing to the gravestones. 'There are over fifty graves here, most of them hold entire families, great grandparents, grandparents, parents, children. Five to a plot and ashes of course. They don't take up any room. It was declared full in the seventies although I believe ashes have been interned here as recently as the late nineties.'

'It's fascinating,' Mr Jones said. 'The circle of life. We come here with nothing and we leave with nothing, only our actions remain.' Mr Jones looked up and nodded. 'What we do during our short time here can have ramifications which echo through time, don't you think?'

'I haven't given it a lot of thought, to be honest,' Clive said, confused. The client was a strange individual. In fact, he was a bit of a knob. 'The graves are the reason it hasn't sold. They are the main problem with the plot being commercially viable.'

'This is a chapel. A place of God. The graves give it the authenticity it deserves,' Mr Jones said. 'Just think about it. Entire families came here for generations. Born nearby, came here to be christened, attended Sunday school, had their weddings here, christened their own offspring in turn and then returned a final time for their funerals. Generations took great strength from being part of this Church. Here they lie, proof of a community lost in time.'

'Quite a profound description, but very true, I suppose,' Clive said, approaching. He wanted to get back to the office. His stomach was grumbling. This was the last appointment of the day. 'Unfortunately, moving them is incredibly expensive and finding living relatives to give permission is impossible. Most of these families are gone. I bet their descendants don't even know who they are, never mind care less if they're moved but the rules are the rules.'

'I can imagine it would be a costly exercise.'

'If they're not relocated, any construction would have to be limited to the footprint of the chapel itself and not everyone wants a graveyard for a garden.'

'When does a graveyard stop being a graveyard?' Mr Jones asked, shaking his head.

'Pardon?'

'I'm sure some of the families would be devastated if they knew their ancestor's resting place was about to be below the bathroom of a holiday chalet.' Mr Jones walked towards the front door of the chapel. 'Imagine knowing tourists were taking a shite above your grandmother's grave. Not a pleasant thought.'

'I never thought of it like that,' Clive said, taking out the keys for the chapel. He wanted to be away from there. His client was clearly a nutcase. 'Shall we look inside?'

'Yes, please. I'm sure no one thought it would ever be anything else but hallowed ground and a place of worship when they buried their loved ones here.'

'I'm sure they didn't.'

'This should be their final place. They laid them to rest,' Mr Jones said. 'Why would they think they would ever be dug up for a profit?'

'None of us can predict the future. It's a sign of the times,' Clive said, becoming irritated. 'Religion is on the decline and the Church is cashing in on its lands. There hasn't been a congregation here for decades, so I guess there aren't many people left to be offended.'

'Decline or not,' Mr Jones said, shaking his head. 'It is hallowed ground and should be treated as such.'

'Obviously, the decision would lie with the buyer.'

'Obviously.'

'What would your plan for the graveyard be?'

'It's a graveyard. I have no plan to move them,' Mr Jones said. 'We will not disturb them too much. They can rest in peace.'

'Really,' Clive asked, confused. 'Are you going to build on the footprint of the chapel itself?'

'No.'

'What are you planning to do with it?'

'Buy it. Make sure it doesn't become a derelict pile of stones.'

'I see,' Clive said, hunching against the rain. He had lost interest in Mr Jones and his cryptic replies. It was like pulling teeth. 'I'll show you inside.' Clive opened the arched shaped door with a huge iron key. The lock clunked. He pushed the door open and the hinges squealed. The smell of damp and decay met him as he stepped inside. It was cold and unpleasant, but at least he was out of the driving rain. He switched on the light. A single strip light flickered; the starter buzzed noisily. Daylight barely made it through the grimy stained-glass windows. Sheets of gossamer hung from the ceilings, blocking the daylight. The windows were narrow and tall. The images depicted within their frames were indiscernible from where they were standing. 'As you can see, there is electricity, but the wiring needs to be replaced. There is no running water and no gas. The chapel has been redundant since they failed to raise enough money to fix the roof. That was in the nineties. The pews are still here and are made from Yew. There's a market for them. The pulpit is oak and might be worth a bob or two as are the windows. Antique auctions are crying out for stained-glass windows, especially if the lead is intact. Apparently, they depict the betrayal of Jesus, the Crucifixion, and the hanging of Judas. All cheery stuff but in demand.'

'Betrayal is a mortal sin,' Mr Jones said. 'Judas betrayed us all and was punished. Hanging has been portrayed in the scriptures for centuries.'

'I'm sure it has,' Clive mumbled, losing his patience. 'There are some worrying cracks at the back of the Church in the chancel and the brickwork is riddled with damp. The walls are crumbling in the corner to the left. I would question if they're capable of holding the roof for much longer without significant structural improvement. The buyer would need a significant amount of cash to keep it upright.'

'Do you want to sell this, Mr Roland?'

'Yes, of course,' Clive lied. He couldn't care less if it sold or not. They didn't take commission from church sales.

'Then you may want to change your selling pitch,' Mr Jones said. Another man entered the nave. He was dressed in a similar fashion to his associate. 'Ah, there you are. This is Mr Roland from the estate agency. We were talking about the decline of the Church.'

'You have had a significant influence on that,' the new arrival said. 'As an associate of Father Creegan, you have directly impacted on how the Church is perceived here in this country and beyond,' the man said, nodding. 'You've sullied the name and reputation of it.'

'Sorry. I've no idea what you've just said,' Clive said.

'I said, your association with Father Creegan is unfortunate.'

'Who?' Clive asked, looking shocked.

'Father Creegan. Father Patrick Creegan,' Mr Jones said.

'I've never heard of him.' Clive looked from one man to the other. They were sinister. Their mannerisms odd.

'You know him, Mr Roland.'

'I do not.'

'You gave Father Creegan access to empty properties in return for invitations to his gatherings. Many of them were held in properties you managed.'

'I'm here to show you around this property. I have absolutely no idea what the fuck you are talking about?' Clive said, angrily.

'You know what we're talking about. You were investigated by the police but there wasn't enough evidence to convict you.'

'Wait a minute. Are you reporters?' Clive said, shaking his head. 'I've told you lot to fuck off a thousand times. I've nothing to say on the subject.'

'We're not reporters.'

'You must be, otherwise, what is this?'

'We're not reporters,' Mr Jones said. 'The accusations have been documented over and over. Unfortunately, accusations alone will not suffice. Without a confession, they're just empty words.'

'If you're not reporters, who are you?'

'Who we are doesn't really matter. This is the time to confess what you did,' Mr Jones said. 'You lied to the police, hence you're free to walk around and be a continuing danger to the public.'

'I don't know what you're talking about.'

'It's very simple. You're a paedophile but there wasn't enough evidence for you to be charged as such.'

'That's a lie,' Clive said, shaking his head. The colour drained from his face. 'Who are you to come in here and make these accusations?' The men looked at him with no emotion in their expressions. 'I've heard enough. Get out. Both of you before I lose my temper.'

'I'm not going anywhere. My name is Mr Jones and I'm going to buy this chapel from the Church, for the Church,' he said.

'I'm delighted for you,' Clive said. 'In the meantime, you can both fuck off. Go on. Get out!'

'I'm also going to accept your confession.'

'I don't understand what the fuck you're talking about,' Clive said. 'You're both mad. Who are you?' he asked the other man.

'I'm Mr Jones too,' he said.

'That figures,' Clive said. 'If you're both Mr Jones, I'm Donald Duck. I don't know what kind of game you're playing but I'm not interested. I'm not telling you again. Fuck off.'

'We're not playing games. I've put an offer in with your office earlier when you arrived. I offered the asking price,' he added. 'It's been accepted.'

'Oh. That's good,' Clive said, confused. 'I really couldn't give a shit if you've bought it or what you do with it. I'll call the office and confirm it.' He looked at his phone but there was no signal. 'When I get a bit closer.' He put his phone away and walked towards the light switch nervously. 'I don't know where you get your information from, but you have the wrong man. And I don't care who you are or what you think you know or what you're going to do with this pile of stones but good luck to you.' Clive looked at both men. They looked back at him blankly. 'You have no right coming here accusing me of anything. I'm an innocent man. Print that in your paper or on your website or wherever you please. Do you have any other fucking nonsense to discuss or can we leave it at that?'

'No more nonsense. We'll need your phone and your car keys,' the first Mr Jones said.

'What are you talking about, you crazy bastard?' Clive said. 'Listen to me. I'm not giving you anything. Get out before I phone the police.'

'Call them if you can, but in the meantime, I need your car keys. The fewer people who can remember seeing your car here, the better.'

'I'm not giving you anything, fucking weirdos.' Clive held the big iron key in his hand and allowed the shaft to poke between his fingers as a weapon. 'I'm leaving. I'll call the police on my way up the road.'

'You're staying here,' the second Mr Jones said. 'I've been digging at the back of the graveyard, next to the brook.' The two men approached him slowly. 'Don't make this more painful than it needs to be.'

'What are you doing?' Clive asked, starting to shake with fear. 'I didn't do anything. I'm going to call the police. Stay away from me.'

'We are the police of sorts,' the first Mr Jones said. Clive didn't give what he said much attention. 'And you're a paedophile and we're going to put you in the ground.'

'Put me in the ground?' Clive asked, astounded. 'Have you heard yourself? You sound like a lunatic.'

'You're going into the Barker family grave next to the wall near the brook, where no one will ever look for you.' Mr Jones shrugged. 'You'll be underneath Mildred Barker's coffin. I'm sure Mildred won't mind her brief visit above ground under the circumstances. She was a mother of four, so she will understand.'

'Stay away from me,' Clive said, raising the rusty key. 'You have no idea who I know. I'll have you both sacked. You can't touch me. I was released. No further action.' The men cut off his escape routes. 'Piss off and leave me alone.'

'The CPS don't always get things right,' the second Mr Jones said. 'They try their best, but their hands are tied. Justice, Clive Roland. We're here to make you confess and bring justice to the dozens of children you and the other scum assaulted. It's ironic you're going to pay for what you did here in a chapel, don't you think?'

The first Mr Jones took a lump hammer from his jacket. The second Mr Jones took a carpet knife from his pocket. He closed the wooden door with a thump.

'This is going to hurt a lot,' he said. 'And it's going to take quite some time but if a job's worth doing, it's worth doing properly.'

Clive Roland ran for the door but his route was blocked. Sweat was running from his forehead.

The men approached from both sides.

He launched himself over one of the pews and tried to hurdle them. His shin caught one of them and there was a loud crack.

Clive felt pain shoot up his leg like a bolt of lightning. His foot hung at an unnatural angle.

He fell to his knees and begged for mercy but mercy wasn't listening.

Chapter 34

Alan was sitting in his office waiting for something to show him the right direction to go in. His conversation with Michaels about the attacker's identity was detailed and interesting but didn't yield anything he could put to his team and get closer to an arrest. Howard Shields was a follower, not a leader. His input to the Justice Asylum website was macho bullshit. His distinction between gay men and straight men and paedophiles was mind-blowingly prehistoric. The lines were so blurred, they didn't exist. Shields thought heterosexual men were the norm. Anything outside of that group were not the same species. He ranted online that homosexual men were responsible for the deterioration of Western society. Apparently, Putin had the right idea jailing them and the Iranians were spot on tossing men accused of being gay from high-rise buildings. He blamed domestic television channels for normalising homosexuality by hiring gay television presenters in the UK. In his opinion, gay television presenters were sending a message that it was okay to be gay, infecting young men everywhere, making them gay in turn. He posted that belief many times and argued his opinion whenever he was challenged. His Facebook account was regularly suspended. Alan found the concept of homosexuality being contagious staggeringly stupid. Shields said it was a vicious circle and the people who employed gays must be gay too. His rhetoric knew no bounds. He hankered for a society that made it a crime to be gay. He had posted that his grandfather and father would be spinning in their graves that gays weren't embarrassed to be gay anymore. Times had changed for the worse.

On the positive side, gay women were acceptable and he liked watching girl on girl pornography, which made no sense at all to Alan, but there was no sense to be made from his ramblings. The man was an idiot. A very dangerous idiot. He was taking credit for several attacks on gay men in Bangor, usually couples. He would stalk them and attack from behind with a baton. Probably the baton which eventually made its way to Father Frank Gamble's home. His ability to morph his homophobia into an equally violent hatred of paedophiles displayed his unbalanced view of the world. Michaels said she could clear up half a dozen unsolved attacks using the information gleaned from his mobile phone alone. The streets would be safer with Shields in a hospital bed.

It was clear Shields wasn't the sharpest tool in the box and it was also clear his hatred of anyone not heterosexual, white, and Christian could be channelled by a leader and pointed like a weapon. The direction didn't matter. He was happy to attack anything he perceived outside of the norm. He could be persuaded to attack a gay couple one day and a Jewish family the next. According to his social media, Muslim students were also on his radar. His discrimination appeared to have no boundaries.

Michaels was interviewing his spouse and workmates. It was difficult to believe he had found someone to breed with. A list of his social media buddies would take more time and preparation to complete. They could make arrests for hate speech but that wasn't the focus he wanted the investigation to go in. They were looking for killers not talkers. Distinguishing who was who would take time.

Bob Dewhurst and April knocked on the door. He waved them in.

'You wanted to see us?' Bob asked.

'I do,' Alan said. 'Take a seat.' The uniformed officers sat down. 'How was Noah's birthday party?' Alan asked April.

'Crazy, as usual,' she replied. 'The kids ate too much, my dad drank too much and started singing, and then he sulked when Sharon told him off for hogging the karaoke. We got it for the kids but you know what he's like.'

'Sounds familiar,' Alan said. 'Anyway, you know we have a video of Father Derek Corbin being attacked,' he asked. They both nodded. 'His attack fits into a string of other attacks, which may be connected to the bodies we found in the woods near Tinto. I'm trying to fit the pieces together. What can you tell me about the report on his car?'

'It was reported missing by a man called Michael Hughes. He called in the information of the tracker and Corbin's description and licence details,' April said. 'Apparently, Hughes is an asset manager for the diocese and works directly for the bishop. He handles vehicle leasing and the Church property holdings and answers to the bishop.'

'What did he say about Corbin?'

'Corbin was allowed to stay at the vicarage under certain conditions. One of them was informing the managers where he was going. He said he was going fishing and never returned, which was unusual. Concern was raised the second day he didn't return and they reported the vehicle missing or stolen as it has a tracker.'

'Did they report him missing?' Alan asked.

'Yes. The people who run the vicarage called us but it wasn't deemed as a missing person incident. He's an adult in good health with a drink problem. They were told to leave it twenty-four hours. I think that's why they reported the vehicle missing, to get us to look for him.'

'Okay,' Alan said. 'If his attack is linked to the others, we have a team of vigilantes focused on attacking the men who walked away without charges at the end of the Creegan case. It could have been a coincidence but in light of the other cases, it's looking like an organised series of assaults.'

'Vigilantes attacking paedos. I'd give them a medal,' Bob said.

'Get in the queue,' Alan said. 'But keep it between us.'

'Aye. Will do,' Bob said, tapping his nose.

'What I can't work out is how did his attackers know where he was?' Alan asked.

'Maybe they followed him?' April said.

'Or maybe they called the vicarage looking for him and they told them where he was going fishing,' Bob said.

'They knew he was going fishing at that spot?' Alan asked.

'Yes. They put it in the missing report for the vehicle, but the tracker had already been traced. They said he was going to Mackerel Rock area fishing,' April said. 'When we got the report, the vehicle had been located and was already found but no one had checked it. It was locked and there was no sign of a break in. Forensics said there was no fishing gear in the vehicle, so we're guessing he did actually set up to fish.' April checked her notes.

'He did set up. The video shows him sitting with a rod in his hand,' Alan agreed. 'How long he was there before he was attacked, we don't know.'

'We've spoken to several regulars who fish the cliffs around there,' April said. 'They said they quite often see him there, usually drinking and smoking and not catching much. One of them said he was sometimes worried about how drunk he was when he headed back to the car, knowing he was going to drive.'

'I checked the rocks and asked around,' Bob said. 'No one had seen any tackle left on the rocks or the headland. The attacker must have tossed it in with him.'

'Can you check with the people at the vicarage and ask if there was anyone who went to see him or called him regularly on the phone,' Alan asked. 'I need to know if these priests were in touch with each other following the trial. Whoever is attacking them appears to know exactly where they are and they definitely have local knowledge of the area. Not just a visitor's knowhow. I think they're from the island. If they are, we should be able to find them by talking to the locals. Can I leave that with you?'

'Yes. No problem,' Bob said.

'Leave it with us,' April agreed.

****

The accident and emergency department was busy. It was always busy. As the day went by, the seats were occupied by a mixture of drunk people and people who had hurt themselves in accidents because they were drunk. Both of which could probably have been avoided if only human beings weren't so reliant on alcohol socially. The massive drop of casualty patients during lockdown highlighted the damage caused when the pubs and clubs reopened. A man wearing a white coat walked through the department with a cup of coffee and a laptop. His glasses were perched on the end of his nose so he could see where he was going. The white coat he was wearing had been taken from the back of a Mazda at the rear of the hospital, as had the stethoscope, name badge, and four pens, which adorned his breast pocket.

He called in at the main reception and asked where Howard Shields was being treated. The receptionist was relatively new, and he baffled her by telling her Shields had been brought in by ambulance and should be in A&E but had been moved and there was no further information. She found him on the system. He had indeed been brought in by ambulance and had been taken straight into surgery and ICU. He thanked her and headed for the lift. The ICU was on the first floor, not far from the lifts. It would be simple enough to identify when he got there. He took the lift with two uniformed officers and three nurses, making sure his name badge was covered with his laptop. The last thing he needed was someone realising he wasn't Dr Lynn Evans. That would be difficult to explain.

The lift doors opened, and he waited for everyone to exit before stepping out. He headed towards the corridor which led to the wards, relieved it was the opposite direction from the policemen. He took just seconds to identify where the ICU patients were. The lights were subdued and the presence of medical machinery sealed it. Nurses whizzed about from ward to ward, talking briefly as they crossed paths. A group of police officers were huddled together in the main corridor outside the ICU. He guessed they were there to monitor Shields and make sure no one spoke to him before they had. That was inconvenient.

He walked down the corridor away from them. He saw a cleaning closet with a row of trolleys outside. They were stocked up with linen sheets and towels. The bottom shelf of each trolley was packed with blue rolls of paper towels. He pushed one of the trolleys into the closet and closed the door. The closet was packed with laundry. He stood on the trolley and covered a smoke alarm with a plastic wrapper from a bundle of sheets. He took a roll of paper towel and pulled the seal free, unravelling it quickly. It made a knee-high pile on the floor. He took a lighter from his pocket and set fire to it. The flames spread quickly. He tossed a bundle of towels onto the flames and pushed the trolley next to it. The shelves caught in seconds and he slipped out of the door and headed for the gents' toilets to wait.

****

Morris Trigg staggered out of the Edinburgh Castle at closing time. It had been a good night. The pool table was busy with plenty of names chalked up, waiting for a game. He loved it like that. The more victims, the better. Trigg was one of the best players in Gwynedd, probably one of the best in Wales. He could have played professionally but that would have involved leaving Holyhead and joining one of the city leagues. Liverpool, Manchester, and London were all stepping-stones to Europe and the USA. Cash players could make megabucks in tournament competitions but they needed sponsors for the entrance money. Trigg didn't have any money. Not that kind of money. Then the kids came along and drained him of every spare penny he could muster. His daughter Nia had been the first on the scene. Then when Brenda fell pregnant the second time, he swore there would be no more. When they found out she was having twins, Trigg got drunk for a week. Everyone thought he was celebrating, but he was drowning his sorrows. He didn't think he could cope with two more children in one dose. Any aspirations he had of leaving the island to play the game he loved for a living were dashed. His hopes of being a professional on the tour vanished before him. The kids were such a drain on his time and his energy that by bedtime he was absolutely shattered. There was no time to breathe let alone practice. Brenda was a fabulous mother, and he did his best to support her. He kept his resentment inside. His family were his life and he couldn't envisage leaving them to follow his dream. He had to drop out of the pub team for a full season until the twins were eating and sleeping through the night properly. Brenda knew he resented the missed opportunity, and that's why she didn't moan if he went to the pub and played pool all night. His winnings paid for all he drank, and he would have twenty-quid on top, which he usually shared between the kids. It was the trade-off they both silently accepted. They had their kids, and they were good kids and they had each other. Trigg was happy enough. Things could always be worse. He walked with practised ease, despite the ale.

'Morris Trigg,' a voice said from behind him. Trigg glanced over his shoulder. He was walking along Turkey Shore Road to avoid the hill. Skinner's monument loomed above him on the cliffs, looking over the harbour like a granite sentinel guarding the town. It was the longer route but easier to navigate after eight pints of Guinness. He didn't recognise the man. 'Do you mind if I walk with you?'

'It's a free country,' Trigg said. He took a better look at the man as he drew level. The man was mid-forties and well-built. His manner was odd. He looked around as if everything was unfamiliar. There was no reason to be on Turkey Shore Road at that time of night unless you lived nearby. The man's accent wasn't Holyhead. 'Do I know you?'

'No. We haven't had the pleasure,' the man said. He had his hands shoved deep into his pockets.

'Yet you know my name,' Trigg said. 'That's a little odd. Are you from the newspapers?'

'Newspapers?' the man asked, frowning. 'Why would I be from the newspapers?'

'Never mind,' Trigg said, eyeing him suspiciously. 'How do you know my name if you're not a reporter?'

'I'm Simon. I won't offer you my hand because I'm here on some unpleasant business.'

'Is that right?' Trigg asked. The hairs on the back of his neck stood on end. There was something about this stranger he didn't like. 'And what business would that be?'

'Nasty business,' the man said. 'Business that involves your kids.'

'You're stepping on dangerous ground,' Trigg said. He walked on to put more space between himself and the man. His hand squeezed his pool cue case tightly. It was maple wood and unscrewed into two sections, jointed in the middle. He carried it in a leather case. 'What do you want, mister?'

'Like I said, I'm here on some nasty business,' the man said. 'Business that should never have involved children, but it does. Unfortunately, your twins witnessed something they should never have seen at their age.' The man shook his head. 'Not at any age, if the truth be told,' he corrected himself. 'Philip and Tom saw a terrible thing and we're sorry for that but they did and it has to be addressed.'

'How do you know their names?' Trigg asked angrily.

'It wasn't difficult to find out.'

'If you mess with my kids, I'll kick your fucking head in.'

The man slipped behind Trigg with elusive speed. He kicked the back of his knees, sending Trigg to the pavement. Trigg lost the cue and lay on his back like a stranded beetle, arms and legs flailing at thin air. The man stood over him and put his foot on his chest. Trigg could hardly breathe.

'Listen to me because I'm only going to say this once,' the man said. 'Your boys are young with all their lives ahead of them. It would be a terrible shame if something happened to them because they were in the wrong place at the wrong time.'

'If you touch my kids…'

'Don't make threats you clearly cannot deliver. You're on your back in the middle of the street,' the man said, shaking his head. 'There are no heroes in this story. This is not a game. This is not something you can stop from happening unless you listen to me carefully.' He stomped on Trigg's chest. Trigg spluttered and a fountain of part digested Guinness spewed from his mouth. He was beginning to choke on it until the man flipped him on his side. 'Get yourself home as fast as you can. If you run, you might be able to save them. If you fuck about, they'll suffocate and burn to death.' Trigg started to panic. 'Tell your boys that they saw nothing, Trigg. Nothing at all,' the man said. 'No matter what the police say or do, they cannot remember a thing. Do you understand me?' Trigg nodded and tried to stand. The man grabbed his wrist and bent it backwards. Trigg felt like it was about to snap. 'Do you understand me?'

'Yes. Get off me,' Trigg shouted. Headlights appeared and a car came around the corner and slowed to a stop. The passenger door opened and the man climbed inside. He opened the window and slammed the door as the vehicle drove off.

'Hurry up, Trigg,' the man said. 'Get home before it's too late.'

Chapter 35

It was nearly midnight when Alan got home. The lights were on in the living room, which was a surprise. His youngest son, Jack, was still in Vietnam. The borders had closed through covid but he didn't appear to be in a rush to go home now they were open again. His middle son, Dan, had a new baby, so it was unlikely to be him. The dogs were not going ballistic in the window, which was unheard of, so someone had let them out on the farmer's field at the back of the bungalow. Alan turned off the engine and climbed out. He tucked a half bottle of Bells into his inside pocket. The boys didn't like him drinking whisky. That wasn't strictly true. They didn't like him drinking all the whisky in the bottle in one sitting. That was the long and short of it. There were days when he could have one and chill out before bed. A big one, granted but just one. Other days, he could finish a bottle and then look for leftover wine in the fridge. Alan said the problem with alcohol is it's moreish and that was the truth. Even the worst hangover ever didn't deter people from doing it again. And again. Stress fuelled his desire for the burn in his throat, the warmth in his stomach, and the numbness in his head that followed. Switching his brain off allowed him to rest and sleep well.

He opened the front door and Kris, the eldest, popped his head around the kitchen door. His girlfriend, Joy, stepped out and waved, her infectious smile beaming from ear to ear.

'What are you two doing here?' Alan asked. 'I haven't got any money.'

'You never have any money. We came to say hello and feed the dogs,' Kris said. 'You're home late. I saw the news and figured you would be stuck at the station and the dogs would be dying for a crap.'

'Bless you,' Alan said. 'Thank you.'

'Is this case a nightmare?' Kris asked.

'Yes. It's a difficult one.'

'There's lots of gossip going around town,' Kris said. 'About who it is and who did it.'

'I can imagine the rumour mill turning at full speed,' Alan said.

'You wouldn't believe the number of people suggesting who it is. Basically, anyone who hasn't been seen since yesterday is a potential victim.'

'That's Holyhead for you,' Alan said. 'We love a good old gossip.'

'Have you found out who the victims are yet?' Kris asked.

'We have a vague idea,' Alan said. 'It's too early to say for certain. I can't say anything. You'll have to make it up if anyone asks you.'

'I've had messages from people I haven't heard from for years asking if I know anything.'

'One of the downsides of having a detective for a dad,' Alan said. 'Probably the only downside,' he added.

'What about none of my friends offer me anything that's fallen off the back of a lorry?' Kris said.

'Nor me,' Alan said. 'I never get offered anything cheap.'

'What about none of my friends invite me to a party where there will be recreational drugs being passed around?'

'Same again.' Alan nodded. 'I never get invited to parties.'

'Shall I carry on?' Kris asked.

'No. You're boring me,' Alan said. 'Go back to the murders. That was a decent conversation.'

'Is it anyone we know?'

'I can't have a conversation about it,' Alan said. 'It's an ongoing investigation.'

'Who is being boring now?'

'I'm amusing myself.'

'Knob,' Kris said, smiling. 'Is it anyone we know?'

'No. I doubt it,' Alan said. He walked into the kitchen and switched on the kettle. Kris frowned. 'Don't worry. I haven't started drinking coffee. I want to do the dishes.'

'I've done them,' Joy said beaming. She was Thai origin and smiled almost constantly. 'You don't have to worry about them.'

'So, you have,' Alan said, smiling. The draining board was full of squeaky-clean crockery. 'I haven't seen this many clean plates since your mum got a cleaner in.' He found his crystal whisky glass under a saucepan and dried it on a paper towel. The glass was from

Waterford, bought on a trip on the ferry to Dublin. He took out his whisky and twisted the top off, pouring a decent measure. 'Would you like one?' he asked them.

'No thanks,' Kris said. 'We had better be off. Do you want me to call the dogs in?'

'No. let them run,' Alan said. 'I'll call them in before I go to bed.' His telephone vibrated. He took it out and put on his glasses. 'A text message, how novel. No one texts me,' Alan said. He read the message and frowned.

Oakwood, Capel Farm estate

'Typical,' Alan said.

'What is it?' Kris asked.

'In the old days, we would call it a tipoff,' Alan said.

'What do you call it nowadays?' Kris asked, frowning.

'A fucking nuisance,' Alan said, emptying his whisky down the sink.

Chapter 36

The first floor of the hospital was transitioning through shift changeover and there were double the number of staff when smoke began billowing from the air vents. The smell of burning plastic filled the air on the first floor. At first, the policemen on duty thought it must be drifting from an incident downstairs or a fire outside but a nurse spotted the cleaning closet was ablaze. The smoke alarms sounded and fire alarms pulsated. One of the policemen grabbed a water filled fire extinguisher and ran towards the cupboard. He grabbed the door handle and in an instant his skin was welded to the metal. He screamed and fell backwards, tearing the skin from his palm and fingers. The smell of burning flesh mingled with the smoke. A male nurse grabbed him beneath the arms and dragged him from the door. Two more uniformed officers arrived, armed with extinguishers. One was foam, one was powder filled. A third officer used a towel to turn the handle and push open the door. A backdraft leapt through the door like a dragon unleashed. The flames engulfed the three policemen, setting their hair and clothing alight. Nurses tried to pull them away and extinguish the flames, smothering them in sheets. Within minutes, the ceiling and floor were blackened by the conflagration. The flames were out of control. Hospital staff cleared the area and sealed the fire doors. They had to contain the firestorm until the fire brigade arrived. There were officers stationed on sight with a limited firefighting capability. They were deployed and were there in minutes. Hoses were used to fight the flames back into the cleaning cupboard and then foam was used to smother the fire and block its oxygen supply. Acrid smoke hung in the air. The hospital was partially evacuated until the full-time fire brigade arrived and checked for any further outbreaks.

The intensive care unit was being prepared for relocation, which was a complicated operation as many of the patients were attached to life support machines. Some of the patients were on a knife edge between life and death. Moving them was the last resort. As the chaos was tackled, status checks were being completed by senior nurses and doctors. The injured policemen were being treated in accident and emergency. Their burns were severe and one of them was being prepped to be flown by helicopter to the burn unit at Whiston hospital, on Merseyside. When the nurses checked on Howard Shields, he had stopped breathing and there were no vital signs. He was pronounced dead. A second doctor pointed out his respirator had been turned off.

Chapter 37

Trigg scrambled to his feet and set off in a panic. He ran as fast as he could. The man's voice echoed around his mind, instructing him to get home before it was too late. What did he mean too late? Too late for what? Was he one of the men the twins had seen murdering two people? The questions were never ending, and he had no answers. None that made sense. He was puffing and out of breath, sweat running down his back. When he reached the boxing club on Ffordd Tudur, he took out his phone and called Brenda, but her phone went straight to voicemail. He tried Nia's number but hers was engaged. She would be able to see him calling but they'd argued, so she would be sulking. She never answered her phone when she was sulking. It was her way of taking control. There was no way of warning them.

He put the phone away and ran as fast as his legs would carry him. His breathing was fast and laboured and he was running out of steam. When he reached his street, he felt like his heart was in his mouth, pounding like fury. The road was full of his neighbours. They were a ragtag bunch, dressed in their nightclothes, staring at his home. He recognised his next-door neighbour, wearing her dressing gown and Dr Martin's boots. There was frantic activity in his front garden and around the side of his house, which was on fire.

He screamed for his family and sprinted towards the burning building. His words were unintelligible, nothing more than desperate grunting sounds. Through his windows, the entire ground floor appeared to be orange. The shadows of flames were dancing on the lawn. He could hear people shouting but he couldn't understand what they were saying. As he neared, the living room windows exploded outwards, showering the onlookers with shards of glass. A skinny woman from the next street fell to the floor clutching her eyes. He couldn't remember her name. Blood ran through her fingers. Flames flickered from inside the house, darting skyward through the empty frames, climbing towards the upper floor. He tried to focus on the bedroom windows, tears blurring his vision. He could see Nia in the window of her bedroom, frantically banging on the glass. She couldn't open it and climb out because the window was screwed shut to stop her sneaking out at night. Guilt gripped his guts and twisted them tightly. You screwed her window shut, you fool.

Trigg shouted her name as he neared the front garden. He could see her lips moving and tears glistening on her cheeks but all he could hear was the roar of the flames and the panicked voices of his neighbours. Nia banged on the window with her fists but the glass was too strong. Keith from two doors away, ran towards the house with his ladders. He put them against the wall beneath Nia's window and scrambled up them. The flames from the living room leapt higher, lapping at his pyjamas. The material of his slippers caught fire. Keith realised his feet were ablaze and tried to put them out with his hands. His sleeves caught fire and his dressing gown burst into flames. He panicked and fell from the ladder like a human fireball, rolling on the grass. Neighbours ran to him with a hosepipe and buckets of water and extinguished the flames, but he was badly burnt. The smell of burning flesh tainted the air, mixing with the smoke. The sounds of sirens wailed in the distance. Brenda appeared in the window where the twins slept, her face blackened by the smoke. She opened the window and screamed for help. The bathroom window exploded, flames jumping upwards to the roof. Brenda screamed for help. Her voice frantic. The fire burnt higher and brighter, and the heat was intense. The onlookers moved back away from its ferocity.

'Drop the twins,' Trigg shouted, gesturing to her. Brenda shouted something back, but he couldn't hear her. 'Lower the twins to me,' he screamed. 'Go and get the twins,' he yelled. 'Lower them down and then jump!'

Brenda disappeared for a second and came back to the window with Tom. He climbed out backwards, Brenda, holding his arms. Neighbours ran to help break his fall.

'I've got him. I can catch him,' someone shouted. 'Drop him to me.'

Trigg looked at Nia's window and she was hardly visible in the smoke. He looked around and one of the men had a crowbar in his hand. Trigg grabbed it from him and ran to the ladder, which was engulfed in flames. The top was leaning against Nia's window ledge.

'Spray me with the hosepipe,' Trigg shouted. The man with the hose looked confused. 'Spray the water on me!'

Trigg climbed towards the flames and the man realised what he was to do. He pointed the jet at Trigg's back. A second neighbour arrived with another hose.

'Aim it at Trigg!'

Trigg climbed through the flames towards the bedroom window. Nia was gone. His eyes were stinging, and his hands blistered and burnt on the ladder but he climbed on regardless of the pain. From the corner of his eye, he saw Tom drop to the crowd of men below but he couldn't see him land and he could no longer see Brenda or any sign of Philip. He screamed for Nia but she wasn't at the window anymore. Trigg aimed the crowbar at the centre of the glass and hit it as hard as he could. The metal bounced off the glass as if it was stone. He aimed it at the corner and it bounced off again. His breathing was frantic, lungs filling with toxic fumes. He hit the corner again and it cracked. A web shaped crack spread across the glass. Several more desperate hits shattered the double-glazing and a black cloud poured through the gap, blinding him. He reached inside the frame and smashed all the glass from it with the crowbar. Thick acrid smoke billowed out, engulfing him. His eyes were stinging and he couldn't suck in any air without burning his throat. His skin was beginning to peel and blister. He felt his lips swelling, the delicate tissue burning.

'Nia!' he screamed. There was no reply but the roar of the fire, tearing through his home, destroying everything it touched in seconds. 'Nia!'

Something exploded downstairs and the blast travelled through the house and up the stairs, blasting tiles from the roof. The force hit him like a steam train and he was blown backwards from the ladder. He fell to the garden, his clothes and hair on fire and the impact with the ground knocked him unconscious.

Chapter 38

Alan rang the number that the text message had been sent from, but it was already disconnected. Not engaged. Not voicemail or the switched off message, disconnected. Only minutes had passed but that identity number was already gone. That confirmed it was a burner phone, the message sent then the SIM card removed, burnt or flushed down the toilet. The result was the same. It was gone and would never be used a second time. Whoever sent the text message was forensically aware. They were also smart enough to use their knowledge of forensics, which wasn't always the case. Alan reread the message. The spelling of the address was correct. That indicated the sender had a working knowledge of the Welsh language, place names and pronunciation. Tourists and visitors working on the island wrote place names the way they pronounced them, which was invariably wrong. It was another indication that locals were involved.

    The address was vaguely familiar and not far away. He decided to investigate himself with back-up from a uniformed unit. Capel Farm was a five-minute drive. Alan called the station but was diverted to a national answering system. Something was up. The diverted system only kicked in when the lines were jammed. That wasn't a good sign. He tried the custody suite number and a uniformed sergeant answered. Alan explained he needed back-up but was informed there had been an incident at Ysbyty Gwynedd, which had taken all available units off the island. There were no police vehicles operating on Anglesey and they were not expected back for at least an hour. That was not what he wanted to hear. It was late and he knew his team would be getting some well-earned rest. His detectives were exhausted but he couldn't risk going alone, so he called Kim.

'I've been trying to ring you,' she said, answering straight away.

'My phone is on silent,' Alan said, sheepishly.

'Why is it on silent?'

'I was planning on going to bed,' Alan said. 'Silly me.'

'Have you heard the news?' she asked, assuming that was the reason for his call.

'I've been told there was an incident at Ysbyty Gwynedd,' Alan said, wishing he hadn't dumped his Scotch down the sink. 'A fire on the first floor near the ICU or something?'

'There was a fire but that's not the half of it,' Kim said. 'To cut a long story short, it was deliberate. Howard Shields is dead.'

'What happened?'

'There was a fire on the first floor,' Kim explained. 'Initial inspections say it was set deliberately in a cleaning cupboard full of linen. All four uniformed officers stationed there were burnt trying to tackle the blaze. It caused mayhem and when the doctors ran their checks on the ICU patients, they realised his respirator was turned off. It can only be done manually, which means it was done deliberately.'

'Fucking hell,' Alan muttered. 'So, the fire was a diversion?'

'Almost definitely,' Kim said.

'It takes balls to walk into a hospital packed with police officers, set a fire and hang around to switch a respirator off in the confusion,' Alan said. 'It also takes training,' he added.

'Training for what?'

'Thinking on your feet,' Alan said. 'They would need to be able to blend in. Maybe wearing a disguise. This isn't the skillset of online keyboard warrior or a thug. This is sophisticated.'

'Okay, who would do it?'

'That's what we need to work out,' Alan said. 'Everything we've seen so far indicates there are multiple players in this game and someone is coordinating their actions.' He sighed. His mind was tired. 'Behind all this is a planner.'

'I agree,' Kim said. 'There's something else.'

'I don't think I can cope with anymore,' Alan said, yawning. He gave in and poured another whisky. A large one. He raised the glass to the empty room. 'Come on. Let's have all the gory details.'

'Don't lose your marbles when I tell you this,' Kim said.

'I've lost my marbles a long time ago.'

'Because of the fire at the hospital, the surveillance unit was taken from the Trigg home.'

'And what?' Alan felt sick.

'Someone set fire to the Trigg house,' Kim said.

'You're fucking joking?' Alan said, sighing.

'No.'

'Which fucking genius made that call?' he asked, swallowing the Scotch. Kim didn't answer. 'I'm guessing it was deliberate?'

'Yes. Definitely. The front and back doors were fastened from the outside with L-shaped brackets screwed to the frames and doors to stop them getting out.'

'These people are professionals,' Alan said. 'That isn't a technique we see outside of organised crime.'

'They were set on silencing the twins,' Kim agreed. 'Whoever set it, didn't want anyone to survive.'

'There were three kids in that home. We promised to keep them safe. Tell me they're okay,' Alan said.

'We don't know yet,' Kim said.

'How bad is it?'

'Bad,' Kim said. 'The hospital have me as the direct contact. As soon as I know, you'll know.'

'This should never have happened. It's no wonder we struggle to get people to testify when we can't protect them properly. I want to know who took my surveillance from that house,' Alan said. 'If that family are not all right, I'm going to personally see to it that they lose their job.'

'Why did you ring me?' Kim asked, changing tack. She knew it would have been a decision made by the ACC or above. The ACC was trying to shave costs at every opportunity but she didn't think it was the time or place to point the finger of blame. There would be time for that later.

'What?'

'Why did you ring me?'

'Oh, that,' Alan said. 'I called the station for uniformed back-up and was informed there are no uniformed officers available. Obviously, I didn't have a clue someone was trying to set fire to all our witnesses. So, much for a nightcap and good night's sleep.'

'No rest for the wicked,' Kim joked.

'Wicked,' Alan said, 'I must have been Jimmy Saville in my last life.'

'He was alive when you were alive,' Kim said.

'Smarty pants,' Alan said. 'This case is beginning to wind me up.'

'Whoever is trying to cover their tracks isn't messing around,' Kim said.

'They're talented but certainly not acting with stealth or caution,' Alan said.

'Meaning?'

'They want the publicity. They clearly don't give a toss about the amount of attention they're drawing to the investigation.'

'Maybe that's the point,' Kim said.

'Someone wants the public to see the rubbish being taken out and disposed of,' Alan said.

'Let's hope we get to ask them soon.' She paused to think. 'Back pedal a few minutes. What do you need back-up for?'

'I've had a tipoff,' Alan said.

'A tipoff?' Kim said, confused. 'From where?'

'I got a text message with an address on Capel Farm.'

'What's the address?'

'Oakwood. Why does that ring a bell?'

'It's the derelict farm at the top of the road,' Kim said. 'It was repossessed a few years back and put on the market but there are problems with the roof and subsidence in the outbuildings. They can't sell it.'

'I know the place,' Alan said. 'Uniform have been there, umpteen times clearing out kids and squatters?'

'That's the one,' Kim said. 'What did the text say?'

'Nothing. Just the address.'

'It could wait until the morning,' Kim suggested, although she didn't sound convinced. 'Is it likely to be life and death?'

'I've got a funny feeling about it,' Alan said. 'I think we should go and take a look.'

'We?'

'Yes. You and me.'

'In light of what's happened elsewhere tonight, I think we should take a look too,' Kim said. 'Unless you want to wait for more muscle?'

'No. You've got more muscle than anyone in uniform,' Alan said. 'I'm scared of you. Bring your big stick and we'll be fine.'

'Baton,' Kim said.

'Nightstick,' Alan said, emptying the glass.

'Nightstick is what they're called in the movies,' Kim corrected him.

'Sometimes I feel like I'm in a movie,' Alan said. 'A really shit one.'

Chapter 39

Ernie has showered for over an hour, shaved and dressed himself in a tracksuit. Now he was staring at the television, even though Naomi had turned it off three hours ago. Earlier on, she told him she was going to bed and he had told her they were going away the next day when the girls had gone to school. The news wasn't received well. It wasn't received well at all. There was desperation behind her eyes. He could see it from a mile away. Her eyes were dilated like a wild animal who suddenly finds itself in a cage. She was panicking inside. That was the human response to fear. It wasn't the response he wanted. If he was honest, it was the response he expected but he had hoped for a different one. He was wrong to hope. Hope was for those who trusted in fate. There is no fate but the one we create ourselves. She had shaped her own by fucking another man in his bed. Slut.

She was quiet at first and tried to portray a calm exterior while she manufactured every excuse she could think of, not to go. Obviously, the girls were her first offering but he told her he had arranged for his parents to pick them up from school and take them for the weekend. They were going to take them to Llanberis on Saturday and they loved the mountains and grandad would ruin them with lunch and ice cream. They loved ice cream by the lake. It would be a nice break for them too.

She didn't give up but eventually, Naomi ran out of practical excuses. Then she argued she wasn't in the right frame of mind to go away. That was a poor excuse. The simple truth of the matter was she didn't want to go away with him. That was crystal clear. He refused to accept no for an answer, which was an emerging pattern that was being repeated recently especially in the bedroom. He needed her to submit. His dominance was his control mechanism. There was no respect for what she wanted. Respect was earned and she'd decimated his reserves of respect. He had none for her. She had no right to say no to anything and if she did say no, he would ignore it. Slut.

Naomi battled on but it was a futile exercise. Once he had deflected every excuse she made, she looked totally deflated and absolutely miserable. She had to submit. Never had he seen such an expression of desperation on her face. There was no hiding her deep unhappiness. It was etched into every line on her face. A tear ran from the corner of her eye but she wiped it away quickly, hoping he hadn't seen it but he had. How things had changed. His beautiful wife was reduced to tears at the suggestion of spending a night away with her husband. That hurt him. It hurt deep down inside where real love hid from the worries of the world. That tear tore him apart.

He studied her face and wondered if he should punch her. His instinct was to do that. It was a strange quandary to consider and he knew it was an unreasonable debate to have yet it was there, in his mind. She has hurt you badly. Punch her fucking face in. If he punched her hard, would her expression change to something more palatable? Would the expression of pain and fear be more acceptable than sadness? Possibly. It was a difficult decision.

The debate was raging in his head. Was there any point in trying to break someone who didn't want to be there anymore? Could she be persuaded by fair means or foul to be his obedient spouse again? The old Naomi was caring, pleasant and cooperative and he was sure she'd loved him once. They talked things through and she usually did as he suggested without too much argument. Had Hal Nelson ruined his wife forever? Would his stink taint her for all time? He wanted things to be how they used to be. He wanted not to see the sadness in her eyes when she looked at him. It broke his heart to see the unhappiness in her, knowing it was him that was the cause of the unhappiness. She wanted to be with another man. Being with him was the root of her sadness. That was impossible to live with. How can you cling on to someone who is already gone?

There was a terrible yearning inside his heart to turn back the clock and fix things before they went wrong. He wanted time to be reversed and normality to be restored. He wanted his beautiful Naomi to love him how she used to. His emotions were like white hot metal running through his veins. The pain was unbearable. He had never loved another woman the way he had loved Naomi and he never would. She was his one true love and she didn't want to be with him anymore. How could he live with that? How could she? Slut.

Everything was unbalanced and spinning out of control. He was struggling to remain calm. The struggle inside him was like two titans battling for his soul. He wanted calm to win the day but the anger inside was so intense, it was taking control. He wanted peace and quiet and his family around him. His beautiful daughters and his beautiful wife. Slut. They were his life. His everything. Don't try to take them away.

Nothing was the same anymore and it wasn't his fault. The turmoil had been caused by the choices she'd made. It was her fault they were in this emotional maelstrom. His nervous system was on overload. He felt like Dr Jekyll and Mr Hyde, battling for the same mind. His mind. Outwardly good and normal, inwardly shockingly twisted and evil. He had taken time from work to try to rebuild their relationship but Naomi was incapable of looking him in the eye. The suggestion that they might go away alone for a short break triggered an expression of absolute desperation on her face. The thought of spending time with him made her dreadfully unhappy. To the point of tears. How could he deal with such a situation, knowing she hankered for another man's love? He loved her. His forever love. He wanted it to be so but his beautiful wife was repulsed by him. Slut.

Ernie thought hard and decided not to punch her in the face. Now wasn't the time. He had to challenge her and ask her to be honest about her feelings. Honesty. Did she know its meaning?

'You are making a lot of excuses not to go away,' Ernie had said, a thin smile touched his lips. His eyes were dark and piercing. 'Is there something wrong?'

'No.' Naomi had answered. 'Nothing is wrong.'

'You don't look very happy about the idea of going away and spending some time together?'

'I'm fine.'

'Fine is a shit word.'

'Happy,' she corrected herself. 'I'm happy.'

'If you're happy, then tell your miserable fucking face!' Ernie had screamed in silence. Inside his mind. On the outside, his expression was one of curiosity. As if he was studying her. Every twitch of her lips, blink of her eyes, word from her lips was proof of her betrayal. Slut.

'As long as you're sure there's nothing wrong?' he had said, calmly. He had smiled but she didn't return his smile. She appeared to be nervous, frightened even. Slut.

Naomi had said there wasn't anything wrong. She said her reluctance was because she didn't like surprises. Who would have known, pretty Naomi didn't like surprises?

Ernie had to admit to himself that he didn't like surprises. Finding out Naomi was taking it up the arse from Harold-fucking-Nelson had been a surprise. That was a big surprise. In fact, as far as surprises go, that was fucking humongous. Probably the biggest surprise he had ever had. Going away for the weekend was supposed to be a nice surprise yet she looked like she was going to puke on her shoes.

The conversation had been one way. She would come up with a flimsy excuse and he would crush it. He had bullied her and berated her excuses and left no avenues for her to escape from the trip he had planned. They were going away in the morning whether she wanted to or not. Maybe slitting her throat was the solution. It would be quick and final. Problem solved. But it would be messy and too quick for the bitch. The trip was the opportunity for him to think straight. There would be no distractions for either of them. He had it all planned and had made sure she would hate every second of it. Naomi didn't like the great outdoors and that was where they were going. She thought people who went camping were crazy. Adventure held no attraction to her. She wanted the comfort and safety of a nice hotel where she could bathe and pamper before going for a nice meal. She was going to get none of those things. There was no definitive outcome to what would happen. It could go anyway. His plan was flexible and had no solid borders. The borders had been crossed in all directions and things couldn't be reversed. Too much damage had been done.

He was going to take her to the middle of nowhere and make her incredibly uncomfortable and then decide if she was going to live or die. That would all depend on her. Could she love him again? Could she choose him? Slut.

One thing was for certain. If Naomi decided she couldn't be with him as husband and wife anymore then she would lose everything they'd built together. Including her life and the life of her daughters. He would have to explain to his daughters why they all had to die and he would make her tell them what she'd done. They deserved to know why they weren't going to have the opportunity to live their lives and have children of their own and fulfil their potentials. It was because their mother was a slut. There was no feasible way of killing them all and remaining at liberty and so, his death was also necessary. He wouldn't go to prison and rot in a cell. If this was the end of the road, he would embrace the finish line like an old friend. His soul was weary of this world and he could leave it when required. That would be a simple task and he would have no problem killing himself. Without his family and the future, he had mapped out in his mind, there was no point in living any longer. Everything was hanging in the balance. If killing them all was the only solution, then others would have to pay the ultimate price. Others had paid the ultimate price. Didn't the innocent suffer for the actions of the guilty? The innocent had suffered since the beginning of time and they would continue to do so.

Harold Nelson would lose everything he held dear to him too. That was only fair and proper. One good turn deserved another.

Ernie looked at the blank television screen and played out things like a cinema in his mind. Images of the past drifted to him in technicolour like digital photographs. The details were incredible. He watched the Afghan couple approaching the group of trainee police officers. The trainees were smoking cigarettes and chatting, oblivious to the approaching danger. Ernie had been training them. The trainees were Afghans, learning to be police officers and enforce the law in a country which was lawless. The Taliban had strict laws. Religious laws. Laws that wouldn't tolerate anything outside of their own. Laws they'd been fighting for since the birth of religion.

He felt sorry for the Afghan cadets. The trainees were stuck between a rock and hard place. They were being trained to uphold a fragile peace when the allies withdrew from Afghanistan. Everyone involved in the occupation knew they wouldn't last five minutes once the Americans left. They would be dead before the last plane took off. Ernest Metcalfe had gone there with a genuine sense of helping the Afghans to help themselves but it hadn't taken long to understand there was no helping them. While the Taliban loomed in the shadows, waiting for their time to come, there was no future but theirs. It was inevitable. And they had time on their side. All the time in the world. Ernie couldn't fathom how he could help people who slaughtered schoolgirls for being schoolgirls. He had been with a unit sent to clean up a Taliban attack. They had attacked a small town and massacred everyone in the school, which had been built with Western money. The bodies of the schoolgirls were laid out in the schoolyard, most of them the same age as his daughters. The massacre unsettled an already unsettled psyche. His mind was sent spinning by the scenes he had witnessed. It had no rhyme or reason to it yet it had profound meaning to the indigenous people. The massacre had deep meaning to the perpetrators. It was a message to anyone collaborating with the allied forces. Take their money and read their books and you will die.

If they'd stayed there for a thousand years, it would make no difference. Imposing Western culture on unwilling people had been tried and had failed for centuries. Ernie soon realised he was wasting his time. Time, he had sacrificed. Time, he could have spent with his family. His beautiful daughters and their beautiful mother. Slut.

Then there were the suicide bombers. The day the suicide bombers had slipped inside the security ring was the day everything began to unravel further. Afghan guards had let the bombers into the base knowing what they were going to do but their families had been threatened by the Taliban, so they did as they were told. Let the suicide bombers in or your families will die. They didn't make idle threats. People did as they were told, regardless of the outcome. The guards allowed a group of Afghan elders to enter the base. An elderly couple and some older men. When the elderly couple approached the group of trainees, Ernie instinctively knew they were acting suspiciously. He pointed his weapon at them and alerted the other instructors of the danger. They were slow to react. Too slow.

The old man had hit Ernie's gun with a walking stick, which was actually a blade and knocked it from his grasp. The Afghan elder had a Kalashnikov under his robes and he machinegunned the Afghan trainees, mowing them down like skittles in a bowling alley. Men dived for cover in all directions. Ernie had watched in terror as the woman revealed a dead-man's switch from her sleeve. He realised she had a suicide vest beneath her clothing and was about to detonate it. Ernie had tackled her to the ground and tried to take the switch but she struggled and held it beyond his reach. A second old man was holding his ankles, stopping him from crawling over her. That's when he picked up the rock and hit her in the face. Once, twice, a hundred times. Panic and self-preservation took over and her head disintegrated beneath the onslaught. It felt like hours until her head was nothing but bloody sludge. One eye stared at him from the mush. It still stared at him today and every day. It stared at him in his sleep and in his waking hours too, always there, never blinking.

With the switch neutralised, he had drawn his pistol and emptied the clip into the second old man, who was still clinging to his ankles. Dozens of lives were saved but Ernie was traumatised by the intensity of the situation. Part of his brain was frazzled, the nerve endings burnt out. His decision making was irreversibly skewed.

His mind had always been different but now it was damaged beyond repair. The parameters of normal boundaries were gone. His vision of acceptable behaviour warped and limits no longer existed. Whatever needed to be done to survive, had to be done. No exceptions. Self-preservation was everything and his world was under attack. Ernie walked upstairs and stopped outside his bedroom door. It was ajar. A nightlight in the hallway cast shadows in the room. Naomi was sleeping peacefully, the covers pulled to her neck. He closed his eyes and imagined Hal-fucking-Nelson next to her.

Chapter 40

Alan and Kim arrived at Oakwood farm and pulled into the yard. The farmhouse was boarded up, metal shutters on all the windows and doors. They had been fixed in an attempt to stop the building being used by local teenagers for impromptu parties during lockdown. No one could be fined if they didn't own the property. It appeared to be secure and the shutters intact and there was no light seeping through the shutters. The barriers were working for now.

'Drive around there,' Alan said, pointing towards the barns, which towered above the farmhouse. They were steel frames with corrugated tin roofs and no walls. The fields beyond them were inky black and the sea beyond them darker still, like looking into the void. 'Point your headlights into the barns. It's cold out there and I'm not walking around with a torch unless I have to.'

'Sounds like a plan,' Kim said, putting the car in first gear. She trundled around the farmyard, using the headlights to search the barns. They were empty. 'There's a tractor shed around the back,' Kim said. 'But we can't drive around there. We'll have to walk.'

'Bugger,' Alan said, fastening his coat. 'Come on then. I hope this is a hoax. Let's do it and go home. I've had enough for today,' he added.

Kim parked up and they climbed out, walking through the barns towards a row of outbuildings. The roof had collapsed, taking the outer wall with it. A workshop and stables were still standing to their right and the larger tractor shed was to their left. They couldn't see the doorway from where they were standing. The ground was muddy and the going was slow. Alan was trying hard not to leave a shoe behind. Their feet squelched and squished as they walked. He felt muddy water leaking into his right sock. It was pointless in trying to retrace his steps. The damage was already done. Kim shone her torch at the doorway and vehicle reflectors gleamed back at them, a yellow number plate between them. They looked at each other and silently agreed to progress.

'A white van,' Alan said. 'Like the one the twins said they saw.'

'That can't be a coincidence,' Kim said.

'There's no such thing as a coincidence,' Alan agreed. 'Not in our world.'

They walked towards the shed and split up without speaking. Alan took the driver's side, Kim the passenger side. When they reached the cab, Alan could see the body of a young man in the driver's seat. His face was grey and the skin sallow, sunk in at the cheeks. A wet patch spread from the groin down the thighs to the knees.

'He's been gone a while,' Alan said. 'A few hours at least.'

'It looks like a suicide,' Kim said. 'There are two disposable barbeques in the footwell, both still glowing. Shall we take a look inside?'

'No. We can't help him now. Let's wait for Pamela Stone to get here. I have a feeling there will be forensic evidence in there and I don't want Pamela on my case for fucking it up,' Alan said. He saw something out of place from the corner of his eye. 'There's an envelope under the windscreen wipers,' he said, pointing. He shone the torch at it. There was writing on it. Neat and capitalised.

'To whom it may concern,' he said. 'It's generic but not the wording I would expect from a man of his age. That's more our generation.'

'Are you going to read it?' Kim asked.

'No. It's a suicide note and there might be prints on there,' Alan said. 'No doubt pointing us in the wrong direction.'

'You think this is a setup?' Kim asked, nodding. 'He didn't send that text,' she added.

'Exactly. I smell bullshit,' Alan said. 'And I can't see any bulls around here.'

'Let's say the note is a confession. They have given us a contrite victim, the van that was possibly at the scene of a double murder and a note saying he did it all by himself and no one else is involved?' Kim said.

'That's my thinking,' Alan agreed.

'It's all very convenient.'

'Too convenient. Case closed,' Alan said, shaking his head. 'We can all go home to bed.'

'Shall we run the plates first?' Kim asked.

'Yes,' Alan said. 'Let's do that.'

Chapter 41

The next morning

The operations room at Holyhead was buzzing with chatter. Dozens of phone calls were being made by sixty detectives, all chasing the information the investigation needed to progress. It was past nine o'clock and it had been a long day already. Alan was tired. Coffee and adrenaline were the only things keeping him going. Kim brought another cup to his desk and plonked it down in front of him. He mouthed thank you and carried on chatting. His face was dour and serious. His desk phone rang and Kim answered it.

'DI Williams desk,' she answered. 'Kim Davies speaking.'

'Kim, it's Carla Michaels,' the DS from Caernarfon said.

'Morning, Carla,' Kim said. 'He's on the other line at the moment.'

'No problem, you'll have to do,' Michaels said, jovially. 'I know it must be busy there after the shenanigans at the hospital last night but I've had a call, which is very odd. I think it's connected to the case.'

'Everything is very odd in this case,' Kim said. 'What was the call about?'

'Bob Parry Estate Agents made a call this morning, reporting their Bethesda branch manager missing. Obviously, the officer asked why the family hadn't reported him missing and they were very vague but said his wife was aware that he was missing. That was followed by a call from his wife about an hour later, saying the same thing,' Michaels said.

'Why the delay?'

'That's what's odd about it. Maybe she wasn't as concerned as his colleagues,' Michaels said. 'His wife called the office last night to ask where he was because he hadn't gone home. Of course, it was getting late and everyone but the assistant manager had gone home. He told her he hadn't gone back to the office following his last appointment and he had assumed he had gone straight home. There's no signal in the Ogwen Valley, so he wasn't worried about it until she called. The office had him listed as showing a client around a chapel in the Capel Curig area yesterday afternoon. It was his last job of the day and he usually goes back to the office before he goes home but he didn't show up.'

'That's all very mysterious. What's his name?' Kim asked, frowning. Her senses were tingling. She had encountered a manager from Bob Parry estate agents. The name was already in her head before she heard it. Roland.

'Roland,' Michaels said. 'Clive Roland.'

'We know him,' Kim said, nodding. 'We looked into him during the Creegan investigation. He was up to his neck in it but he had covered his tracks going back decades. He was a sly bastard, never putting his signature on anything. We actually thought he was part of the organising group working closely with Creegan himself.'

'I know you did,' Michaels said. 'I'm a detective, you know?'

'Of course, you are,' Kim said, embarrassed.

'How did he slip through the net?'

'We know he gave Creegan access to some empty properties, which were used for their gatherings but the case against him fell to pieces. There just wasn't enough evidence against him for the CPS to proceed. We were gutted. He was in my top ten wankers list. If anyone needs to be doing life, it's Roland.'

'Well, he's vanished. There's no sign of him,' Michaels said. 'His mobile is switched off. The wife is saying she has no idea where he might be and that he's never not gone home before but she's being very sheepish. Probably because of the Creegan investigation. If her husband was implicated the way he was, she may be wary of us. She's a strange fish if you ask me.'

'She stuck by him all the way, despite knowing the evidence against him was powerful. They have three kids of their own,' Kim said. 'That's strange in my opinion.'

'He's an estate agent,' Michaels said. 'They are professional liars, trained at painting a better picture of a shit situation. He probably has her wrapped around his fingers.'

'There must be a shadow of doubt in her mind,' Kim said. 'She wouldn't be human otherwise.'

'It might be nothing. He may have buggered off with the cleaner for all we know but something tells me he hasn't. You might want to check his car registration and bank accounts,' Michaels said. Kim chuckled as she listened to her advice. 'Apologies. Am I teaching my granny to suck eggs?'

'Yes,' Kim said. 'Thanks for the tipoff.'

'You're welcome. I thought you would want to know sooner rather than later.'

'Much appreciated. I agree it's too much of a coincidence not to follow up. Are you going to send someone to the property where he was last reported?' Kim asked. 'You said it was a chapel.'

'I have a detective there already but there's no phone signal in the Valley. I'll expect to hear from him when he's on the way back,' Michaels said.

'Do you know who he met with?'

'Yes. Roland was booked in to see a client called Mr Jones.'

'Is that genuine?' Kim asked.

'Yes. He appears to be. He subsequently made a cash offer and has purchased the chapel subject to contracts.'

'Have we spoken to him?' Kim asked.

'No. We've left a message with an answering service but he hasn't returned them as yet,' Michaels said. 'Bob Parry Estate Agents are communicating with him via email. Apparently, he's uncontactable any other way at the moment.'

'Roland could be in trouble,' Kim said.

'My thoughts exactly.'

'The worrying thing is, although he fits our victim profile, he wasn't employed by the Church.'

'Were the employees listed separately to non-employees?'

'Yes. He's on the list from the wider investigation. Our pool of possible victims just got a whole lot bigger.'

'That was my concern exactly,' Michaels said. 'I'll call you when I have anything else you should know.'

Kim hung up the phone and waited for Alan to end his call. He slurped his coffee and gestured to his phone.

'Who was that?'

'DS Michaels,' Kim said.

'The wicked witch of Caernarfon?'

'Does that make you the tinman with no brain?'

'The scarecrow had no brain,' Alan said. 'And neither have you.'

'Are you sure?' Kim asked. 'Or was it the tiger?'

'Lion.'

'What lion?'

'Never mind. It was before your time,' he added. 'What did she want?'

'The estate agent, Clive Roland has been reported missing.'

'Roland Rat,' Alan said. 'I would love five minutes in a room with him. When was this reported?'

'This morning. His wife said he never returned home yesterday evening. His office in Bethesda had him showing a client around a chapel in the Capel Curig area. The client made an offer and bought the property, so he was legit but Roland hasn't been seen since.'

'Maybe he's gone on a bender to celebrate,' Alan said.

'What, overnight in Bethesda?' Kim asked, shaking her head.

'Good point.' Alan sipped his drink. 'He's not dancing the night away there.'

'Seriously. He's vanished and he fits our victim profile.'

'That's great news,' Alan said, nodding.

'Great news?'

'Yup. Another one bites the dust,' Alan hummed. 'And another one's gone and another one's gone and another one bites the dust,' he sang tunelessly. 'Hey, I'm going to get you too, another one bites the dust.'

'Alan,' Kim said, sighing. 'Really?'

'Really,' he said. 'Roland is a horrible bastard with an arrogant smirk permanently fixed to his fat face. I would never get bored of punching him.' He paused.

'Have you finished?' Kim asked, shaking her head.

'Yup. I don't know anymore of the words,' Alan said. 'Has she sent someone to the chapel?' Kim nodded, making another call. 'We need to run his plates and his bank accounts.'

'Already doing it,' she said, grinning and pointing to the phone.

'You should be a detective,' Alan said, slurping his coffee. 'We need to go to Pentraeth,' he added. Kim frowned. 'That's where our suicide victim is from. That was Pamela Stone. I need to give the team an update first,' he said. 'Make your calls and then join us.'

Alan left his office and clapped his hands. The detectives in the room stopped chatting and wrapped up their calls. Everyone paid attention to the DI.

'Good morning everyone. I hope you all got as much sleep as I did,' he said. Tired faces answered him.

'Any news on the Trigg family, guv?' someone asked.

'They're all alive at the moment,' Alan said. 'But it's touch and go. Brenda and the twins were taken to Bangor with smoke inhalation and superficial burns. Philip had to be sedated because of lung damage. He was inside longer than his brother. Only for a few minutes, but it was enough to make a difference. They'll be kept in for a few days at least for observation. Morris Trigg and his daughter, Nia are in a bad way. They're being taken to specialist burns units on Merseyside but the prognosis isn't good.'

'What happened to the daughter?'

'Nia was trapped in her bedroom and Morris tried to climb a ladder to rescue her. He was burnt trying to break the window and reach her. There was an explosion and he was blown off the ladder. The fire brigade got her out but she wasn't breathing and she's burnt pretty badly.' Alan shrugged. 'They are all under surveillance and hopefully no one with pips on their shoulders will decide they don't need to be protected.' He waited for any more questions but there were none. 'Okay. Let's crack on. You all know the plates on the van we found last night were false but we have an ID on the chassis number,' Alan said. The operations room fell quiet. 'The van belongs to Gethin Rankin from Pentraeth.' His image appeared on the screens. 'You will be pleased to hear he has a tattoo on his hand. A compass and a skull.

'Like the twins described.'

'Yes. Tom Trigg described that tattoo on the hand of one of the men at the firepit. The chassis number on the van relates to a Ford van registered to Rankin and Rankin is the suicide victim. Pamela Stone says there's forensic evidence in the back of the van. A tooth, some blood, hairs, and fibres. They ran the bloods straightaway and it matches Rupert Blackstone.' A murmur rippled through the crowd. 'She has also sent the details of the hip joint recovered from the firepit. It was fitted to one of the firepit victims by Gobowen hospital. Chod's team has some information on that,' Alan gestured to Chod.

'We have traced the medical records of all the men investigated in the Creegan investigation,' Chod began. 'Several of them have had hip operations but only one of them is missing. Father Griff Trimble.' His mugshot appeared. It was obviously taken in the custody suite. 'He was last seen in his local supermarket in Conwy. The local uniform have been there and his property is empty, the RSPCA took his cats away and there's been no activity on his phone or his bank account and we all know what that means.'

'Thanks Chod,' Alan said. He pointed to crime scene images of the firepit. 'We have blood in the van and the hip joint from the firepit. We can safely assume Rupert Blackstone and Griff Trimble were the victims in the firepit. Agreed?'

'Agreed,' the group replied, nodding.

'It would be hard not to come to that conclusion.'

'The men investigated by us during the Creegan case are being targeted, probably by members of the Justice Asylum website.

Gethin Rankin frequently posted on there as did Howard Shields, both now deceased in dubious circumstances,' Alan said as images of them appeared on the screen. 'Father Derek Corbin and Frank Gamble are both dead.' Some of the detectives looked surprised. 'Read your notifications and updates if this is news to you,' Alan said, smiling.

'Like you do?' Richard asked.

'Shush,' Alan said. 'Gamble died this morning following extensive surgery to remove cement from his stomach, which makes four victims from the Creegan list that we know of for sure and another possible attack in progress.'

'Who is the possible, boss?'

Alan typed a name into the laptop and the image of Clive Roland appeared.

'This is Clive Roland, the estate agent. Most of you will remember this slimy bastard from the Creegan investigation. We affectionately called him, Roland Rat.' Nodding heads agreed with him. 'He was reported missing by his wife last night, which means he has either been attacked or he's on the run,' Alan said, looking around the room. 'Word of these attacks is already out there. It's all over the Internet and the press and the other men investigated by us must realise they're possible targets. They could be next. They're going to be getting very nervous. Some of them will be in the wind already. Roland may be one of them. Until we have a body, we keep looking for him.'

'Could he be involved in attacking the other suspects?'

'What would be the point in silencing them now?' Alan said. 'We investigated them and failed. I don't think this is about suppressing historic evidence unless someone has stashed videos or photographs, we haven't seen yet but I doubt it. I see the attacks as punishments and now whoever is responsible is cleaning house. They're tying up loose ends,' he added. He changed the images to pictures of the Trigg home. 'Last night they tried to wipe out our witnesses. The Trigg home was torched because our surveillance unit was taken to attend another fire started at Ysbyty Gwynedd where another potential witness was. Four of our officers are in hospital, one of them is badly injured.' He changed the image to the scene at Oakwood farm. 'Then we have the suicide. Ladies and gentlemen, they're leading us a merry dance and pulling our pants down and leaving us with a trail of bodies along the way.' The detectives were quiet. The situation was dire. 'They left us a trail of destruction last night and we have to admit we're struggling to keep up,' Alan admitted. 'This is a well-organised group of nutcases but we can't underestimate them and I'll tell you why. They're nutcases with forensic savvy and undercover training.'

'Undercover police training?' someone asked.

'Or military,' Alan said. 'Look what they did. They entered a busy hospital to silence a member of their own group, who was under police protection. They set a diversion and had the confidence to wait until the opportunity appeared to turn Shields off at the wall.' Alan shrugged and looked around the room. 'That takes balls of steel and knowhow. This is covert stuff, not a couple of troggs from the mountains. They are cool and calculated and we're reacting to whatever they do, always two steps behind them.'

'Are you suggesting hitmen are controlling this?' Chod asked.

'All options are on the table but I think they have a plan and they're using local members of Justice Asylum to carry out the attacks. They're working to a schedule and we're stumbling around in the dark waiting for them to make a mistake,' Alan shook his head and looked annoyed. 'If we keep waiting for them to make a mistake, we could be waiting a long time. I'll tell you why we're chasing our tails and that's because we haven't managed to identify where all their potential targets are yet. What is taking us so long?' Alan asked.

'We're being fobbed off by the Church.'

'We're the police,' Alan said. 'If you think someone is withholding information, arrest them. Drag them in here and throw them into cell six. It always stinks of piss,' Alan said. Subdued laughter rippled through the room. 'We're not looking for these men to arrest them, we're looking for them to verify if they're dead and if they're not dead, we're going to try to make sure they stay that way. How many of them have we traced?'

'Five,' Kim said.

'We need to do better,' Alan said. 'We have killers on our island and they're not acting randomly. They are assassinating men we investigated during the Creegan case. They are using a list that we created.' He pointed to the screen. 'We made this list. We know who their targets are, so where are they?' The room stayed silent. 'If Clive Roland has been abducted, the list has expanded to nearly fifty and we only have five so far. We need to know where everyone is, today.'

'Caernarfon are looking at the Justice Asylum website, so what do we know about the website users? Has DS Michaels made any progress interviewing members of Justice Asylum?'

'She's shared what they have. It's all online. Kim has a detailed list of everyone who has posted on that site in the last twelve months but we all know most of that will be utter shite,' Alan said. 'We need to filter out what is irrelevant and prioritise. I want to know the names and addresses of everyone on that list who resides in North Wales. Let's take a look at their records and start with the ones with form for violence. Look at their profiles and identify who has been posting aggressive or threatening stuff online. Idiots like this love to shout the loudest. Shields took his own phone to an assassination. Most of them are morons being manipulated by a puppet-master but we need to be swift and surgical to catch these vigilantes before they do any more damage.' Alan pointed to the image of Rankin. 'But don't be blinded by the website members. They're pawns in this. I have a hunch we're being groomed into thinking they're solely responsible for all the attacks.'

'You think someone is pulling the strings,' Kim said.

'They are staging everything. Enter from stage left, Gethin Rankin,' Alan said, pointing to the image of the man again. 'Gethin Rankin is a Justice Asylum member. Last night, he drank half a bottle of rum, put two disposable barbeques into the passenger footwell of his van and sucked all the oxygen out of the air, suffocating himself while listening to his favourite radio station.' Alan shrugged and looked around. 'At first glance, Gethin Rankin killed himself and conveniently left us a note waffling on about how the courts let all the victims down and so he took vengeance but can't live with himself.' Alan tapped the screen again. 'When his tox-screen comes back I bet there's something in his bloodstream that shouldn't be there. Flunitrazepam or similar.'

'You don't think it was suicide?' Chod asked.

'Do you?'

'No.'

'It makes sense,' Kim said. 'They kill two birds with one stone. We have a scapegoat and they tie up another loose end.'

'Exactly. The fact a lot of the men we investigated were never charged is a scandal but it doesn't justify making them drink cement and setting fire to them,' Alan said. 'They want us to believe this young idiot left us a note admitting his guilt for killing Blackstone and Trimble.' Alan shook his head and looked around the faces in the room. 'Are we having that?'

'No, sir,' someone said.

'I'm not swallowing it, sir,' another agreed.

'It's all too easy,' Richard said.

'They must think we're a bunch of yokels living on a big rock in the Irish Sea,' Alan said. 'How fucking stupid do they think we are?'

'Not that stupid, boss,' a detective said. Another murmur passed through the detectives.

'Absolutely right,' Alan said. 'The way I see it, they sacrificed Rankin as the scapegoat, hoping we will bugger off and leave them alone, unfortunately for them, we're not done yet.' Alan looked around the room again. 'We're far from done here. We have our victims and we have the motive. Paedophiles or not, it's against the law to cremate them before they're dead and we're here to enforce that.' Alan pointed at the list of names on the screen. 'We need to up our game. I want to know where every man we spoke to during the Creegan case is living and where they are today, what they're wearing and what they had for breakfast, and I want to know today. That's our focus.' He looked around the room. 'Are we clear?'

'Yes, sir,' the room replied.

Alan changed the image to the remnants of the Maltese bank cards found in the pit. 'Where are we with the items from the rucksacks?'

'I'm struggling with them,' Richard said. 'Every time I get close, it's a dead end.'

'Okay, Richard. Take another five detectives and get deeper into the Maltese connection because there is one. We just can't see it yet.' Alan tapped the screen again. 'Where are these two priests?' Alan asked. 'We found their rucksacks in that pit. Where are they?' No one replied. 'The Trigg twins told us there were three men in those woods and one of them had a tattoo on his hand, just like the one on our dead guy Rankin. He was one of the three. He has to be.' Alan shrugged. 'That leaves us two men, who are out there wanting us to think Rankin has admitted doing this and then topped himself. Do those rucksacks belong to the other two men the twins saw?'

'If so, why did they burn their belongings?' Kim asked.

'Exactly,' Alan said. 'Go to the top of the class,' he added.

'Do you think the Maltese priests are involved in the murders or are they possible victims that we haven't found yet?' someone asked.

'Richard. What can you tell us?' Alan asked.

'I can tell you that there are more questions than answers about them,' Richard said, puffing his cheeks. 'I've hit nothing but brick walls. There are no facts about these two men or their journey. They travelled across Europe allegedly heading to Dublin where they're supposed to fly to the USA. There are no flights booked in their names from Dublin Airport at any point in the future. So, I have two names and a Maltese bank, which won't disclose if they have accounts there or not. They are not on any modern-day payroll list I've managed to acquire.'

'But you have them on an historic payroll?' Alan asked,

'Yes,' Richard said. He blushed. 'But it's not relevant.'

'Why do you think that?' Alan asked.

'Ganni James and Arturo Troisi were employed by a Maltese merchant seaman with connections to the Vatican,' Richard said.

'That sounds relevant to me,' Alan said.

'They died in the eighteen-hundreds.'

'Ah, I see. So, we know it's not them?' Alan asked, joking.

'I'm going nowhere with it. I know they were guests at the Vatican for roughly a month before stopping off at various places across Europe but no one will confirm or deny their existence.' Richard shook his head, and his jowls wobbled. 'Are they really on a charity mission, raising money?' Richard shrugged. 'I can't see any evidence of donations. No web page to give funds. Nothing. With extra hands, we might be able to cover more ground.'

'What do you think?' Kim asked Alan.

'I don't have a clue but I know if something looks like a duck, walks like a duck, and tastes good in plum sauce, it's a duck.' Kim looked confused. 'The entire thing looks like a smokescreen to me but I don't know why,' Alan said. 'I don't think they're here riding bicycles around the island to raise money for a leper colony somewhere,' Alan said. 'Something about those two men stinks, and if we find out who they are and why they're here, we'll be a lot closer to cracking this. They're not going to give us the run around anymore. Like I said before, how stupid do they think we are?'

Chapter 42

Corporal Mamood was eating an egg muffin and drinking a latte when the call came through from the Air Commodore's office. Pauline Verwood wasn't at work. She was a creature of habit and was normally at her desk before seven o'clock. She hadn't arrived at her office and wasn't answering her mobile or landline. Her secretary had called the RAF Police station and reported her absence, informing them that she'd received abusive messages the previous day and that her new Mercedes had been damaged by her abuser. Mamood could see why they were being cautious but doubted anything had actually happened. She had probably had a drink or two and decided to have a lie in. It would all be a fuss about nothing.

The corporal pulled up outside the Commodore's home and parked his vehicle. He turned off the engine and looked at her house. The curtains were open downstairs but closed upstairs. He finished the food he was chewing. Best not to knock on a Commodore's door with a mouthful of unfinished breakfast. Wiping the crumbs from his uniform, he straightened his hat and got out of the vehicle. He walked to the front door and knocked. There was no answer. He tried again with the same result. The house was silent. He lifted the letter box and peered inside. His breath stuck in his chest and he stepped backwards, forgetting the doorstep. He tumbled and banged his head on the concrete path. His fingers reached for his comms.

'This is Corporal Mahmood. It's a triple nine. Get the police here pronto.'

'Calm down, Mahmood. What have you seen?'

'There's a pool of blood at the bottom of the stairs and some teeth, I think.'

'Have you looked around the back of the house?'

'No.'

'Ring me on your mobile,' the control sergeant said, annoyed. The corporal tutted and took out his phone. He called the station. The sergeant answered.

'I don't want every man and his dog listening to you panicking on an open comms link. Get a grip, man. Tell me exactly what you can see.'

'I can see what looks like blood and bits of white,' the corporal said.

'Are you certain it's blood?'

'Not absolutely.'

'Could it be red wine or ketchup?'

'I suppose so, but spilling wine doesn't stop you going to work, does it?' the corporal said, sarcastically.

'Don't get funny with me. You have no fucking idea what has happened,' the sergeant said. 'Can you see a body?'

'No. Of course not. I would have said if there was a body.'

'Do you want the civvies to arrive and find her in the kitchen with a cup of coffee and a sore head and think we're a load of muppets?'

'No. Of course not.'

'Then get your fat arse around the back of the house and take a look. When you know for sure what we're dealing with, call it in.'

Corporal Mahmood swore beneath his breath and made his way around the side of the house. A pathway led to a large fence and wooden gate. He tried the handle and the gate opened. A scraping sound made him look down. There was a clawhammer on the floor behind the gate. There was blood and hair on the face. The hair was still attached to a piece of scalp. The grip and shaft were soaked in blood. He ran back to the car and retrieved some evidence preservers. The exercise had him out of breath. He placed one of them over the hammer in case it rained and called in to the station again.

'I've found a clawhammer with blood on it,' the corporal said, puffing. 'Get the police and an ambulance here.'

'Roger that,' control said without questioning him.

The corporal tiptoed around the side of the house to the back garden. It was a huge lawn with Cheshire stripes in the grass. There was a patio and a jacuzzi. It had been covered for the winter. He followed the path to the back door, which was open. A trail of blood ran from the hallway across the tiles to the back door and down the steps. It was beginning to congeal. He could see the pool of blood at the bottom of the stairs and he could confirm it was blood. A quick scan of the kitchen from the doorway told him there was no body. The Air Commodore was badly injured and missing.

Chapter 43

Detective Constable Harris parked his car on the patch of gravel near the chapel. He could see the village of Capel Curig to the south in the distance. A new van was parked in the only other available space. There was a man wearing safety equipment, hard hat, and goggles and bright green overalls, strimming the grass. It looked like it would be a thankless task. It was knee deep, except for some of the graves. The machine had a high-pitched whine, unpleasant to the ears. Harris got out of the car and walked to the gate. It had been taken off and was leaning against the dry-stone wall. The workman acknowledged him but didn't stop working. DC Harris approached him and gestured he turn off the strimmer. He showed his warrant card.

'DC Harris,' he introduced himself. 'Are you the supervisor?'

'Not me, mate,' the workman said. He pointed at the chapel door, which was open. 'The boss is in there. I just cut the grass.'

'Thanks,' Harris said. He walked into the chapel. The pews had been moved to the right-hand side of the nave, piled on top of each other, exposing the stone floor, worn smooth by time. The sound of a jet-spray echoed from the walls. A plume of water was cleaning cobwebs and dust from the stained-glass windows and the mortar beneath. The smell of detergent filled the air. A man in overalls saw him and walked over.

'Can I help you?'

'I'm looking for the estate agent,' Harris said. 'Clive Roland.'

'Never heard of him, boss,' the man said. 'We're here to make the place safe before the builders come in. Apparently, it's being restored but the rear walls are weak. We're looking for cracks in the mortar so we need to clean the crap off first before we put jack posts in to support the back of the structure.'

'Who hired you?' Harris asked.

'Some guy called Jones.'

'That's a big help,' Harris said.

'What do you want me to say?' the man asked. 'That's his name.'

'Just for my records, who are you?' Harris asked.

'Callum Barker. We're from Cleani-King based in Chester,' Callum said, showing his business card. Harris studied it and handed it back. 'Anything else because we're on a tight schedule?'

'No. I'll have a look around outside myself,' Harris said. A beam of light shone through the clean stained-glass, exaggerating the colours and refractions. 'Those windows are amazing,' he added as he left.

Harris picked his way through the overgrowth to the uneven path which circled the chapel. The gravestones were higgledy-piggledy, different heights and different angles. Some were leaning so far back, they defied gravity. The sound of the strimmer whirred, annoyingly.

At the rear of the chapel, he leant over the wall and looked at the stream. It was full and babbling loudly. He noticed the name on the gravestone closest to the water. Mildred Barker. He felt guilty for standing on the grave.

'Sorry, Mildred,' he said, stepping back onto the path. He took out a cigarette and lit it, drawing deeply on it. 'I should give these up or I'll end up where you are,' he said to Mildred. Mildred was long past listening. 'It's a nice spot,' he added, walking away. He went back to his car and checked his phone. There was no signal. DC Harris started the engine and reversed onto the road. He decided not to go straight back to Caernarfon station. His favourite chip shop was on the bridge at Betws-y-coed. If he took his time, he could be there for when it opened. He could sit on the bridge and watch the waterfall for an hour or so.

Chapter 44

Hal Nelson woke up with a banging headache. The empty bottle of rum rolled from his chest onto the floor. It made a splash instead of a thump. He didn't want to open his eyes. The pain would be increased by the light. He felt cold, despite the heating being on full blast. Condensation ran down the windows. He could hear the endless drip, drip, drip of water from downstairs. The floodwater was evaporating. It would take months to dry the building out. The floors would have to be taken up and the walls and ceilings would all need to be replastered. Most of their belongings would need to be replaced. They were beyond repair. It was difficult to process the true extent of the damage while most of his property was floating around downstairs. They were insured but it wouldn't be a quick process. Everything would be complicated by the fact Maisy and the kids had gone. That had been a hammer blow. His heart sank when he thought about them getting into Caroline's car with the kids' rucksacks packed. Luckily, the kids weren't there to witness the devastation. Maisy was going to pick them up and take them to Caroline's house. He contemplated what a colossal event this was. What he did next would shape the remainder of his life. Would he forgo being a father to his own children and a grandfather to theirs to be with Naomi and her children. Children he had never met. This could be the biggest mistake of his life. Naomi Metcalfe had rocked his world, but there was a niggling doubt that being away from his kids would rip his heart out. If Maisy took them to London, he would hardly see them and he wasn't sure he could live with that. He wasn't sure he could live without them.

A bang on the front door surprised him. He opened his eyes and immediately wished he hadn't. He wondered if it was Maisy come back to apologise and make up. Apologise for what? he thought. The room was spinning. He felt like he was going to vomit. Another three loud bangs on the door reverberated up the stairs, much louder this time.

'Harold Nelson,' a voice boomed through the door. 'Open the door!'

'That's not Maisy and it's not Amazon,' Hal muttered, standing up. 'Fucking noisy, whoever it is.'

He had kicked his shoes off in his sleep. His feet touched the floor and immediately his socks were saturated. The water was freezing cold. It made his toes ache. Another three bangs reverberated up the stairs, and he suddenly felt frightened. The sound was threatening.

'Harold Nelson, open the door!'

'Oh, for fuck's sake. I don't believe this is happening to me.'

The front door exploded and he heard glass shattering. Heavy footsteps thundered through the house. Hal was trying to put his shoes on over his saturated socks when the police burst into his room. They swarmed in and dragged him to his feet, shouting in his face. A baton was jammed into his ribs. It took his breath away. In seconds, he was handcuffed and dumped face down on the bed.

'Will someone please tell me what the fuck is going on?' he shouted, catching his breath.

'Where is she?' a voice asked. Alan entered the room.

'She's at her friend's house,' Hal muttered. 'Someone trashed the house and flooded it, so she took the kids and went to stay with her friend. It's not fit for children.'

'Is that right?' an officer snapped. 'Arsehole.'

'You're the arsehole barging into my home when I haven't done anything. She is with her friend. Her name is Caroline Greenman. I have her number,' he said. 'Ring her if you don't believe me.'

'Are you trying to be funny, you sick bastard?' a voice growled.

'I'm not trying to be anything,' Hal said, trying to stand. A punch in the kidneys persuaded him to stay put. 'There's no need for this. It's so unnecessary. Fucking hell. There's no need for this at all.'

'I'll ask you one more time,' Alan said. 'Where is she?'

'Are you deaf?' a dig in the ribs winded him.

'That's assault. What's the fucking problem?'

'Where is Pauline Verwood?' Alan asked.

'Pauline Verwood?' Hal asked, confused. 'The Air Commodore?'

'The woman you harassed on social media and then wrote off her Mercedes.'

'I've no idea what the fuck you're talking about,' Hal said. His mind began to spin. 'Why would I know where she is?'

'Okay have it your way. We'll do it all at the station,' Alan said. 'Harold Nelson, I'm arresting you for the murder of Caroline Greenman, Maisy Nelson, Noah Nelson, and Jessie Nelson. You do not have to say anything…'

Hal didn't hear the rest of the caution. Ice-cold shivers ran through his body, and the names of his dead wife and children echoed through his mind.

Chapter 45

Alan and Kim returned to the crime scene. It was a tough one to process without losing their sense of balance. Everyone was innocent until proven guilty on paper. This one wasn't so easy to accept. Caroline Greenman had a detached house in Gwalchmai. The postman had alerted the police when he found the front door ajar. When the police arrived, they were met with a scene from the darkest depths of hell. Alan and Kim were not the first detectives there but were told to take control immediately. They had identified the victims and a series of communications with the senior personnel on the airbase, led them straight to Harold Nelson. He was under investigation for the sexual harassment of several women on the base and was looking at criminal damage to one of the victim's vehicle. Nelson was in their sites immediately.

Pamela Stone was already processing inside the house. When they arrived, two uniformed officers were in floods of tears near the front door and Sergeant Bob Dewhurst was organising the cordon. They parked and approached the house from the driveway. Bob met them and gave them forensic suits and overshoes. His face was thunder.

'You've arrested the husband?' Bob asked.

'Yes,' Alan said.

'I think you should send those men back to the station,' Kim said. The first responders were clearly shaken. 'They're a photographer's dream,' she added. 'I can see the headlines already.'

'She has a point,' Alan said. Bob agreed with a nod but didn't comment. He went to speak to the distraught officers. 'This must have affected him. He hasn't come out with any witty inappropriate comments.'

'He's a grandfather,' Alan said.

'Let's go back and see if we've missed anything, shall we,' Kim said. Her face was pale and her eyes sad. She didn't want to see the crime scene again. She knew she would never be able to unsee it.

Alan nodded, and they stepped inside the front door. The coppery smell of blood tainted the air. Caroline Greenman was behind the door. At least her cashcard identified her as Caroline. There was no chance of a visual identification. Her facial features no longer existed. Pamela Stone approached.

'Hello,' she said, flatly. 'I know you've done a walk through but I would appreciate your thoughts.'

'No problem.' Alan gestured to Caroline Greenman. 'She opened the door unawares and was attacked immediately,' Alan said, looking at her position in the hallway. 'There are no defensive wounds on her arms. She didn't have time to defend herself. The first blow probably knocked her senseless. It was a blitz attack. She was overwhelmed in seconds.'

'I agree,' Pamela said.

They carried on further down the hallway. The home was bright, the walls and ceilings white. The floor was tiled with grey marble. The smell of urine and excrement became more prevalent. Noah Nelson was in the doorway of the living room. The detectives didn't speak for long minutes, taking in the scene.

'Noah came to look at who was at the front door. Typical for an inquisitive young boy,' Kim said. Alan agreed. Bloody handprints ran along the wall and door frames and splatter had reached the ceiling. They followed the blood trail. Maisy Nelson was lying on the stairs, face up. Her features were unrecognisable as human.

'At first I thought she may have run and been caught?' Pamela said. 'What do you think?'

They crept past her body and climbed the stairs as if they might wake her from a peaceful slumber. 'She tried to fight him here,' Kim said. 'She sent Jessie up the stairs and put herself between the attacker and her daughter.'

'Because she's face up not face down?' Pamela asked.

'Yes,' Kim said. 'And her fingers look broken and twisted. She fought back.'

'We're all agreed on that,' Alan said.

At the top of the stairs, the blood trail stopped. Alan could see the battered body of Jessie Nelson. She was face down near the bed. There were circular bruises on her ankles.

'She was hiding under the bed and he pulled her out by the ankles?' Pamela said.

'Yes,' Alan said. He studied the splatter for long minutes before retracing his steps. 'The level of rage in this attack is unreal. These injuries have not been caused by a man on a mission to kill. This was a man on a mission to dehumanise them. He wanted to make them unrecognisable. That means he had to revisit each victim after he had killed them to inflict more damage on their dead bodies. This is unhinged.'

'This is hatred personified,' Kim said. 'Pure evil on a scale I've never witnessed.'

Chapter 46

An hour later, Alan and Kim met DS Michaels at the Nelson house a few minutes before the detailed search team was deployed. Harold Nelson was on his way to St Asaph station. His behaviour had been strange. He didn't put up a fight while being restrained in his bedroom, but he had a confused arrogance about him, which Alan associated with suspects who were sure they couldn't be convicted of anything. That was usually because they were innocent or they'd destroyed any forensic evidence. Alan had read him his rights and ordered he be taken to St Asaph to be held there until they were ready to move him.

'Are you two just back from the scene?' Michaels asked.

'Yes. Pamela Stone is there now,' Alan said.

'What are your thoughts, so far?'

'This guy is unhinged,' he added. 'He's completely off the nutcase scale.'

'Killing your wife and kids is a reasonable sign of some mental detachment,' Michaels said. 'What state of mind do you think he was in?'

'Deranged,' Kim said. 'It was a blitz attack.'

'How was he when you arrested him?' Michaels asked.

He was acting as if he didn't have a clue what was happening to him at first,' Alan said. 'He looked hung-over and stank of booze. I suspect you would need a drink after what he did.'

The detectives went into the house. Water dripped from the ceiling in a hundred places. The house had been ransacked. There would be no evidence to gather from the downstairs of the house. Water had destroyed everything. The devastation was total.

'Nelson had obviously lost the plot,' Michaels said. 'It appears he destroyed his home because his wife found out he was sexting other women. She confronts him and leaves, taking the kids.'

'How do you know she confronted him?' Kim asked.

'A woman from further down the road drove by last night and saw Maisy and another woman arguing with Nelson on the doorstep. I reckon she left him and he lost control and then murdered his family.'

Alan thought back to when his wife, Kath, had left him and the impact it had had on his mental health. It was a difficult thing to deal with. The most difficult thing he had faced in his life yet he got over it. Most people do. Break-ups happen every day and while they're devastating at the time, people can move on. Some people cannot. Nelson had reacted with rage and the rage became violence and violence became retribution. Male suicide is the biggest killer of men under fifty-five. Nelson couldn't handle it. Some men can't handle rejection.

'I guess something snapped inside,' Alan said. They were waiting for the search teams to be given instructions. 'I need some fresh air.' Alan went back outside and walked around the hire car.

'The ACC said he's going to need a chief inspector as the SIO,' Alan said. 'Because serving RAF officers are involved and because the missing woman, Pauline Verwood, is an Air Commodore. It's a political hot potato. Too big for us, apparently.' He paused. 'Plus, this guy is out of control. Way out of control. There's an insanity defence in the making.'

'What makes you say that?'

'Because he's fucking insane,' Alan said, shaking his head. 'What he did to his family is beyond description.'

'The press will be all over this,' Michaels said. 'With a bit of luck, he'll admit everything and we can lock the bastard away without too much fuss.'

'Or he might hang himself,' Alan said. 'We can live in hope. This is a hire car.'

'Yes.'

'Apparently, he crashed his car into the back of Pauline Verwood's Mercedes and claimed it was an accident,' Alan said. 'Now, Pauline is missing and there's sand on the wheels of this car.'

'Where is the nearest beach?' Michaels asked.

'Rhosneigr,' Alan said. 'There are miles of dunes there accessible by car,' he added.

'I'll get a search team over there,' Kim said.

'Is the DI there?' an officer shouted from the side of the house.

'I'm here,' Alan shouted. 'What is it?'

'The garden shed is locked and there's blood on the padlock,' the officer said.

'Get some bolt cutters,' Alan said. 'Come on. This could be a breakthrough.' They walked into the back garden. The shed was in the far corner against the fence. A huge oak tree towered above it. A child's swing hung from a bough. A poignant reminder of the family who lived there yesterday. Alan looked at the lock. It was a Yale. Congealed blood encrusted the metal. Alan put an evidence bag around the housing of the lock. An officer approached with bolt cutters. 'Cut the shackle there,' he said.

The lock was cut free and sealed in a bag. Alan opened the shed door and stepped inside. It was very organised. Everything was on a shelf or in a pigeonhole. There was a pinboard fastened to the wall, which held tools. Each tool was hung on the board where its outline was clearly marked. There was an empty space where the outline of a hammer was marked.

'A hammer was found at the Verwood home,' Kim said. She pointed to two heavy duty rubble sacks. They were sealed with zip ties. 'They don't belong in a shed this tidy,' she added.

'Cut them open, please,' Alan said. One of the search team cut the ties free. Alan looked inside. 'Wellington boots covered in blood splatter. Gloves and a balaclava. What have you got?'

'A jumpsuit of some kind, covered in spatter,' Kim said. 'It's a murder suit.'

'Signed, sealed, and delivered,' Alan said. 'This guy is going away for good.'

Chapter 47

Ernie was driving across the Britannia Bridge with Naomi. They decided to use the Jeep. The boot was loaded with camping equipment. A decent family tent, which they'd bought years ago and used once. Naomi wasn't the outdoors type. She tried it and didn't like it. It was simple to put up and it was only for one night. He had packed a rucksack with a few supplies. There was nervous tension between them. She didn't want to be there and he knew it but was pretending everything was normal. At least on the outside. Inside was a cauldron of anger bubbling and boiling over. It was taking all his energy to restrain himself.

Naomi was miserable. Her entire being oozed misery. It was difficult not to get angry with her. He wanted to shout at her and make her snap out of the dark mood she was in. It was breaking his heart to see her so unhappy to be with him but he couldn't break the spell. There didn't seem to be any light at the end of the tunnel. The future looked black. Jet black. He hankered for a different time when they were happy together. A time when they loved each other. He wished he could turn back the clock and look into her eyes and see a welcoming glint in them but it had dissipated and gone. He felt like his heart was being squeezed by a giant hand. The emotional pain was debilitating. Naomi's phone rang but she ignored it. The colour drained from her face. Ernie glanced at her phone.

'Aren't you going to answer it?' Ernie asked.

'It's a switchboard number,' Naomi said nervously. 'It's not going to be anyone I want to speak to. It will be a sales call or something.'

'Answer it,' Ernie said, glancing at her. His eyes drilled into her.

'I don't know who it is,' Naomi said. 'So, I don't want to answer it.'

'Answer it.'

'I don't want to answer it,' she said. The call cut off. She stared out of the window and a tear ran from her eye. She wiped it away quickly. 'Stop bullying me.'

'Are you crying?'

'No.'

'What's the matter,' Ernie asked, his voice strained.

'Nothing,' she said. Turning her face away from him.

'You look like you're upset about something?' Ernie said. 'What on Earth would you have to be upset about, I wonder?'

'I'm not upset,' Naomi said, trying to pull herself together. She sat upright in her chair and tried to smile at him. it didn't work properly. 'Can we stop somewhere, please? I want to use the toilet.'

'Sure,' Ernie said. 'How about I drive down to Betws?'

'Okay,' Naomi said. Her phone started ringing again. She pressed the reject button. Ernie kept looking at her phone as if it was going to explode. She looked out of the window and pretended not to notice his angry glances. The message icon appeared on her screen; the phone beeped. Naomi looked terrified.

'Someone has left you a voicemail,' he said.

'I know.'

'Don't you want to know who it was?'

'No.'

'That's very odd,' Ernie said. 'Are you hiding something from me?'

'No. Of course, not.'

'Have you got your brush in your bag?' Ernie asked.

'My hairbrush?'

'Yes.'

'Can I borrow it, please?'

'Now?'

'Yes.'

Naomi searched her bag and found it. She handed it to him. 'What do you want that for?'

Ernie took the brush and dropped it in the footwell near his left foot. 'Oops. Butter fingers,' he said, shrugging, his expression blank.

'What?' Naomi asked, shaking her head. 'That wasn't an accident.'

'Yes. It was.'

'Why have you thrown my brush on the floor?'

'I didn't,' Ernie said. 'You did.' Naomi looked baffled. 'Play the message on your phone.'

'I don't want to,' she said, folding her arms across her chest.

'Play the message,' Ernie said chirpily.

'No.'

'Play it.'

'No.'

'Play the fucking message!'

Ernie grabbed the back of her head, grasping a fistful of hair. He twisted it hard and accelerated.

'Get off me,' Naomi shouted, crying. 'You're hurting me. Stop it!'

'Play the fucking message or I'll hurt you more than you can imagine,' he said calmly. He twisted her hair again. 'Play the fucking message!'

'Okay,' she sobbed. She opened the message and played it.

'Put it on speaker,' he said. The message played.

Naomi, it's me, Hal. I've been arrested. I only have one phone call, so I can't call you back. They're saying I murdered my family. You need to get away from him as quickly as you can. He's lost his mind. He's killed Maisy and my children. Get away from him...

'Delete the message,' Ernie said, shaking his head. Naomi did as she was told. Tears streamed down her cheeks.

'What have you done?' she sobbed.

'What have I done?' Ernie said, frowning. 'You did this, slut.'

Ernie let go of her hair and grabbed the phone. He tossed it into the passenger footwell. Naomi was frozen in fear. Ernie reached down and pressed the release on her seat belt. She was clueless as to what was about to happen. He accelerated and steered the Jeep towards an oak tree.

The impact was catastrophic.

Naomi had a millisecond to regret her mistakes before she was catapulted through the windscreen at sixty miles an hour.

Chapter 48

Alan and Kim had been on their way back to Holyhead when they got the message that a body had been found in the dunes at Rhosneigr. The victim matched the description of Pauline Verwood. They drove in silence until they reached the area where she'd been found. Several police vehicles were already there and the search teams were being dispersed. Alan parked up and they eyed the scene through the windscreen.

'I'm not in a rush to see this,' Alan said. 'Enough is enough for one day.'

'I thought we might have found her alive,' Kim said. 'At least I hoped as much,' she added.

'There are no happy endings in this one,' Alan said, climbing out. The sun was beginning to drop towards the horizon, melting into the sea. He pulled on his beanie hat. The temperature was changing quickly. They walked across the sandy flats, following the natural paths between the lower dunes. Sharp grasses grew in clumps between the paths. A forensic team and four uniformed officers kept the scene safe from ghouls and photographers. They were led to Pauline Verwood's naked body. She was hogtied, hands behind her back, face down in the sand. Her head had been buried completely.

Kim circled her and walked back to Alan. He didn't need to see any more. It was obvious what had happened to her.

'The last message he sent said, *I want to tie you up and smash your back doors in*. It couldn't be any closer to what he sent to her,' Alan said, nodding. 'He's signed his own work.'

'The man needs to be executed.' Kim looked thoughtful. 'Who's going to be leading on it?' Kim asked.

'A chief inspector from Wrexham. Georgina Moran,' Alan said. 'I've met her a few times. They're lining her up for ACC. This will be the interview that seals the deal.'

'It's not like we need a confession. This had been handed to her on a plate,' Kim said. 'Nelson might as well say nothing at all. The evidence is overwhelming. He's going down, regardless.'

'It should play out that way,' Alan agreed.

'Who's she partnered with for the interview?' Kim asked.

'The ACC asked me if you're okay to do it,' Alan said.

'When did he ask that?'

'Earlier on.'

'What did you say?'

'I said you wouldn't want to do it,' Alan said. Kim nearly snapped her neck turning around. 'Joke,' Alan added.

'Not funny.'

'I said you would be keen to do it,' Alan said.

'I am,' she said, nodding.

'Don't fuck it up,' Alan said. 'You'll embarrass me.'

Chapter 49

Richard and his team were ploughing through pages of useless information. The Maltese priests were like ghosts floating across Europe, leaving nothing but silence behind them. There were dozens of posts trumpeting their imminent arrival on the tour but nothing to follow them up, as if they never arrived or if they did, it was hushed. When they approached the people who posted anything about the charity ride, they were fobbed off and the posts were removed. Nothing made sense. It was a coordinated cover-up, but of what?

'This is a waste of time,' Richard said, shaking his head and hanging up the phone. 'That was the dean of a catholic school in Calais, who set up a page on their Facebook account supporting the charity ride, six months ago. Now he doesn't know anything about it. The page was set up by a student on placement, who has since left. Another dead end and another person in authority denying any knowledge of our Maltese friends.'

'Was there any activity on the page?' Sharna asked. She was a black DC from Bangor.

'Nothing. It was another non-event.'

'You should look at the school,' Sharna said.

'I'm not sure what we should be looking for but if the DI is right, there may have been some historic abuse there,' Sharna said.

'That's worth looking into,' Richard said, googling the school. 'Maybe that's the approach we need to take.'

'You have been searching for something current when what we might need to do is take a different approach,' Sharna said.

'A different approach? Different, sounds interesting,' Richard said. 'Run it by me.'

'Rather than follow up where we think they've been, we need to start again. I think we need to deconstruct what we have.'

'That sounds like *Masterchef*,' Richard said.

'I've never watched it,' Sharna said. Richard shrugged. 'We need to start at the end and work backwards.'

'Okay. I'm open to ideas,' Richard said, not fully grasping her theory. 'I've been banging my head against a brick wall. What do you suggest?'

'If we look at what we have right now, we can trace it back,' she began. 'We have an online group targeting the perpetrators of historical abuse carried out by employees of the Church. The DI indicated he thinks someone is directing the Justice Asylum activists to mobilise and attack anyone connected to the Creegan case, right?'

'In not so many words,' Richard agreed. 'What's your point?'

'Let's say he's right,' Sharna said.

'Heaven forbid,' Richard muttered.

'Let's say these priests are responsible for provoking the locals, acting as the catalyst and puppet masters.'

'Okay. I'm following you.'

'Let's assume they're here on a mission to clear up the mess left behind from Creegan and his arsewipes.'

'For what purpose?'

'Damage limitation. They might be trying to limit any further damage to the reputation of the Church caused by its own employees. Rather than brushing the crap under the carpet, which hasn't worked, they're taking the rubbish out completely.'

'Okay. It's plausible.'

'But they're not getting their hands dirty,' Sharna said. 'They're getting the locals to do their dirty work for them.'

'It's definitely worth looking at,' Richard agreed.

'But that theory begs another question,' she said.

'Which is?'

'If that's why they're here, why not get on a plane in Malta and get off in Manchester?' Sharna said. 'Why spend months crossing Europe to get here?'

'That question has been on my mind from day one,' Richard said. 'If there is some wider conspiracy going on, why invent the charity marathon at all?'

'That's my point exactly. They invented the charity ride because they might need a cover story as to why they were in certain places at a certain time. Like your school in Calais,' Sharna said. 'Which means they didn't come here directly because they had things to do along the way.'

'Things like what?' Richard asked, nodding.

'The same things they've been doing here.' Richard looked baffled. 'It's simple.'

'It is?' he asked.

'Yes. Paedophile priests are not unique to the UK,' Sharna said. 'There have been scandals across the planet. This could be damage limitation on a global scale.'

'You're saying there could be similar websites to Justice Asylum across Europe?' Richard said, finally following her. 'Generating similar attacks?'

'That was my rationale. I thought there could be similar groups,' she said. 'So, I had a look using Google Translate and when I searched for paedophile hunters across Europe, there are hundreds, Austria, Switzerland, France, Spain, Italy, Portugal, Belgium, Holland, and Germany. Obviously, when I searched in French, the sites that come up are French and so on, so we would have to translate their posts to spot patterns or similar activity to what we've seen here.'

'So, if we search the areas where they've travelled and look for idiots bragging about attacking paedophiles, we might find a pattern that could confirm what they're up to.'

'Yes. And maybe who they really are. I think we are likely to find Arturo Troisi and Ganni James have been encouraging similar groups to clean house along their way,' Sharna said. 'They spent a long time in Rome before setting off, correct?'

'Yes. I know they were in Vatican City for weeks,' Richard said.

'They were probably taking instructions and prioritising their targets,' Sharna said. 'If they're doing what we think they're doing, this could only come from the top.'

Chapter 50

Georgina Moran and Kim walked into the interview room where Harold Nelson was waiting. His brief was a young man from Chester called Lewis Holding. He looked like a fish out of water, sent by his practice to defend Nelson, as a test of his ability. One look at the evidence would make them think he couldn't successfully defend the case. The best he could do was make the prosecution think twice and make them earn their money. It would be a huge test of character and ability. This was being seen as a slam dunk for the prosecution and there was little to no sympathy for the accused.

Harold Nelson had claimed dog faeces was put into his food, which was denied profusely by the custody sergeant. He was a child killer, so no one was surprised. A uniformed constable had been sent on a food run to McDonalds and it was claimed Nelson's food was contaminated at some point before it got to him. No one was overly concerned about it.

Nelson would be interviewed and then shipped to HMP Risley in Warrington. It was geographically suitable and had the facility to segregate and protect him while on remand. It had been explained that he had no chance of bail. When they walked into the room, he looked like a rabbit in the headlights of an oncoming truck. There were dark circles beneath his eyes, and he had a haunted look about him.

'Detective Chief Inspector Moran and Detective Sergeant Davies.' Moran switched on the cameras and the system began recording. 'This interview is with Harold Nelson and he's represented by Lewis Holding from Gladstone, Brookes. It is a preliminary hearing under caution. We are going to ask you questions about the murders of Pauline Verwood, Caroline Greenman, and your family,' Moran said. 'This is a very distressing situation and we need to be clear that you're in a fit state of mind to be interviewed. Are you okay if we call you, Harold?' Harold Nelson stared at her blankly. His eyes were bloodshot from crying. 'Is that okay with you, Harold?'

'Hal,' he replied. His voice was no more than a whisper. 'Everyone calls me Hal.'

'Okay, Hal,' Moran said. 'I know the doctor's been to see you but I need you to say you're feeling well enough mentally and physically to answer our questions.'

'I'm not a crackpot, if that's what you mean. I haven't killed anyone. I'm sorry about Pauline Verwood but I had nothing to do with that.'

'We'll talk about it in more detail shortly,' Moran said.

'I need you to tell me what has happened,' Hal said.

'I need you to answer my question,' Moran said.

'They won't tell me what happened to my family,' Hal interrupted. Moran and Kim exchanged glances. 'What happened to my family?'

'Your brief hasn't gone over the evidence with you?' Moran asked.

'Yes.'

'He has?'

'Yes, but I don't think he has all the facts,' Hal said. His eyes filled up. 'He said they were all beaten to death with a clawhammer?'

'Can you answer my question first, Hal,' Moran said. 'Then I'll answer yours.'

'Yes. I'm well enough to answer your questions,' Hal said, nodding. He wiped his nose with the back of his sleeve. 'What happened to my family?'

'Your brief was correct in what he said. They were beaten to death with a clawhammer,' Moran said.

'But what were the circumstances?' Hal asked. 'No one will tell me the circumstances. I need to understand what happened to my family. Where they were and who died first?' he asked. 'It's important to me.'

'Are you asking this question to aid your defence down the line?' Moran asked. 'Playing games will not help you in the long run.'

'I thought I was innocent until proven guilty?' Hal said, shrugging. He looked like someone had sucked the life from him.

'That's for a jury to decide but at this stage, I have a weight of evidence to balance, and the evidence is pointing to the fact that you killed Caroline Greenman and your family, hence explaining the circumstances of their deaths to you, feels like we're playing a game.'

'This is beyond games to me,' Hal said. 'Way beyond games. My wife and kids are dead, and you lot think I did it. I'm confused as to why you would think that. Surely, you can understand my predicament here?'

'My client has asked a reasonable question, Chief Inspector,' Holding said, removing his glasses. 'Assuming my client is innocent, it would be right and proper to explain the circumstances in which his wife and children lost their lives.' Moran looked down at the desk for a moment too long. 'Unless you're going to charge my client already?'

'We're not making any assumptions at this stage,' Moran said, smiling. It was the smile of a skilled negotiator. 'To answer your question, Caroline Greenman was killed first. She opened her front door to the attacker and was overwhelmed in seconds, then your son Noah was next. He was in the hallway, and we think he probably wanted to see who was at the door,' Moran said, looking up at Hal. 'That could be because he recognised the attacker's voice?' Neither Holding nor Hal rose to the bait. 'Maybe the attacker was someone he knew, and he was excited to see them,' she added. Hal stared at her but didn't react. 'Your wife, Maisy was found on the stairs where we think she tried to stop the attacker going upstairs, where Jessie was hiding under the bed. Jessie was found upstairs. The attacker pulled her from under the bed and bludgeoned her to death.' Hal broke down, sobbing like a child. 'Obviously, this is very upsetting for you. To summarise, they were all killed the same way by one attacker using a clawhammer.' Hal was broken. He couldn't lift his head from the table. 'I'm going to suggest a five-minute break,' Moran said. 'To allow your client to compose himself.'

'I'm okay,' Hal sobbed. 'I just need a minute. It's hard to hear it.'

'I think a break is in order,' Holding said.

The detectives left the room. They walked to the coffee machine and Kim bought a latte for herself and a tea for Moran. Moran leant against the wall and sighed. She looked frustrated.

'What are your first impressions?' Kim asked.

'He's either in complete denial or he thinks he can blag his way out of this. Either way, he's mistaken if he thinks he can squirm out of this,' Moran said.

'Now you've seen him how are we going to play it?'

'He's clearly going to deny it. We won't react to his denials. We'll let him talk. He'll talk himself into knots. I don't want to cause conflict with him yet. We'll put the evidence to him and listen to his answers. The CPS will make their decision based on that and the evidence is powerful. There's no way to twist out of this. He can sit there until doomsday denying it.'

'I'm morbidly interested in how he thinks he can deny it without claiming demonic possession or aliens did it,' Kim said.

'Let's go back,' Moran said. They walked back into the room, and Moran restarted the recording and explained the legalities once more. 'Are you okay to continue?'

'Yes.'

'I want to start by asking you about a series of messages you sent to several women on the base on the night of the thirteenth of November,' Moran began.

'I didn't send them,' Hal said. 'That's the whole point. I didn't do any of this. I'm being set up.'

'Okay, but we need to get the facts straight,' Moran said, nodding. 'You agree they were sent from your accounts?'

'Yes, but not by me,' Hal said, leaning forward to emphasise the point.

'And you would agree they were sent from your device?'

'Yes. But not by me,' Hal said, again.

'Can you explain how the messages were sent from your accounts on your device if you didn't send them, please?'

'We're not allowed mobile phones or tablets on shift, so we leave our belongings in the changing rooms. We're all allocated lockers. My locker was broken into and my phone was stolen.'

'Your phone was stolen?' Moran checked the details on her laptop. 'But you have your phone now?' Moran said.

'Yes. He put it back.'

'Who did?' Moran asked.

'Ernest Metcalfe,' Hal said. 'He's a sergeant at my station.'

'Did you report the break in at the time?'

'No.'

'Okay,' Moran said. 'You're suggesting Sergeant Metcalfe broke into your locker, took your phone, sent a string of abusive messages to women on the base and then put your phone back in your locker?'

'Yes.' Hal shuffled uncomfortably.

'Why?'

'He's a nutcase,' Hal said, blushing. 'He should be in here not me. You have got the wrong man.'

'Why would Sergeant Metcalfe do that?' Moran asked.

Hal took a deep breath and whispered to his brief. Holding nodded and scribbled a note on his pad.

'Because he found out I was having an affair with his wife, Naomi,' Hal said, putting his head in his hands.

'You were having an affair with Naomi Metcalfe?' Moran asked.

'Yes. It had been going on for a few months. All this is because I had an affair with his wife. I shouldn't have gone near her but these things happen. I don't know how he found out but he did and he's lost his mind. I never thought it would go this far.' Hal tapped the table with his fist. 'Ernie Metcalfe is damaged. He killed my family,' Hal said, his voice breaking. His lips trembled. 'He is deranged and you need to lock him up.'

'Sergeant Metcalfe works the same shifts as you?' Moran asked, frowning.

'Not always,' Hal said. 'We work swing rotas.'

'So, you wouldn't have arrived at work at the same time?'

'No. He was at work when I arrived.'

'How do you know that?' Moran asked.

'His Jeep was in the car park.'

'Your wife said you had left home early that day to work overtime but you didn't go in early on the thirteenth,' Moran said.

'No.'

'Where did you go?'

'What has this got to do with anything?' Hal asked, agitated.

'It has everything to do with the investigation,' Moran said. 'You lied to your wife about going to work. So, we need to establish the timeline for that day,' she said. 'Where did you go?'

'I was with Naomi,' Hal muttered.

'At her home?'

'Yes.'

'How long were you there?'

'About two hours,' Hal said.

'Okay, thank you,' Moran said, smiling again. She looked almost reptilian when she smiled that way. 'You went to work and you put your mobile into your locker and secured it?'

'Yes.'

'When you returned, was the lock on your locker broken?' Moran asked.

'No. But there were scratches on the keyhole. He must have used a lockpick.'

'You noticed scratches on the lock immediately?'

'No. Not immediately. The lock wouldn't open. I had to wiggle the key and when I opened it, my phone had been switched off. I never switch it off.'

'When did you know he had broken into your locker?'

'The apps had been wiped from my phone, so I suspected something had happened but I wasn't sure until the next day when the accusations started,' Hal said. 'My apps had been wiped from my phone. I didn't realise the extent of what he had been up to until the damage was done.'

'Once you realised what had happened, did you report it?'

'No. I didn't want to have to explain why he would do a thing like that,' Hal explained. 'You can understand that, surely.'

'I'm not here to understand what you did,' Moran said. 'I'm here to find out the facts as you present them to us.'

'You need to understand what happened,' Hal said, agitated. 'Clearly you don't understand or I wouldn't be here.' He glared from Kim to Moran and back again. 'If you understood, Ernest Metcalfe would be in here, not me.'

'We have to follow the evidence,' Moran said. She half smiled. Hal looked like he was going to speak but he thought better of it. 'One of the women messaged from your phone was Air Commodore Pauline Verwood,' Moran said. Hal nodded. 'You were interviewed by human resources about that?'

'Yes.'

'She made a formal complaint,' Moran said.

'Yes,' Hal said, nodding. 'She would, wouldn't she. I don't blame her for making a complaint. But I didn't send the messages.'

'That must have been embarrassing?' Moran asked.

'Embarrassing isn't the word for it,' Hal said. 'I was mortified. It was very confusing. I didn't have a clue what they were accusing me off at first. I couldn't believe what they were saying to me.'

'There's no mention of Sergeant Metcalfe stealing your phone in the interview,' Moran said. She looked him in the eye and smiled again. 'The interview notes are very clear.'

'I didn't want them to know about the affair.'

'But that would have been the perfect opportunity to come clean and clear your name?'

'I was protecting Naomi and my family,' Hal said. Moran looked up at him when he mentioned his family. It made him feel dirty, violated by the accusation in her eyes.

'They asked you to surrender your devices, to clear things up but you refused,' Moran said.

'Yes.'

'You didn't tell them you knew who had sent the messages,' Moran said. 'You refused to allow them to look at your devices and apparently, you became abusive?'

'I was annoyed,' Hal said. 'I knew the amount of trouble I was in and I was embarrassed. I didn't know where to put myself. With hindsight, I should have told them there and then but I had no idea he was going to turn psycho on us. I knew he was a psyche ward case but I didn't realise how far gone he is.'

'You say you were annoyed,' Moran said. 'So annoyed that you rammed your car into the back of Pauline Verwood's Mercedes?'

'That was an accident,' Hal said, shaking his head. 'There were screws in my tyres. The breakdown mechanic said they'd been put there on purpose. He did that, knowing they would cause a blowout.'

'Sergeant Metcalfe?' Moran asked.

'Yes.'

'Did you report this to anyone on the base?'

'No. I've explained that to you. I didn't want anyone to know about the affair,' Hal said, frustration in his voice.

'Yes. You said that earlier,' Moran said.

'I've said that already but you're not listening,' Hal said, trying to remain calm. 'Ernie Metcalfe sent those messages and put screws in my tyres. It was pure coincidence I crashed into Verwood's car.'

'I'm not a big fan of coincidences,' Moran said, smiling. Hal's expression darkened. 'It must feel like a very unfortunate coincidence,' she added.

'I know how it looks,' Hal said, shaking his head. 'I can see how all of this looks but I need you to see past the superfluous facts and dig deeper into reality. I didn't kill anyone,' Hal insisted.

'You appear to be getting angry now,' she added. Hal shook his head and took a deep breath. 'Do you have anger issues?'

'No.'

'In summary. You said Sergeant Metcalfe broke into your locker, stole your phone, sent Pauline Verwood abusive messages from your phone, which led to you being interviewed by senior officers from human resources, and then he sabotaged your vehicle causing you to crash into the back of her vehicle and yet you said absolutely nothing to anyone about it?'

'Yes.'

'You didn't talk to anyone about this?'

'No.'

'So, no one can verify what you were thinking at the time?'

'No.'

'Not a soul?'

'Naomi,' Hal said, sighing. 'Obviously, I told Naomi. Ask her if you don't believe me.'

'Why did you tell Naomi?' Moran asked, frowning.

'It's complicated,' Hal said, rubbing his hands together. Moran waited for him to expand. He knew the technique, but he was struggling. 'Ernie took my phone from my locker and he had a text conversation with Naomi, pretending to be me. He wiped her phone too, so we spoke about it. We were worried he had found out about us,' Hal explained. 'Ask her. She will confirm that.'

'We will,' Moran said. 'Going back to the messages sent from your phone. They were pretty lurid to say the least.'

'I didn't send them,' Hal interrupted.

'There seems to be a pattern to the messages involving tying women up?' Moran said. Hal shrugged. 'We found Pauline Verwood tied up in the sand dunes at Rhosneigr.' Kim placed crime scene photographs on the table. Hal went pale. His brief went paler still. 'She was found in this position, head buried in the sand, kneeling, tied, and gagged. The cause of death was suffocation. Her airways were full of sand. She'd been sexually assaulted and beaten with a clawhammer.' Hal stared at the photographs and bit his lip. 'We found the clawhammer used to beat her at her home.' She stared at him. Hal withered beneath her glare. 'It's your hammer.'

'What?' Hal asked with a sharp intake of breath.

'The hammer is yours from your shed,' Moran said, placing a photograph of the tool board with the hammer missing. 'It has your prints on it.' She pushed the photograph closer to him. 'We don't have the DNA results yet but there's hair and skin and blood all over it. That's the murder weapon used to kill, Pauline, Caroline, your wife, and your children.' She paused. There was deathly silence. 'They were all killed with your hammer.'

'I don't fucking believe this,' Hal shouted. His face flushed red with anger. 'Ernie Metcalfe did this. He stole my wife's keys and went to my home. He trashed the place,' Hal said, angrily. 'He must have taken the hammer from the shed. This is a set-up. Can't you see this is a fucking set up?'

'I think you need to calm down,' Moran said. Hal sat back in his chair and closed his eyes tightly, the nerves in his neck twitched. 'Do you need a break to control your anger?'

'Fuck off,' Hal said.

'Charming,' Moran said, smiling.

'Someone will wipe that smile from your face one day,' Hal said, pointing at Moran.

'That sounds like a threat to me,' Kim said.

'It's not a threat, just an observation,' Hal said, looking at Kim. 'She's trying to push my buttons and it's working.' His brief took off his glasses and whispered in his ear. Hal ignored him. 'I can see what you're doing. You're making me angry and making a big deal of it. You want it to look like I'm the lunatic, not him.'

'I'm not trying to do anything,' Moran said. 'I'm showing you the evidence as we see it and judging by your reaction, we've touched a nerve.'

'Bullshit. You're trying to make it look like I was so angry I went on a killing spree. Well, that's not what happened. You have the wrong man in here. Ernie Metcalfe did all this and he's stitching me up because I banged his wife.'

'You banged his wife. I see. So, it was a casual fling,' Moran said, half smiling this time. Her expression and tone were deeply patronising. It was having the desired effect. 'You banged her, so it wasn't a serious relationship?'

'I didn't mean to say it like that,' Hal protested. 'You're making me say things I don't mean. I'm not thinking straight. It wasn't just about sex. Maybe in the beginning but after a while, it was much more than that.'

'You said you banged his wife. They were your words.' Moran paused for a few seconds. 'That doesn't sound like a loving relationship to me.' She paused again. Hal was simmering. 'Did you want to bang Pauline Verwood?'

'No,' Hal snorted. 'You're trying to provoke me.'

'What about Jamillia Squire?' Moran asked. 'Did you want to bang her as well?'

'What has she got to do with the price of fish?'

'She received a similar message from your phone.'

'I didn't send those messages,' Hal said.

'Maybe not on the night of the thirteenth, but you've sent her others, haven't you?' Hal shrugged and looked down. 'We spoke to Jamillia and she said you had been stalking her on social media for months,' Moran said. 'Liking her photographs going back years, especially holiday pictures when she was wearing a bikini?'

'I don't know what that has got to do with anything,' Hal said, blushing purple. 'Are you going to say anything?' he said, turning to his brief. 'You're supposed to be supporting me.'

'Is there a point to this?' Holding asked.

'Your client is pinning everything on his claim that someone else sent those women lewd messages, when the fact is, he has been bothering women on the base for years.'

'I didn't bother her,' Hal argued. 'We were chatting.'

'You stalked her photographs and told her how hot she looked in a bikini. That is crossing the line, and she changed her security settings so you couldn't see her photographs,' Moran said.

'She took it the wrong way.'

'I'm not sure she did. Did you want to bang Jamillia too?'

'Fuck you!'

'This line of questioning is provocative and uncalled for,' Holding said.

'I'll dictate the line of questioning,' Moran said. 'Shall I read you one of the messages you sent to her from your phone. *I want to tie you up and smash your back doors in.* Not a classic approach to make to a woman but it seems to be a favourite of yours.' Moran read from the laptop. 'You seem to have a problem with approaching married women on social media and Maisy found out, didn't she?'

'I didn't send the fucking message!'

'That's the message she received from your phone and this is how we found her, face down in the dunes.' Moran tapped the photograph. 'Is that a coincidence?'

'You're not listening to me,' Hal muttered, trying to contain himself. 'I didn't send the message in the first place. Ernie Metcalfe sent those messages.'

'So you said but I don't believe it,' Moran said. 'You send messages like that all the time.'

'I didn't send those messages on the thirteenth,' Hal said. 'Ernie Metcalfe stole my phone and sent them.'

'Sergeant Metcalfe didn't ram your vehicle into the back of her Mercedes,' Moran said. 'You did that. You were driving.'

'That was an accident,' Hal protested. 'You're not listening to me.'

'Your car was taken away, wasn't it?'

'Yes.'

'They gave you a hire car,' Moran said. Hal nodded. 'There was sand on the tyres of your hire vehicle,' Moran said.

'So what?' Hal asked, frowning.

'We're testing it but I'm certain it will come back as matching sand from the dunes at Rhosneigr.' She paused. Hal looked shocked. 'Where we found Pauline Verwood's body.'

'I drove to the beach after work,' Hal said, shaking his head. 'I had a really bad day. My head was banging, so I went for a walk on the beach.'

'Alone?'

'Yes.'

'Did anyone see you?'

'No.'

'Did you tell anyone you were going there?'

'No.'

'Then what did you do?'

'I went home and Maisy was there with Caroline Greenman,' Hal said. 'She was in her car because Ernie Metcalfe had stolen her keys and slashed her tyres.'

'One of your neighbours said you were arguing on the driveway,' Moran said, looking at her laptop. Hal didn't reply. 'Did you argue with Maisy when you got home?'

'It wasn't an argument,' Hal said. 'She had been told about the messages Jamillia received, so she was understandably pissed off. I explained that it wasn't me who sent them and then we went inside. That was when we saw that the house had been trashed.'

'Tell me about the damage to your home,' Moran asked. Hal looked confused.

'What about it?' Hal asked, frustrated. 'He turned on all the taps and blocked up the plugs and smashed the place to bits. That man is batshit crazy.'

'How do you explain him doing all this without being seen by anyone?'

'I don't know,' Hal said. 'I told you. Maisy went to Tesco and her keys were stolen,' Hal said, calming down slightly. 'That's how he got into the house. That's how he got into the shed and took my hammer. That's how he has made this look like I killed my family,' he pleaded. He put his hands together in prayer. 'He took her keys and went to my home. Her tyres were slashed so he knew he had enough time to trash the place. He's done all this to hurt me. This is revenge. Please tell me you can see what is happening here?'

'So, you want us to believe everything is down to the fact you were having an affair with Naomi Metcalfe and her husband, Sergeant Metcalfe found out, started a smear campaign against you, sabotaged your vehicle, and then went on to murder five people and frame you for it?'

'Yes,' Hal said, nodding. 'That's exactly what's happening. He's a raving nutcase. The man is dangerous.'

'But he doesn't have any issues on his record,' Moran said, reading from her laptop. 'Historical behaviour is important when we're investigating a crime. In the cold light of day, we have to investigate previous behaviour to predict how a suspect would behave in any given situation. People tend to repeat their behaviour and we have to look for patterns.' Moran looked at Kim and nodded. Kim placed a photograph on the table.

'Do you recognise this profile picture?' Kim asked.

'No,' Hal said, shaking his head. He blushed.

'It's obvious to me by your reaction that you do,' Kim said. 'Her name is Felicity Car and you approached her three months ago on Facebook.'

'I may have done,' Hal said, shrugging.

'You did and she chatted to you until some of your messages became sexualised and she asked you to stop,' Kim said. 'You didn't, so she blocked you but she took a screenshot of the messages for security in case anything happened. Does that ring any bells?'

'I was just messing around, flirting,' Hal said. 'What has this got to do with anything?'

'This is the message that made her block you,' Kim said. '*I want to tie you up and smash your back doors in*,' she read. 'Does that sound familiar?' Hal shrugged. Kim placed another photograph on the table. 'This is Jess Tate. You approached her on Facebook about four months ago and told her how pretty she was and then it went downhill from there,' Kim said. 'She blocked you following this message. *I want to tie you up and smash your back doors in*. Again, does that message ring a bell?'

'Where are we going with this line of questioning?' Holding asked. He looked uncomfortable.

'I have six profiles belonging to females on the airbase who have come forward since Pauline Verwood made her complaint. An online campaign has encouraged women to come forward if they've ever been approached by Corporal Harold Nelson. I have a list of women on my desk that's going to take some time to explore,' Kim explained. 'Hal has been bothering women most of his life by the looks of it. There are several incidents on his personnel record. They all follow the same pattern.'

'So, I enjoy chatting up women,' Hal said, angrily. 'So what?'

'You approached Naomi Metcalfe online, didn't you?'

'Yes. So what?'

'This is the initial string of messages between you and Naomi Metcalfe. *I think you're the prettiest woman on the island.* Very romantic. Things get a bit more sordid in the fourth week but Naomi was responsive.' Kim shrugged. 'I suppose if you cast your net often enough, you'll eventually catch a fish.'

'Is there a question here?' Holding asked.

'There's a pattern of behaviour,' Kim said. 'Can you tell us why you were transferred from your last posting in Germany a year earlier than contracted?'

'There was a misunderstanding,' Hal said, looking at his brief for support. 'Can they ask me about this?'

'Yes. If it relates to a pattern repeated in this case,' Holding said. 'I assume it does?'

'Yes. It does. Would you like to tell us about it?' Kim asked.

'No.'

'For the recording,' Kim said. 'You were interviewed and reprimanded for a string of harassing messages sent to females on the

Hamburg airbase. You had an affair with one of the women, Laura Bates. She contacted the police and claimed you sexually assaulted her by handcuffing her and forcing her to have anal sex,' Kim added. 'You were arrested and interviewed about the assault.'

'I was never charged with anything,' Hal said. 'That was a misunderstanding,' Hal said, shaking his head. 'In the heat of the moment, these things happen. I misunderstood what she was saying.'

'You misunderstood that when she said no, she meant no?' Kim asked.

'It wasn't like that.'

'You threatened her when she made the complaint,' Kim said. 'It's all on record.'

'She lied,' Hal said.

'So, it didn't happen?'

'Not how she said it did.'

'What about Maria Kipling?' Kim asked. Hal didn't answer. 'You gave her a lift in your car and drove her to an empty car park, where you tried to molest her. Do you recall that?'

'She wanted to go but got cold feet,' Hal said.

'She withdrew her statement because she said you had threatened her?'

'She's a liar.'

'Another liar?'

'I know what you're trying to do,' Hal said, shaking his head. 'I didn't kill my family. I didn't kill anyone.'

'You don't handle rejection well, do you?'

'They would have kicked me out of the RAF if I'd done what she said,' Hal argued.

'You made threats of violence but you made them verbally, so it was he said/she said.'

'She exaggerated what had happened. It was rough sex gone wrong.'

'Why do you think you're still a corporal after ten years of service?' Moran asked.

'Fuck you,' Hal said.

'You haven't been promoted because of your behaviour. Ernest Metcalfe had no part in what happened in any of those cases,' Moran said. 'You can't blame him for your pattern of behaviour.' Hal glared at her. 'We spoke to Maisy's mother and she said she nearly broke up with you over the incident in Germany.'

'Her mother is a drunken tart,' Hal said angrily. 'She has nothing to do with my family.'

'She's been speaking to Maisy and Maisy wanted to go back to London with the children,' Kim said. 'You knew that and you couldn't handle it.'

A knock on the door interrupted them. A detective handed Moran a note and she read it and checked an email on her laptop. She showed it to Kim. Hal looked terrified and his brief was clearly losing the will to live. Kim took a moment before starting again.

'You were solely responsible for sending hundreds of menacing text messages. This is a long-term problem for you, isn't it?'

'I'm a bloke. I like women and they like me,' Hal said. He shrugged. 'I've never hurt anyone and I didn't kill my family.'

'You're a serial sex pest but this time, it went way beyond what you could control. Maisy said she was going to leave you and take your kids away. Pauline Verwood is a high-ranking officer and wanted you kicked out of the RAF. You lost control and you killed Pauline Verwood, Caroline Greenman, and your family, didn't you?'

Hal folded his arms and sat back. He shook his head and closed his eyes.

'No comment,' he muttered.

Moran turned on the screen in the room. She cast images from her laptop onto it. It showed a pair of wellington boots and a jumpsuit.

'We've just had some forensic results back from the lab,' Moran said. 'You have a copy of the report on email,' she said to Holding. Holding clicked through to his email and opened the file. 'These are items found in a bag in your shed, which was locked. The wellington boots have your name written in them and contain your DNA. Sweat and skin samples match yours. There's sand in the tread and multiple blood traces on them. The DNA matches your children and your wife.' Hal shook his head and closed his eyes. 'Fibre analysis put them at both the Greenman and the Verwood residence.' Hal put his head on the table and covered his ears. 'The jumpsuit has also been identified as yours and the blood spatter on the sleeves matches all five victims, so far. There are more samples being analysed but these are the initial findings.' Hal looked up at the ceiling. 'Have you got anything to say?'

'Ernie Metcalfe had the keys to my home,' Hal said. 'You haven't listened to a word I've said. He took those things from my home and the hammer from the shed and he killed my family and those poor women and then he put the evidence in my shed to frame me.' Hal shrugged. 'You're raking up a few slaps on the wrist from the past to back up your accusations. Ernie Metcalfe is setting me up. This is not rocket science. Why can't you get your head around this?'

'We have listened to what you've had to say all the way through and there's a team of detectives listening too,' Moran said. 'As soon as you mentioned Sergeant Metcalfe, my team were looking at him. An initial search of his phone records and GPS puts him at home in his house when these murders took place.' Moran smiled again. 'I think we've heard enough. Charge him,' Moran said. She stood up and left the room.

Chapter 51

Richard knocked on Alan's door and waited for a second before walking in. He carried three cups of steaming hot coffee and put them down on the desk. Sharna followed him.

'Hello, Sharna,' Alan said. 'How's Richard looking after you?'

'Sharna's looking after me,' Richard said. 'I've needed looking after for a while now.'

'Can't say I've noticed,' Alan said.

'The team has gelled,' Richard said.

'Good. Are you making progress?'

'Definitely. Sharna has brought a different approach to the search. I couldn't see the wood for the trees but we've changed tack and uncovered some remarkably interesting incidents on the continent.'

'Related to ours?' Alan asked.

'Let's say they're so similar, we can't ignore them.'

'That sounds encouraging. We need something to break on the case,' Alan said. 'Show me what you have.'

'I was concentrating on the charity ride and getting frustrated with being fobbed off by everyone I spoke to. I found a post from San Francis Xavier. A catholic school in Calais. It was promoting the arrival of Maltese priests but like all the others, there was no follow up and no social interaction. I rang and spoke to the headmaster about the post, but he said he didn't have a clue what I was talking about. I told him it was about a charity bike ride from Rome to New York and had been posted on the school's social media,' Richard began. 'He fobbed me off with a story about an intern who had posted it and since left and that he had no knowledge of any such event. Sharna made the point that there had been social interaction on the post. It was another dead end,' Richard explained. 'But Sharna came up with the idea of digging deeper into the places we know our Maltese priests visited, so we looked at Calais and the school. San Francis Xavier School for Boys. It's a fee-paying school attended by the children of wealthy people from across Europe. Lessons are taught in four different languages, including English. We scratched beneath the surface and found what we were looking for.'

'Which is what?' Alan asked, slurping his coffee.

'We uncovered some incidents of historical abuse, allegedly carried out by the school padre over a period of a decade or so. His name was Pierre Basset. Basset was prosecuted and over thirty boys made statements against him but the investigation was flawed and rules had been broken. Basset walked on a technicality.'

'Sounds familiar,' Alan said. 'Where do our priests come into the story?'

'Basset was found hanged in a wood near the school six weeks ago, which was the week the charity ride was due to arrive,' Richard said. 'The timing is too perfect to ignore.'

'That's spooky,' Alan said, smiling. 'What a coincidence.'

'We don't do coincidences,' Richard said. 'There was no note and the suicide went virtually unnoticed. Of course, the school wouldn't make any comment. They wouldn't even confirm Basset had ever worked there. This is where Sharna comes in,' Richard said.

'I checked for paedophile hunters online in Calais and there are four active groups on Facebook,' Sharna said. 'One of them had chatter about the Basset suicide.'

'What type of chatter?'

'Chatter claiming it wasn't a suicide,' Sharna said. 'I contacted the Calais police and spoke to a detective who investigated the initial abuse case. He has retired, so I contacted the detective who investigated the suicide and asked him if it could have been staged to look like a suicide.'

'I bet that went down well,' Alan said.

'He called me an idiot and hung up,' Sharna said, shrugging. 'So, I went onto the Europol information sharing pages and there were questions being asked by the MIT in Florence. They are thinking along the same lines as we are.' Sharna showed Alan some news articles. 'The remains of an accused paedophile priest were discovered by a diver in the river Arno, south of Florence. Louis Abruzzo. He was part of a paedophile ring, prosecuted eight years ago. Only one of the twelve men accused was convicted. He's doing life. The rest of them walked. When Abruzzo was identified, a murder enquiry was initiated and only two of the remaining men were traced. The rest are missing.'

'That's scarily similar to what we're dealing with,' Alan said, sitting forward. He gulped his coffee. 'This is excellent work, both of you.'

'You haven't heard the best of it yet,' Richard said.

'Louis Abruzzo had cement in his stomach and intestines. The detectives said he had been forced to ingest it. It was to weight the body down,' Sharna said. 'The fact the victim had cement in his stomach set all the alarm bells ringing.'

'Ah, you superstars,' Alan said, clapping his hands. 'That's a signature to remember, especially when you consider who the victims were. Have you contacted the detectives in Florence?'

'No,' Richard said. 'I wanted to run it by you first. There are four other potential cases similar to ours. Sharna has been translating chatter on websites in Paris, Salzburg, Porto, and Rotterdam. They all have historical abuse cases that collapsed, and they were all visited by our charity cyclists. That's as far as we've gone. The next step is trawling through the news reports for each area at the time of the visits.'

'How long do you need to verify if they're connected or not?' Alan asked.

'Give us a few days,' Richard said. 'The abuse cases are simple enough to find. Sorting through the suspects who walked takes a bit longer. We've identified several abusers in Paris, who are missing, going back about seven months.'

'Are they all linked to chatter on relevant websites?' Alan asked.

'Yes.' Sharna nodded. 'Obviously, it's idiots bragging and implying they were involved, but it reenforces what we have.'

'Absolutely, it does. I'm going to put a few calls in to Europol with what we have so far,' Alan said. 'I think there will be someone there already looking into this. I bet they're wondering where our Maltese friends have got to. Well done, you two.'

Chapter 52

Kim was driving back from St Asaph when she missed a call from Georgina Moran. Harold Nelson had been indignant and abusive when she charged him. It was a relief to get out of the station and breathe the fresh air away from his stink. She had taken the route over the Denbigh moors to Pentrefoelas. It was a narrow, winding road, but the views over towards Snowdon were stunning. Snow covered the higher peaks. It was a mesmerising vista. She stopped at the Sportsman's Arms for a coffee and a sandwich. The signal was sporadic, so when the missed call icon showed on her screen, she rang her back.

'Did you go over the moors?' Moran asked.

'Yes. Why?'

'The team were following up on the Ernest Metcalfe accusations made by Nelson,' Moran said. 'His number plate has come up on the system as being involved in a fatal RTA.'

'When?' Kim asked.

'This morning,' Moran said. 'Apparently, it's in the Capel Curig area. You're heading that way, aren't you?'

'Yes. I'm going towards Betws now,' Kim said. 'I'll stop and see what I can find out.'

'Call me back,' Moran said.

'Will do,' Kim said, ending the call.

The road to Betws was clear. There were no caravans or campers crawling up the A5. Tourists were in short supply, which suited the locals when they needed to get somewhere quickly. She drove through the village without stopping. There were a handful of visitors, most wearing hiking gear, hats, and winter jackets. Fifteen minutes later, she was in the Ogwen Valley and she could see an incident ahead. A thick oak tree stood stoic at the corner of a small graveyard. The road was narrow and one side had been closed. There were three traffic police cars and an accident investigation van. She could see a Jeep being dragged onto the flatbed of a recovery vehicle. The front of the Jeep was squashed like a concertina into where the backseat should be. Kim pulled across the road and parked behind an interceptor outside a small chapel. A uniformed officer marched towards her, gesturing furiously for her to move on. She got out of the vehicle and showed her ID.

'DC Davies, Holyhead MIT,' she said. 'Who's in charge?'

'Inspector Mather,' the officer said. 'He's around the other side of the chapel having a cigarette. Couldn't organise a piss up in a brewery,' he added.

Kim ignored the remark and headed towards the chapel. She watched the Jeep being fastened to the flatbed. Jeep versus a hundred-year-old oak. There was only one winner. As she neared, the accident investigators were leaning against their van chatting. She approached them and showed her ID.

'DC Davies, Holyhead MIT,' she said. 'Have you finished your investigation?'

'Pretty much.'

'Was it a fatality?' The investigators looked at each other unsure if they should be divulging anything at all. 'I know the vehicle belongs to Sergeant Ernest Metcalfe,' Kim said. The officers looked surprised. 'He's implicated in a murder case we're working on.'

'Ah, I see. I thought you were just being nosey,' one of the investigators said. 'The wife was killed instantly. She wasn't belted and went through the windscreen. She hit that oak tree skull first, didn't stand a chance. The husband is lucky. His legs were crushed. They had to cut him out but he'll live. He won't be dancing for a while.'

'Any idea what happened?'

'We're speculating until we speak to Sergeant Metcalfe, you understand. So, anything we say is off the record.'

'Yes. I won't quote you,' Kim said.

'There was a hairbrush in the footwell, her handbag was open and she wasn't belted,' the investigator said, shrugging. 'Maybe she dropped her brush, husband tries to catch it and bang. It only takes a split second and it's curtains. This road is dangerous at the best of times.'

'Poor woman,' Kim said. 'Thanks for your help.' She walked past the investigators and through the chapel gate, which looked new. The grass was neatly cut and the graves were well groomed. Most of the headstones had been laid horizontal on the graves, probably for safety reasons. She followed the path around the chapel and saw the inspector. He saw her coming and looked flustered. 'Inspector Mather,' she said. 'I'm DC Davies, Holyhead MIT. Have they taken Ernest Metcalfe to Ysbyty Gwynedd?'

'Yes,' Mather said, crushing his cigarette with his foot. He picked up the butt and flicked it over the wall into the stream. 'The poor bugger was out of the game when they got him out. He was pumped full of painkillers, high as a kite. The firemen had to cut him out. His legs were trapped. It will be a nasty shock when he comes around and finds out his missus didn't make it.'

'It will be a nasty shock for her kids too,' Kim said.

'She has kids?'

'Three girls,' Kim said. The officer shook his head. 'Thanks for the info.' She took out her mobile and headed back towards the road. Scaffolding had been erected at the back of the chapel. The stained-glass windows had been cleaned recently and glinted in the weak winter sunshine. It was a pretty chapel. She dialled the custody suite at St Asaph, and the desk sergeant answered after a few rings.

'Has Harold Nelson been transferred to Risley yet?' she asked.

'Not yet. The transfer unit is stuck in traffic at Holywell.'

'Can you give him a message,' Kim said.

'Of course,' the sergeant said.

'Tell him Naomi Metcalfe was killed in an RTA this morning.'

'Okay. Was she family?'

'No. She wasn't family but she had one once, before that bastard came along,' Kim said.

Chapter 53

A month later

Alan accepted a meeting request from a French inspector, called Pierre Ricci who was on secondment to Europol. He had arranged a conference call with a detective from Florence, called Aldo Bonnetti. They were both investigating the aftermath of revenge attacks by online paedophile hunters. The similarities were uncanny. His screen changed and the two men appeared in separate boxes. Alan hadn't used the zoom app before, but it appeared to be simple enough. Even for a technophobe like him.

'Good afternoon, gentlemen,' Alan said. The other officers were adjusting their camera angles and chair height. He was glad they looked as unfamiliar as he was with the app.

'Hello,' Ricci said when he was comfortable.

'Ciao,' Bonnetti said. Alan thought he looked like Brando in the Godfather. His cheeks were puffy. He looked like he was storing food in them. 'Thank you for inviting me. I hope I can help.'

'Thank you for meeting with us,' Ricci said. 'It seems we all have a problem with priests from Malta. Inspector Bonnetti is somewhat of an expert on them,' he added. 'Isn't that, right?'

'I wouldn't say expert,' Bonnetti said. 'I would say I've had the unfortunate opportunity to deal with them before.'

'You have dealt with Troisi and James before?' Alan asked.

'In a roundabout way, yes,' Bonnetti said. 'Let me explain something to you. Arturo Troisi and Ganni James are buried near the Basilica Saint Peter in a graveyard called Campo Santo. I'm not sure of the exact date they died but they were in the original Swiss Guard in the fifteen hundreds.'

'Swiss guard as in the Vatican security force?' Alan asked.

'Yes. It was formed in fifteen hundred and six, to protect the Pope from assassins. It is the oldest army and the smallest. Only one-hundred and fifty men are employed at any one time. Troisi and James are revered as founders of the force and that's why their names are taken whenever the protection of the Pope or the Church comes into play. The priests from Malta are not Troisi and James, neither are they priests. Their identities are a mystery. I'm not sure they're Maltese, to be honest.'

'But you said you've dealt with them before,' Alan said.

'No. I've dealt with men like them,' Bonnetti said. 'These men are themselves assassins, employed by a company owned by the Church in Malta. There is no direct link back to Rome. The names Troisi and James have been used before to create a shield to protect the Church and its reputation.'

'Arturo Troisi and Ganni James are false identities?' Alan asked.

'Yes. Used many times in defence of the Pope.'

'So, you have no idea who they are?' Alan asked.

'No. No one has. These men are hired to provoke violence on behalf of powerful people. Their secrecy is paramount. Nothing can be allowed to be linked back to the Church. The purpose of their employment is to protect the reputation, not cause more damage. Stealth and propaganda are their weapons. They mobilise the people on the fringe of society, who want to take the law into their own hands.'

'Stealth? They have caused chaos,' Alan said. 'Chaos and anarchy.'

'No. I must disagree with you,' Bonnetti said, shaking his head. His jowls wobbled in a Brando-like way. 'The chaos has been caused by people local to the crimes. Citizens of your country, not those men. Those men were gone before you knew they were there.' He paused for it to sink in. 'The chaos you have seen, they will deem regrettable but what they've actually achieved is unknown. We will never discover a fraction of what they have done because they inspire others to do their work for them. Most of the victims will never be found. Nothing can be traced back.'

'But they have done this before?' Alan asked.

'Yes. We will never know how many times.'

'When did you last encounter these men?'

'Twenty years ago,' Bonnetti said. 'They're not the same men of course, yet they use the same names. The Church is having a purge, getting rid of all its embarrassing baggage. It looks to me like they've done a good job so far,' he added. 'Let's not lose sight of who is being removed from society.'

'I can't argue with the sentiment, but I can argue with their methods.' Alan felt robbed. 'They're not infallible. We found Maltese ID in a firepit. That's how we knew they were there,' Alan said. 'We know they're aiming to fly to New York from Dublin. But we have no idea where they are now.'

'They're already gone,' Bonnetti said, smiling. 'You found things that no longer matter. They lose their identities before they move onto the next phase.'

'I'm not so sure,' Alan said, feeling disappointed. 'They may be still around.'

'No. They're gone. That's the way they operate,' Bonnetti said. 'Everything is smoke and mirrors. Those men were never involved in any crimes, I can tell you that. If you found them tomorrow, you would have nothing to charge them with. They provoke locals to do work locally. I can guarantee they're already in the USA. There's an awful lot of work to be done there. I think their journey there will take years, not months.'

'You sound sympathetic to their mission,' Alan said.

'Maybe a little,' Bonnetti said. 'It is not so long ago we executed people for much less. We burnt people at the stake when the real power lay with the Church. The Church has dominated Europe for centuries. Why are we surprised it's still protecting itself?'

'Because the world has moved on,' Alan said. 'We can't have vigilantes running riot through our communities. What is Europol planning to do about it?' Alan asked.

'What would you have us do?' Ricci asked. He shook his head. 'We think we know what's going on but who do we arrest?' He shrugged. 'The Pope himself?'

'That's not a bad idea,' Alan said. 'Surely, you can trace them back to whoever hired them?'

'There are no links to follow, no money trail, no identities, no evidence that they actually communicate directly with the local activists. They light the fire and move on before it burns out of control. They leave nothing behind. The best you can do is arrest the perpetrators in your area. No one forced them to do what they did. They did that because they wanted to do it. Telling them the paedophiles should be murdered isn't a crime,' Ricci said. 'The majority of citizens would secretly agree. I'm sorry we're not telling you what you wanted to hear, but this is the reality of the situation.'

'Okay,' Alan said. 'The Church is cleaning house. Why now?'

'Money,' Bonnetti said, shrugging. 'As simple as that. The coffers have never been lower. Congregations are at an all-time low and shrinking and paedophile priests have a lot to do with people's disillusionment. Millions used to be left to the Church in wills but not anymore. The concept of buying forgiveness on your deathbed has long since died. No one has a priest at their bedside anymore. There are no last-minute confessions in return for a share of the family fortune. The Church has sold its property and its silver and its soul. The Vatican is desperate to make good its reputation. Wiping out an entire generation of paedophiles is good public relations, even if they can't take the credit for most of it.'

'Maybe people are just becoming wise to what a load of bullshit it is,' Alan said, nodding. He felt a niggling sense of failure. 'Thanks for your advice,' he added. 'Please keep in touch with any further developments.'

'You're welcome,' Ricci said.

'*Scaramanzia*,' Bonnetti said.

'You too,' Alan said. He finished the call and sat back in his chair. '*Scaramanzia*. I've no fucking idea what that means but it sounds good.'

Chapter 54

Twelve Months Later

Alan was waiting for the new ACC to arrive. Georgina Moran had been in her new position for six months. She had brought in changes, which Alan agreed with. They were moving away from league tables and results were being measured fairly. Not every case is solvable and not every case can be closed in a week. Some take years. Kim came into his office and sat down opposite him.

'Good afternoon, Detective Inspector Davies,' he said.

'Good afternoon, Chief Inspector Williams,' she replied. 'Sounds good, doesn't it?'

'It does but do you know what I like better?'

'The extra money?'

'Bang on,' he said, nodding.

'Why haven't you traded in your crap car?'

'It's still going,' Alan said.

Georgina Moran appeared in the doorway and knocked on the frame. She smiled. Alan thought she was a very pretty woman. Not as pretty as Kim, obviously but pretty.

'Did I overhear you talking about a wage increase?' Moran asked.

'No,' Alan said. 'We're not motivated by money. I would do this for nothing. Just for the rewarding feeling we get when we solve a case.'

'You need to work on your bullshit face,' Moran said. 'That one doesn't work.'

'I will work on it,' Alan said.

'Where are we on the Justice Asylum investigation?' Moran asked.

'We have four of their members in custody. None of them are talking. We can't trace nine of the men we investigated during the Creegan case,' Alan said. 'They were mostly solitary characters who avoided other people. Their families and friends had disowned them years ago, so when they went missing, no one noticed.'

'We don't know if they were attacked and disposed of or they ran and are in the wind,' Kim added. 'The nine missing have had no phone and no bank activity, which is odd because they're technically still on the Church payroll.'

'But they've stopped paying them?' Moran asked.

'We spoke to Bishop Hansen,' Alan said. 'He told us that if they don't maintain contact with their handlers, their wages stop. He brought it in last year, apparently. All the men missing had a meeting with Hansen in the months before they disappeared and they all requested a cash settlement to walk away but none of them were given a deal. Hansen refused to pay them off. All those men wanted money to disappear and keep quiet. They were refused and disappeared. I put that to Hansen but he said it's purely a coincidence.'

'No surprise there,' Moran said.

'I asked him about the Europol theory that the Vatican employed people to provoke attacks on discredited employees and he laughed.'

'Bishop Hansen and you are never going to be best friends,' Kim said. 'He hates you.'

'Hates me?' Alan said, 'That's a bit strong.'

'You hate him,' Kim said.

'When you put it that way, it makes sense,' Alan agreed. 'He's an arsehole. He said the thought of the Vatican putting human lives above the reputation of the Church was absurd.' Alan shrugged. 'Haven't they been putting themselves first for centuries?'

'Yes,' Moran agreed. 'What did you say?'

'I told him to fuck off out of my office,' Alan said. 'And he did.' Moran rolled her eyes to the ceiling.

'You're not good for our relationship with the Church,' Moran said.

'They are in this up to their necks,' Alan said. 'Do you remember the chapel in Capel Curig where Clive Roland was last seen?' Alan asked. Moran nodded and looked at Kim.

'It was also where Sergeant Metcalfe crashed his Jeep,' Kim said. 'Although I didn't know it at the time.'

'What about it?' Moran asked.

'It's been renovated and reopened as a wedding chapel,' Alan said. 'The father who will perform the ceremonies is a young man called Stephen. He told me the chapel was bought and renovated by a charity that restores historic religious buildings with European lottery money.'

'And?'

'It was the last place Clive Roland went to,' Alan said. 'The chapel was viewed by a man called Mr Jones. We haven't been able to trace him. The purchase was made by a holding company in Malta, paid with lottery money.' He shrugged. 'The European lottery won't confirm that,' Alan said. 'I thought that was odd. So, I went back through the case files and found the report made by DC Harris from Caernarfon the day after Roland went missing. He spoke to the supervisor on the job. Callum Barker handed him a business card. I tried to speak to the company he said he worked for. They were contracted to do the initial clean-up. They renovated the graveyard, cut the grass, fixed the gate, lowered dangerous headstones and the like,' Alan said. 'Cleani-King was the name of the company. Guess what?'

'What?'

'There is no company in Chester called Cleani-King, so there is no way I can speak to Callum Barker,' Alan said. 'I find that odd.'

'Maybe they were cowboys,' Moran said. 'Did the job for cash and vamoosed.'

'I checked around and Cleani-King renovated the graveyards of eight churches in North Wales during a three-month period. None of them were told work was scheduled. They just turned up and renovated them. The graves were renovated. Now the company isn't there,' Alan said, shrugging. 'Doesn't that seem odd?'

'What do you think?' Moran asked Kim.

'I think they were cowboys. Did the job for cash and vamoosed,' Kim said laughing.

'Is that how you got promoted?' Alan said. 'Seriously, there is something not right there. Graveyards are a great place to dispose of a body. We can't take cadaver dogs in there. Their heads would explode. Most of those graves are full. Five coffins or more.'

'What are you suggesting?' Moran asked.

'Nothing,' Alan said. 'I'm just pointing out a mystery to go with our other mysteries.'

'Are you suggesting there are dead paedophile priests buried in graveyards across North Wales?' Moran came to the point. 'Because if you are, I'll have to follow up on it and that would mean desecrating hundreds of graves at a cost of millions on a hunch and whoever was responsible for suggesting there are bodies buried, would be crucified.'

'I didn't suggest anything of the kind,' Alan said. 'That's a ridiculous idea.'

Chapter 55

Ernie Metcalfe was in Llanberis with his parents and children. Helen, Hannah, and Hilary were growing fast. They were having lunch and enjoying the mountains. Snow covered the upper slopes. It was postcard beautiful. Every time he looked at them, he saw Naomi. Her smile, her facial expressions when they laughed and when they cried. They were doubles of their mother in so many ways. Naomi would always be with them. Slut.

Life had settled down. The insurance money from Naomi's death had cleared the mortgage and left him comfortable. His legs were permanently damaged, and he needed a stick to walk. He was in pain every day but he was alive when he shouldn't be. No one should have got out of that crash. The RAF pensioned him off, and he was enjoying his time with his daughters. His parents had been a great help and supported him through his injuries and his grief. Losing his wife had been devastating. Slut.

The accident investigators had accepted his account of what happened. Naomi had undone her seat belt to brush her hair. He remembered that because she was making a fuss about it. She dropped her brush and demanded he passed it to her. She went on and on. Eventually, he reached for it. That was all he remembered. It was very sad. People from the base had rallied to his aid and no one gave a second thought to the ridiculous allegations made by Harold Nelson. He was a pervert and a psychopath. He got five life sentences and was to be held at Her Majesty's pleasure, which meant he would be dribbling and sitting in his own piss before anyone contemplated releasing him. That was what he deserved. Karma had repaid him tenfold. Since he had been incarcerated, his parents had been killed in a fire at their home. The police were sure it was arson but had no suspects. And his brother had fallen from his motorbike in what looked like a hit and run. His sister and her family were due to have a fatal accident soon. Probably a gas explosion. Hal Nelson would find his bad luck would continue to haunt him. Ernie would make sure of it.

The girls came back from the counter with ice cream. Hannah was sulking because they didn't have her favourite flavour, and she was making a fuss. Ernie listened to them arguing for a few moments. Hilary was adding fuel to the flames, calling her sister a baby, which wound her up. Ernie thought about punching her in the face, but decided against it. It was a constant battle. She was so like her mother. Slut.

Epilogue

Alan was standing in the graveyard looking at Mildred Barker's resting place. He went there sometimes and walked around the graves. There was no rhyme or reason to it. He felt drawn to the place. Barker was the surname the Cleani-King supervisor had used. That bugged him. The stream was roaring, swelled by recent rain on the mountains. It had rained for weeks. The graveyard was pristine, despite how old the plots were. There were a lot of graves, and it was just a small chapel. Some of the bigger graveyards in North Wales were huge. There was no way they could be dug up and searched. Searched for what, anyway? Dead paedophiles. Who cared?

Inspector Bonnetti had called the day before to inform him of a double shooting in Chicago. It had been a sting operation by the FBI investigating the production and distribution of child pornography. An undercover agent had been drawn to a meeting with two men. It turned out to be a trap and the agent was attacked by a group of men, calling him a paedophile. They were paedophile hunters and had mistaken him for a priest of the same name. The agent shot three of the men. One was local, but two of them could not be identified. It appeared they''d entered the USA from Dublin using false identities and they had no idea who they were.

Alan walked through the graves, reading some of the names and how old the occupants were when they died. It made him think how fragile life was. One minute we're here and the next we're gone without the chance to say goodbye. He made a mental note to phone his sons when he got into the car. It didn't matter what he did in life, they would be his legacy. The pain in his bad knee further reminded him of his mortality. The clock is ticking.

Tick tock, tick tock, tick tock.